The Scott and Laurie Oki Series
in Asian American Studies

paper bullets

a fictional autobiography

kip fulbeck

UNIVERSITY OF WASHINGTON PRESS

Seattle and London

This book is published with the assistance of a grant from the Scott and Laurie Oki Endowed Fund for the publication of Asian American Studies, established through the generosity of Scott and Laurie Oki.

Library of Congress Cataloging-in-Publication Data
Fulbeck, Kip.
        Paper bullets : a fictional autobiography / Kip Fulbeck.
            p. cm. — (Scott and Laurie Oki Series in Asian American studies)
        ISBN 0-295-98078-8 (cloth : alk. paper) — ISBN 0-295-98079-6 (pbk. : alk. paper)
        1. California, Southern—Social life and customs—20th century—Fiction.
2. Autobiographical fiction, American. 3. Race relations—Fiction. 4. Ethnicity—Fiction. 5. Racially mixed people—Fiction. I. Title. II. Series

    PS3556.U33 P36 2001
    813'.6—dc21   00-048434

Certain portions of this book have been published previously in slightly different form: "It Never Tastes Like It's Supposed To," *YOLK* 5:1 (Winter/Spring 1998), 22–23; "Prostitution, Massages, & Apologies," *YOLK* 5:2, *(Summer 1998), 22–24.*

for the ways she makes me feel

contents

preface	ix
acknowledgments	xi
introduction	3
sunflower	5
One	6
Two	13
Three	20
Four	24
Five	29
violet	41
Six	42
Seven	50
Eight	61
daffodil	67
Nine	68
Ten	79
Eleven	84
carnation	97
Twelve	98
Thirteen	103
orchid	111
Fourteen	112
Fifteen	121
Sixteen	138
delphinium	145
Seventeen	146
Eighteen	156
morning glory	175
Nineteen	176
Twenty	185
Twenty-one	192
Twenty-two	198
iris	203
Twenty-three	204
Twenty-four	216
impatiens	233
Twenty-five	234
Twenty-six	247
Twenty-seven	259
sources	272

preface

Occasionally in this text I've had to modify the truth a bit. Please
forgive me. I did it for you.

acknowledgments

I have no idea how to thank people to begin with. But putting it in print creates a whole new set of problems. Am I supposed to just thank the people whose lives I drew on for material? Or do I just thank people who actually helped with the actual editing and production of the work? What about supporters who kept believing through all the rejections? Then there are people like Eleanor Antin, my grad school advisor, who inspired two whole chapters about art and life that got cut out entirely somewhere in the fourth edit. Do I thank her? What about my life mentors and people who pulled me through college, like my academic counselor B. J. Barclay? What about my role models? Ex-lovers? People who let me stay over and use their computers? Friends who read the text and gave me feedback for nothing more than a burrito dinner? The guys I go fishing with? The people whose art inspires me? And then there's Jeff Enright, who really had nothing whatsoever to do with this work but kept insisting I put him in somewhere—quite annoyingly, really—even including me in his wedding party as some sort of bonding insurance towards this goal. That's got to be past some sort of line.

This artwork and I depend on a lot of people, and I'd like to recognize some of them here. Thanks to my mother and family, and thanks to my friends: George Avelino, Xavier Callahan, Sucheng Chan, Candy Mae Estalilla, Karen Gee, Trang Lai, Teresa Williams-Léon, Victoria Namkung, Larissa Nickel, Naomi Pascal, Harry Reese, Sandra Reese, Selene Steelman, Gretchen Van Meter, Michael Velasquez, and the staff of the University of Washington Press. I'd also like to thank Ayinde Chong and Shawna Fildes, not only for inspiring me as students but for letting me adapt their work here. Special thanks to Ted Lai (my fearless editor), Ben Northover, Paul Spickard, and my father, who taught me how to write.

I guess that wasn't so bad.

Kip Fulbeck
Santa Barbara, California
March 2001

paper bullets

a fictional autobiography

kip fulbeck

introduction

It comes out of movie scripts, deejay signature playlists, a repeating four-color poster set edge to edge to edge to edge along plywood construction barriers and iron scaffolding. Advertisements for magazine subscriptions and androgynous singers and closer, better shaves. It comes from a throwaway Hollywood rag with stir-fry-sauce styrofoam stains at its edges, another failed late-night talk show attempt despite much hype, a resampled pop song getting its second and third incarnations on suburban college radio. Canceled seventies sitcoms and old commercial slogans rising from the dead. Music videos getting played so often you no longer hear the sounds without seeing the images. That's just the way it is with me. Blessed or cursed, I remember everything.

I soak up television and comic books like a sponge, keep 20,000 random melodies, lyrics, and guitar solos idling too high at traffic lights, replay monologues and shot sequences in my daytime sleep. Over time, everything slowly mixes together like so many nondairy smoothies at your local juice bar. Four dollars. Buy ten, get one free. Orange juice, bananas, blueberries, spirulina, and assorted bodily fluids—my every recollection filled with random names and phrases.

Marsha Marsha Marsha!

Steve Austin, a man barely alive.

Jill, Kelly, and Sabrina. They work for me. My name—is Charlie.

Sometimes everything in life, and everything on TV, is just one big fiction.

sunflower

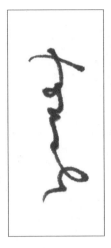

One

If what you're hiding is valuable enough, sooner or later someone will come looking for it. That's just the way it's played. Red light, green light. Ready or not, here I come. Hidden treasures only matter if you're looking, and if you're in the right place. Sometimes it all comes down to a matter of timing and perception. You notice certain things along the roadside. Some you stop for. Some you take with you. Some you drive by.

If you take the 101 north past Montecito, you get into a semi-hometown of mine. I've never come to terms with Santa Barbara as a place to call home because I've never gotten away from its image as some kind of beach playground for rich white people who live here and sometimes-rich white people who are just visiting from L.A. to get away from all the smog and all the heat and all the guns. The air is better here, but it's actually colder than people and postcards let on. We get a few shootings here and there, and a few murders here and there, but it's not anywhere close to L.A. Then again, you can't get *dim sum* or decent Korean food here so there's a trade-off. Given the choice, you can order me the *dim sum* with guns any day.

This semihometown north of Santa Barbara, called Goleta, basically revolves around the adjacent university where I teach. I wouldn't really call it a college town, though, since it doesn't really cater to the students, even though it depends on them to exist. I wouldn't call it an old-fashioned town either, since it's still got a few high-tech firms that every now and then talk of joining the mass industry flight out of California long enough to get their employees nervous and some letters to the editor written. Deep down, though, we all know it's a farce. I mean, who really wants to move to Arizona? You just end up here on summer vacations anyway, and it's a longer drive. Sooner or later, to much fanfare and celebration, these engineering firms announce they'll brave the odds and stick it out here, while a thousand workers pack away their pins and needles and wait for their lives to be teased again. These firms are like a pretty high-school girl— cheerleader, ASB, the works. The type with a constant entourage of admiring lettermen, all lined up waiting for a date that will never happen. Everyone knows it but the guys in line. There's a Carrows. A Honda dealership. A hardware store that doesn't carry any lumber. I'd just call it a town.

Teaching here at the university level has always been a little tricky for me. I was lucky enough to get hired at twenty-six, which made me the youngest faculty on the campus. It also put me in the predicament of having to regularly prove I really was who I was, and I really did what I did. A lot of my students assumed I was one of their peers during my first couple years. This still happens occasionally, but not as often. I still have a baby face. I still get carded. And I still don't look like a professor, which is all fine with me. I'm not quite sure what a professor is supposed to look like, but I know I don't fit the traditional bill. My skin is dark from both my Cantonese genes and a love of the sun, and my black hair falls to the middle of my back—though I almost always tie it back in a ponytail when teaching. Basically Axl Rose minus the bandanna, hair color, skin color, leather pants, and tenor voice. For better or worse, I've spent a lifetime in athletics, and that continues here. In most ways I still do what I do. It's not uncommon for me to see my students as often in the weight room, pool, or basketball court as I do in lecture. Which means someone somewhere is spending too much time in the gym or too little time in class. Take your pick.

I started living in the married-student housing complex, which is essentially like freshman dorms but instead of seeing who can play their stereo the loudest, we see who can get away with parking in the twenty-minute zone the longest. I figure when you get older your methods of civil disobedience and posturings of independence and rebellion get a little more subtle and a lot more sad. It just sneaks up on you. Everyone's watching VH1's "Where Are They Now?" and laughing at random Billy Idols and David Lee Roths without realizing we're just a DV cam and an interviewed former lover away ourselves. More reasons for me to blast my stereo when I get home. A random grab out of 500 CDs.

Power on. Track 1.

You wanted the best and you got the best! The hottest band in the world . . . KISS!

Good enough.

We have a community laundry room and mailbox compartments that you locate by row number and letter. I'm at Row 4, Box F. Good seats at the Staples Center, but bottom corner here. Full bent back and all. Interchangeable kids run around constantly. I play Nerf football with the ones under ten or eleven. I watch single moms go off to night classes leaving their fourteen-year-old girls to dye their hair, smoke, and hang out with horny skateboarding boys with baggy pants under the trees on hot September Fridays. The kids all say "fuck" a lot. I imagine the parents do, too. People say hi to each other for the most part and sometimes decorate their patios with potted plants and holiday decorations. Crepe paper pumpkins. Turkeys. Leprechauns. Holy Mother of Mary manger scenes.

Born and raised Eurasian, Amerasian, and Hapa in dry, inland SoCal, I grow up watching a city called Covina turn from orange groves and cows into condo complexes and mini malls like some silkworm caterpillar turning into a moth. Someone somewhere makes these decisions, but no one seems to know who and we're all pretty busy. People buy five-gallon baby orange trees from nurseries to plant inside condo dirt patches built over orange-tree graveyards. Someone somewhere's got to think that's funny. We pay $2.79 for carcinogen-filled Enzo mothballs to try and rid ourselves of condo mini mall moths, while cedar chips and Ivory soap are free or nearly free. Real oranges would probably work just as well. I grow up in a suburbia youth of white debutantes and white trash, checking "white" on ethnicity questionnaires because there's no box for mixed-blood Cantonese, English, Irish, and Welsh. Still isn't. Peter Frampton look-alikes mutate into urban cowboys, L.L. Beans, punks, rockabillies, Goth freaks, and mod revivalists at the various stages of an L.A. suburban lifetime, with no one, including me, ever worrying about things like oranges or ethnicity questionnaires. Someone somewhere must worry about these things. Maybe it's God.

I have the typical parents of a Hapa kid. And when you're a kid, everything is typical. By the time I got anything remotely figured out, all I understood was that my father had already done a bunch of things I'll never ever do. Edit a newspaper. Fly a plane. Play college football. Go hungry. These are never gonna be part of my present life. It's a different time now, a different place. No one waits for the truth anymore. We'd rather watch real-life reenactments, made-for-TV movies, and syntho-news. Dad's the complete English professor, quoting a lot of prose, telling a lot of jokes, and sharing very few true stories. And, like anyone else, he turns his head at traffic accidents.

Three gents walk into a bar . . .

Oral history isn't passed down in my family. It just kind of seeps out. Like a taste for coffee or a widow's peak. I remember Depression-era stories of a family of five sharing a single potato for dinner, cross-cut like a ham. Ketchup in water becoming tomato soup. Sugar and ice becoming popsicles. Imagination becoming oral fantasy. Dad's father emigrates from England with a seventh-grade education and takes a job cleaning floors. His Irish mother housekeeping. The stories we've heard before stay the same. Wages are drunk, jobs are lost, children are abused. Some stories need to be told. Some you just figure out yourself. Some get passed down from generation to generation. Aren't all of our fathers storytellers? Aren't all of our fathers alcoholics?

My father graduates from his family without commendation. The first to attend college, the first to earn a Ph.D, he leaves for college hearing promises of his father sending him $1 a week "just to help out." The first time he receives the dollar he's surprised. He smiles slightly, but doesn't expect any more, and doesn't receive any more. It's that way with him. He says you can spend your life looking forward to things that never come—lottery tickets, gold medals, princes and princesses on galloping white stallions—or you can prepare for the worst. If you prepare for the worst, you're either ready for it or you're pleasantly surprised. And sometimes being pleasantly surprised is a nice thing. I find myself checking door locks at night, unlisting my phone number, and viewing introductions with suspicion. Early inheritance from my father.

Dad flies in WWII. Even gets shot. Closer in my real world to a John Wayne rerun or *Tora! Tora! Tora!* than anything near my own experience. I look at a scar and I hear a story. Basically, you don't get a Purple Heart if the guy shooting you is your own squadron mate. Small detail. The kind of detail that ruins an otherwise good story. Sorry about that, I guess. Accidents happen. Dad's squadron visits him in the hospital, and he only has to see their faces walking in the door to know who did it. Four men walk in and one is pale as a ghost.

Three of these things belong together,
Three of these things are kind of the same,
Strafing over the Everglades on a training mission, my father finishes his run, peppers the target, and prepares his climb. Behind him, the next pilot nervously opens fire too soon. There is a slap at my father's back. Some smoke. No flames. My father looks at himself and his plane, confused. He transmits, "I think I've been shot," and spends a lifetime chuckling over this phrase with each sequential telling of the story. He uses his left hand to compress the bullet's exit wound and flies the thirty miles to the training airstrip one-handed, because bleeding and flying one-handed is still better than parachuting into the Everglades. You have enough to worry about without thinking about Discovery Channel reptile episodes.

One of these things is doing its own thing,
Thoughts of death, maiming, impotence, and paralysis disappear when he has to land. His left hand leaves its station, wet and warm, and two trembling hands guide the SNJ down to a perfect landing. "Painted it on," as he says. The ambulance is waiting. An orderly pulls him out of the cockpit, pale as a ghost. On a rough dirt road a medic plugs an IV

into him and says, "You've used up all your luck, mate." What is that supposed to mean? Pardon me?

Now it's time to play our game.

There is an investigation, a court martial, and many apologies. But there is no anger in my father for this. There are other angers, and other places for them. He just says, "Poor guy didn't mean to . . ." and leaves it at that. For the longest time, I thought everyone in WWII got shot, flew planes, held their pain in, and kissed nurses in Times Square. I've been to Times Square, but I've never kissed a nurse. The entry and exit wounds have almost healed over half a century, but not quite. You can still see them. We all have our own sets of entry wounds, and some of them haven't found their exits. We hope they do, and sometimes all you can do is hope. The body naturally repels splinters, passes foreign bodies, and relinquishes tears, but some bullets stay embedded indefinitely. Like my father, I carry them in my organs and gut, occasionally flinching at a physical memory and setting off certain metal detectors. Prepare for the worst, a sense of occasion, control your pain, store your anger. These are things I learn from my father.

Coming back from VJ Day he enrolls at USC in the Comparative Literature Doctoral Program. He T.A.'s a small ESL class where my mother, fresh in from China, is a student. As they say, the rest is history. And as they say, history repeats itself.

But it doesn't work out that way for either of us. Ma's English is too good for the class. Dad kicks her out after the first day. Too much the ringer or maybe just too beautiful to deal with. I know what that's like. A week later she runs into him on campus. Dad's a complete stud. Tall. Single. Clean-cut. War hero, even if it was friendly fire. He turns heads wherever he goes. Still wearing his hair in a crew cut, Dad sports tight sunglasses like Jack Lord on *Hawaii Five-0,* black zoot-suit pants, and argyle socks. The locking leather briefcase completes the ensemble.

Ma walks straight up to him and asks if he wants to attend her Methodist church luncheon. That's pretty gutsy in its own way, but Ma's never been one lacking for guts. These cute meets are funny, because you'll bend over backwards to make the situation work. Ma's Buddhist. Dad's atheist. A Methodist luncheon. You do the math. Dad looks at my mother—a complete princess—and agrees. I don't think it was much of a decision, really. Atheist who? They go to the luncheon. She introduces her "niece and nephew," who become my brother and sister later along the line, once the ties are on. Lock, stock, and two smoking barrels. A woman knows, a man supposes. They date, get engaged, and marry. Dad prepares for the worst and is occasionally pleasantly surprised along the way. And the rest, as they say, is a new history. I don't know if new histories repeat themselves or not. I'll let you know.

ㅏ

People meet my father and respect him. People meet my mother and love her. I'm more hit-and-miss. More love-or-hate.

I get uneasy telling Ma's story. Because Ma's story fits too easily into some kind of *Joy Luck Club* old-school legend, some kind of food staple for white America. But to understand why it is I write, you have to understand some basic and not-so-basic boundaries. You have to believe in fabricated stories. You have to understand how it is I came to be who I am. It'll all make sense in the end. That's what they tell me anyway. Relax.

"Hey, Bishop, do the thing with the knife!"

Oh, please.

"Hey . . . what are you doin', man? What are you doin'? C'mon, quit messin' around, Drake! C'mon! Bishop? Hey, man! Hey, not me, man! Hey! . . ."

Bishop places his hand over Hudson's.

Trust me.

Back in rural China, Ma's first husband works in the salt industry. China isn't that industrialized yet, so there's no refrigeration and salt is a crucial commodity. My mother's first husband is a good man. Honest, she says. One day he discovers a syndicate in the salt mining industry. Some network shaving profits or smuggling or embezzling or stealing. A salt Mafia. He reports the crimes, and several lower-end guys get arrested and punished. This is basic Organized Crime 101. Bosses never do the dirty work, so bosses never do the time. Not then. Not now. Not ever.

My mother and her first husband go for a walk in the village. A woman from down the road approaches them with a plate of fried fish. River fish or king fish or minnows. She begs my mother to buy some, because company just came over and she's out of rice with no money to buy any. If Ma will buy the fish, she can buy the rice and serve her guests.

Ma doesn't want any fish. She doesn't need any. But the woman looks so desperate my mother says she'll buy the fish to help her out.

The woman thanks her and Ma goes back into her home to get some money. While she is inside, a soldier from the salt mines approaches her husband and salutes him. Then the soldier continues walking past, turns around, and shoots her husband in the back, killing him. My mother and her rice money come running out to find her husband lying face down on a dirt road, and a soldier, who looks back at her once and keeps on walking. This is beyond what I am able to write or feel. This is beyond my present life. It is a different time now, a different place. But this isn't what I remember when Ma tells me the story. I remember Ma telling me she was supposed to be killed also. I remember her telling me she was spared because she had decided to help this woman out of kindness. I remember her telling me everything comes around.

I'm only able to write this because my mother wanted to help out a neighbor. If she doesn't help her, she gets killed. If she is killed, my sister's mentally retarded students never learn, my brother's patients never recover, I never write or speak a word.

Quid pro quo, Agent Starling.

Maybe because Ma chooses to help a woman, my sister can touch a particular student, and this student can visit a nursing home and take an inmate to a movie. My brother can take the extra time to be with a patient's family, and later that afternoon one of these family members can pay for the person behind him on a toll bridge. I can write a text that someone reads before making their parents dinner or sending a friend flowers or smiling at someone on the street or campus or at work. My mother's story operates like a chain letter, except it doesn't make you angry when you get it in the mail or online. It goes back a generation and a generation before that. It remembers favors and kindness and justice.

Months later, investigators lead my mother to a beaten man in shackles, waiting to be executed on her identification. She looks in the man's eyes and sees the man who killed her husband. And even though she recognizes the man, she tells them she has never seen him before and they release him. What's the point, she says. Her husband is already dead. That's the way it is. That's the way it works out.

This is my first exposure to a woman.

Two

I grow up in a Chinese household with an out-of-place American father. Ma's "niece and nephew" become my half-brother and half-sister. They are fullblooded Chinese from Taipei. My first cousins, who play with me every day, are from Hong Kong—Alan, Bobby, Carl, Diana. ABCD. Chinese do things like this.

We play Chinese games where everyone understands the rules but me, and I can't ask my dad about it. Maybe I can ask Ma. We play *tien gao* on weekends after the adults are done gambling and before the dominos are put away, shuffling the click-clack tiles over a green felt table cover. You stack the tiles in stacks of four. You stack the stacks of four in a row of eight. You cut it cross-cut like a ham or skin it off the top to deal. For eight-year-old kids there's no money to play with. Chinese have plenty of time for money later. Too much money. Too much jade. Too much gold. Too many Gucci bags, black Mercedes, eye jobs, and bad suits that cost too much.

The sun and chlorine have turned our skin to a deep chocolate, dry and bitter like the last one left that no one wants to eat in after-Christmas See's Candies boxes. Never, ever take the last of anything. We play in the pool on hot summer days without thought of the first-, second-, or third-degree smog alerts that pepper the San Gabriel and Covina Valley Unified School Districts. At school on a first-degree recess, you're not supposed to play running games—no Greek dodge, no kickball, no Smear the Queer. On seconds you can only play Four Square or hopscotch. On thirds you just stay inside and read comic books with the lights out. This is our recess and P.E. We go home after school and swim till we can't breathe, our lungs jammed with leaded fuel from the blood and bones of all the burning dinosaurs. I learn about them in school. I know their names. I feel them in my lungs. Diplodocus. Brachiosaurus. Archaeopteryx.

"It hurts to breathe, Dad."

"You get used to it."

I wake up going in the water. During summer we have days and months on end without shirt or shoes for me and my cousins. Days before sunscreen. We stay at the pool playing Marco Polo or Silent Night, getting stung by bees and rescuing sow bugs from the bottom of a nine-foot pool. Breathe the breath of life into them and watch them come back from the dead. Primitive organisms, primitive needs.

My father loves the tropical heat of Covina summers, but his skin has betrayed him. He can only stay out a few minutes without burning, so he has to swim in the early mornings or late evenings when the shade of avocado trees casts over the pool. Avocado trees are too brittle to climb, he says, but I still build tree houses and they don't collapse. My mother also swims these early mornings and late evenings. It is one of the few things they do together, though she does it for different reasons. While my father loves the sun even as it burns, my mother hates the sun even as it tans. My father, like me, sees a tan as beautiful. My mother sees it as primitive. Is it any wonder my parents live separate lives under the same roof? This Chinese prejudice on skin tone passes on from generation to generation. A preference for alabaster and porcelain and an absence of hand calluses. As an adult, I overhear my sister telling her daughter she's forbidden to do junior lifeguards in the summer. Too much sun, she tells her.

"You'll look like him," she says, motioning in my direction.

I admit it. You are better than I am.
"Then why are you smiling?"
Because I know something you don't know.
"And what is that?"
I am not left-handed.

Dad works in an oak study at the end of the hall with a lockable door. Inside are a marble fireplace, an enormous rosewood desk with an electric Smith-Corona typewriter, and bookshelves filled with classical verse and prose, and various knickknacks from around the world. Edith Hamilton's *Mythology.* Don Quixote figurine. Mayan statue. Japanese Geisha doll. There are ashtrays full of Muriel Coronella cigar butts and soggy toothpicks used to keep their stems clean. A remote-control television sits across the desk on top of a file cabinet and is left on constantly. A college roommate visits and asks me why my parents watch the same program on separate televisions in separate rooms. I never thought about it before. I tell him, "They just do."

I was always scared of the dark as a kid, and scared of being alone. This is unusual for a kid growing up in the southern valley avocado groves, where summer days spent alone catching frogs or hunting fruit rats with a BB gun is part of life. I stayed sleeping in my parents' room until eight or nine—long after my schoolmates had left the den, and plenty of reason to fabricate elaborately detailed stories to tell at school, of having my own room, along with the stories of me not needing training wheels and camping out in the backyard. Some stories over time get told again and again, each time becoming more detailed and more true, while some stories never get told at all. These are the stories that are too close, too deep, too real, or too far down to remember. Maybe we think no one wants to hear. Maybe we think no one will believe us. As young boys we claim independence from parents and fear. As older boys we claim independence from women and fear. Both times we're usually lying. To this day I have never camped out, I don't need training wheels anymore, and I always sleep alone. Believe me?

We have three twin beds in "our" room. My mother's and mine are pushed together to form a mock king. My father's sits across the bedroom against the wall by the window. There are teak nightstands with imported lamps on either side of my mother and me, while my father has a nightlight next to him that stays on constantly—a small circle that plugs directly into the outlet and glows a dim orange. It is never completely dark here. My father checks the double locks on both bedroom doors before going to bed.

Click click. Click click.

Sometimes in the middle of the night he gets up to urinate. I hear his bed creak with his movement. I hear his footsteps across the room past my bed, and his stop at the toilet. The seat is already up. It is almost always up in this house. I hear his soft stream in the water. It is loud in the dim orange light, and if you hold your breath you can hear it even louder like the ocean. It sings and cascades and fluctuates pitch like music, starting quickly but soon growing slower and weaker. It tries to keep in tune but soon begins to break up, unable to hold its note. I hear his shake and dribble, a few solitary drops echoing in the bowl and the bathroom-tile auditorium. There is an awkward silence now. No one knows if we're supposed to applaud or not. The maestro has his back to us and isn't moving. One second. Two seconds. He flushes the toilet, and through the noise of the flowing water I hear him walk to both doors and recheck the locks.

Click click. Click click.

Slow footsteps sound from my left to right and stop at his bed. It creaks at the pressure of his body as he gets back in, rustles in the covers, and takes a deep breath. There is another silence here, but it is not as awkward. One second. Two seconds. As my father's breath slows and the tank refills, I begin to hear the crickets again. Maybe they were there the whole time. Maybe I just didn't hear them. You get used to some sounds. I get used to the sounds of checked door locks, and to the restlessness of my father at night. When there is no complete darkness everything is okay. When there is no complete silence we can both sleep. When the crickets stop chirping, that's when you worry.

Shhhhh . . . shhhhh . . .

At night, cuddling up to my mother, I can smell her scent but can't sleep. I am four, maybe five years old. Dad is snoring across the room. It is loud and fitful. I'm scared by the anger in its intake, by the sudden rush out of the darkness when he suddenly inhales. It is almost, but not quite, violent. I wake my mother by nudging her. I whisper that Dad's snoring is keeping me awake. I don't tell her it's scaring me. She gets up and goes across the room slowly. Next to his bed I see her quietly stop, then gently nudge him. A soft midnight touch in the middle of his dreams and space and locked doors. He reacts abruptly to this touch in the night. He bolts up stone-awake, screaming, "What are you doing?"

Ma doesn't know how to react. I'm in bed alone without my mother. I don't care about the snoring anymore. I'll never complain about your snoring again, Dad. I won't. I won't. I won't. I won't.

"The boy . . . the boy was having trouble," she mumbles, " . . . you were snoring . . ."

"What are you doing?" he repeats, sitting upright in the dark. *"What are you doing?"*

ー
ﾄ

A childhood morning. I wake up to the smell of my mother, but different this time. I am five, maybe six years old. I roll over to my right to see her. She is always to my right. Today, women sleep only to my left. I open my eyes and see my parents lying together in the twin bed pushed next to me. My father has his arm around my mother. They are both clothed and both a bit uncomfortable. Partly because of me, but more I think because of the touch itself. Like the forced family portrait at the local photography shop, Dad's arm is over-rehearsed and somewhat self-conscious. Ma's lean into it is stilted and aware. I see the physical contact as unnatural and forced, yet I still smile and feel a warm morning with my parents. The sun is just coming in through the east window and the jacaranda trees. My dad's solo canary has begun his daily song with the incoming light. It is the only time I have ever seen my parents touch. It is the only morning I remember.

I, like any man, am scared of marriage. Mostly because I see it all around me as a mutual tolerance and dependency rather than as any kind of spiritual intimacy and union. The few times I see older couples glowing in each other's presence are anomalies, more like four-leaf clovers, Ferraris, or bank errors in your favor. Sure you desire, but it's not like you can really do anything about it. You can spend your life looking forward to things that never come. Why bother?

As a child, though, marriage sounds like a wonderful thing. I was never at the "girls = cooties" stage like most boys. There are constant hopes and fantasies, but instead of knights on white horses or princes from frogs, it is coming home to a kiss in the doorway, or waking up to each other in the morning. My sun now comes in from the southeast, over the edge of the Pacific through mini blinds and a potted ficus. There is no canary here, no song. I could never keep one after finding out they only sing to find their mate. Something's wrong there. You should never celebrate loneliness. You should never hide your emotions when you wake together. There are other times and other reasons for hiding feelings. Morning is not the time to play games. It is not the time to force. It is not the time to pretend. If you can't trust a person when you wake, when can you trust her?

From kindergarten on, I love and desire—physical contact, love letters, initials in trees, the touch of hands or lips or feet under desks, the folded note. It pushes further. I see it. There are senses there beneath the indifference, beneath the just-a-night-out-with-the-boys, like so many pillows impersonating human beings underneath down comforters and throw pillows and stuffed sock monkeys. Do you clutch your pillow at night in passion or in the morning during your overwhelming sadness? Do you understand or do you know how to sleep alone?

I see, even as a child, the thought of being with a partner as more than the sum of A + B. As more than dinner companionship, midnight sex, or a date for the next *Jurassic Park* sequel. I see the idea that you can count on each other, that phone calls each day are part of your everyday experience, like checking door locks or feeding your fish tank or breathing. I see the idea that another's safety, well-being, and happiness are as essential to your own as yours are to her. Call her each night to make sure she's okay. Greet each other with a kiss and embrace—not for your body needing hers, but for the draw, the movement towards the safety, love, and security she offers. Check the map. Restrooms. Escape routes. Food court. Security. *You are here.*

Each classroom photo, from kindergarten through sixth grade, carries with it the promise, within a pixilated, 1/4-inch face, of a nameless, interchangeable little girl. It is before erections and sexual fantasy. It is before locker-room talk and male bravado of whose hands have touched who where. It is before learning about how to see, treat, and fuck women (in that order)—before hollow fixes and beliefs that some experimentation of positions, some sharing of bodily fluids, is satisfying anywhere beyond the recurring physical hunger and fear of being alone. It is fourth grade before I have my first kiss, underwater in my swimming pool with Kelly Sullivan. It is seventh grade before I taste my first tongue, so nervous I run all the way home afterwards, replaying it in my mind. It is tenth grade before I enter my first woman—a fourteen-year-old girl, really. Fumbling and overanxious in my father's study with our pants pulled to our knees. I had asked her over to watch *Enter the Dragon* on television. No lie. Even I couldn't make that one up. She said she had seen it before, but she came anyway.

Sixteen years and a million martial arts movies later, I am no less scared of women and no less focused on the search. It just seems that way. The special effects and stunts have improved. The dubs are more realistic. Our scripted dialogue seems more improvisational. Flirtations seem more natural. Kicks look more real. I understand the game better, but sometimes understanding a game better doesn't make you like it any more. I celebrate a Magic Johnson no-look pass, a Michael Chang backhand, a Jimi Hendrix lick, but knowing how to crossover dribble or play a minor pentatonic only satisfies a small part of me. It's nowhere close to what I see, and what I want to celebrate. It's no French Open at seventeen, no "Little Wing," no elderly couple holding hands in the park, no absolute truth and trust in the morning. Relationships come factory-direct now, loaded with all the options. I can choose any color I want, any interior, any trim, and still have no idea whatsoever about what I'm doing or why I am where I am. I just go through the motions, hearing the same question over and over again.

Anyone else would be happy.
Why aren't you?

I figure there's got to be something more out there than just being satisfied, than having things go okay. There's got to be something more than wondering what to do on a Saturday night together. I mean, who came up with the idea the two of you have to *do* something? You want to get something to eat? You want to see a movie? You feel like staying home? Are you listening to me? There's got to be something more out there than dozens upon dozens of little partnered honeymoons that never live up to their beginning promises. I've never felt like this before. I've never been able to talk like this before. I've never loved someone like this before. There's got to be something else there beneath all the smiles and all the red ribbons and all the early laughter you share together in bed and bagel shops. There's got to be a reason to keep looking.

I never asked anyone for sight. I never thanked anyone for it either. It's just there.

Three

As a two-year-old I'm taken to toddler swimming lessons at Highlands Swim School. I walk in with Ma and recognize the water. I remember the way it smells, the way it tastes, the way it touches. It's the first day. Ma and I are with thirty other toddlers who don't know how to swim and mothers who want them to. The mothers are in line filling out forms and paying for the five-day program. Ma lets go of my hand and opens her purse to look for a pen. Inside her purse is a mound of safety pins, coupons, compacts, lipstick, emery boards, toothpicks, and a joint-account checkbook. She's ready for *Let's Make a Deal* with Monty Hall. Ma is busy digging through her purse, not wanting to lose her place in line. I'm at her side, feeling the familiar touch of her polyester sundress. It feels slick and tingly on my fingers. I smell tablet chlorine and locker-room smell and wetness. Ma digs up a metal pen with the name and address of a bank on the side of it. I let go of her dress.

"You shouldn't play this game."

I don't have a choice.

"You're in over your head."

I know.

"I've got a book to write. I'll see you around, Shooter."

I look at the pool, walk to the edge, and jump off the steps into the deep water. The water instantly envelops me and my senses as I go under. For a wonderful moment I am touched and held everywhere at once. The water is all around me again. I feel and hear the adults panicking and yelling, but my feeling and hearing is different now. I understand it and I'm not scared. I feel the thumping of adults running on the pool deck and yelling, getting louder as they come towards me. I hear splashing and feel the water change as they jump into the pool next to me. It becomes defensive like a dog, raising its hair at the intruders. My eyes, ears, nose, and mouth are open and taking it in. My fingers are spread on both hands. Someone suddenly grabs my arm and yanks me back up into the frenzy and the yelling and the air. The person holds me completely out of the water by both shoulders, as if somehow the higher they hold me, the safer I am. Ma is screaming something in Chinese from the pool deck, but I don't understand. It's like all the adults are caught somewhere between fear, relief, and anger. They don't know whether they should hug me or spank me. Maybe both. I feel the water leaving my eyes unprotected, and the familiar cool slap of wind starting again. Stay away from me.

Once they realize I'm okay, the panic fizzles out like warm Coca-Cola. The situation slowly calms down. No one even wants a sip anymore. The police, paramedics, firefighters and SWAT teams go Code 4. The mothers start filling out their forms again and talking to one another about what they'd do if that was their child. I'm pulled out of the water and toweled off. The towel is warm and fuzzy. Ma yells at me in English so I and everyone else on the pool deck can understand her. That's it. Show's over. The rest of the lesson settles into the typical monotony you'd expect at swimming lessons for two-year-olds.

Days two and three are more uneventful. All the instructors watch me like a hawk. I can't get near the water without someone's arm on me somewhere. Part of the reason is my earlier AWOL fiasco. Part of it is that I can't swim worth beans. I mean I can't swim at all. I suck. I'm a rock with arms. All the other toddlers can hold their breath and blow bubbles and kick on the wall. I just sink underwater with my eyes and mouth open. Ma is threatening about getting her money back. What kind of swim school is this? The people running the school tell Ma that I just don't seem to understand how dangerous the water is. They tell her I don't seem to have a natural fear of it, so I don't instinctively hold my breath or try to stay on top like the other kids do. Sometimes I don't even hold on to the wall during kicking. I just go under. They tell her she should keep the fence up around our pool a couple more years. We don't go back for days four or five.

At home Dad buys me an inflatable float ring so we can unlock the fence and I can go in the pool. I guess they've given up on swimming lessons for a while. Dad gets the ring at Thrifty Drugs on Grand Avenue. It's clear with colored animals on it, mostly hippos and alligators and otters and stuff. Water animals. I get it. It's called a Toddler Water Safety Ring. It's the full safety gizmo—untippable, puncture-resistant, hypo-allergenic, the works. Seems like everything's toddler-something these days. Kind of stupid, if you ask me. But if you ask me, I don't need the ring to begin with. What's the problem?

Dad opens up the package and blows up the ring on a late Saturday summer morning. He inches me into it and puts me in the pool. The ring holds and floats me. I slowly drift out into the deep end and get caught up in the circulation pattern of the water. Dad sits down on some patio furniture and looks at the sports section. I don't have much to do. I'm just floating around. The bottom half of me is underwater, the top half of me is dry. I just bob in clockwise circles around the pool.

It's like doing laps. I can move my legs around a little and reach the water with my hands. Sometimes I can grab a bug or a leaf. I can spin in circles. That's about it. Where's the touch? Where's the feeling? Where's the safety?

Dad puts the paper down and goes inside the house for something. Maybe another section of the paper. Maybe a glass of wine. Maybe a phone call or a sandwich or a glance at the football game on TV. In the pool, I reach for something just beyond my reach. Probably a drowning bug. Maybe a leaf or a stick or something. I struggle and stretch and reach. I kick with my feet and press my body forward. It is almost there . . . just beyond my fingertips.

The Toddler Safety Ring shifts its balance point and suddenly the untippable ring flips completely over, inverting me. My head goes underwater. My feet go in the air. My eyes stay open. I hold my breath. I'm kicking my feet in the air and paddling my hands in the water, but I can't right myself. Partly because of the untippable safety ring. Partly because I can't swim worth beans. Ma is in the kitchen making lunch. Maybe tuna sandwiches or chicken salad or hot dogs. She feels a blur in the next room and glances over. She sees Dad flying down the stairs.

I've never seen your father run so fast.

Underwater, I hear Dad's footsteps approaching. I'm holding my breath with my eyes open. My hands are spinning me in circles. Hurry, Dad. The footsteps stop and for a moment I think he's not coming. He's not coming. He's stopped. Then I feel and hear the splash as he lands in the pool next to me. I feel his hands grab me and instantly flip me over. I feel water rush past my face, then air, then drops and splashes and yelling. I gasp in a breath.

Gasp

He holds me high out of the water with my eyes open. His fingers are buried into my arms. It hurts. The look on his face scares me. There's no anger in it—only pure fear and concern, pure anxiety and guilt. Daddy look I'm breathing. I'm breathing Dad. I'm breathing

(Inhale)

(Exhale)

(Inhale)

(Exhale)

He sees me breathing and is overcome with a wash of relief. His face and fingers relax. Ma is on the pool deck, yelling in Chinese again. Neither of us understands her or is paying any attention. My father is holding me in waist-deep water in our swimming pool with all his clothes on. I'm not crying. I'm not even upset. I don't know how long I was underwater or how close I was to drowning, but I don't think it was that long or that close. And if it was, somehow I think that would be okay, too. Sometimes we're supposed to drown.

Make no mistake about it, my friend. It is a gift from me to you, so you'll always remember us.

The pool fence gets locked up and swim lessons start again immediately. Somehow this time I catch on much faster. "He really is picking it up well now," the instructors say. One of them even calls me a natural. She says I have the instincts of a fish, and Ma just shakes her head.

It makes me smile. I take lessons for five weeks, until they finally tell Ma there's nothing left to teach me at my age. I've done the full YMCA routine, going from Guppy to Pollywog to Minnow to Shark, and I'm not old enough for swim team. Ma says okay and takes me home. The pool fence comes down and the Toddler Ring gets tossed in the trash. I know something now. For the rest of my life, summers and love are about water.

Holden stares ahead, then swerves the wheel to the right. The car pulls to the side of the road. The rain is a bit heavier now. He throws the car into park. Close up on Alyssa.

Why are we stopping?

"Because I can't take it."

. . .

Can't take what?

At two and a half, I swim in the deep end alone. At three, I dive to the nine-foot bottom and pick up pennies. And at four, I touch the ocean for the first time. I never want to come out.

Four

I take my shoes off at home. My father tells me it is a good tradition that makes sense, although he doesn't do it himself. I think he's too old, too lazy, or doesn't really believe it. *Don't smoke, son. Don't drink.* My mother taught me to remove my shoes indoors, although she does it only sporadically herself. I guess if one person isn't washing their hands when making *won ton,* it all gets contaminated anyway, so what's the point?

My father watched his father die a drunk with a TV remote control in his hand. My father's father watched his father die a drunk with a bible in his lap. Say that three times fast and spin your partner.

5 . . . 6 . . .

5, 6, 7, 8 . . .

We talk, as many men do, through a series of codes and behaviors. Laughter, jokes, NFL football, professional boxing, or Mexican bouts on channel 34. Politics and Larry King and *L.A. Times* editorials. Women become objects first, measured by the size of their breasts and length of leg. Sports highlights are circled in *TV Guide* as weekend parameters to work around. Everything else comes second. You tease the pain and fear of others as a way to cope with wanting to actually talk, to actually communicate with each other as men. We ridicule women to hide our own desperate fascination and bewilderment. We lose ourselves in primitive challenges of physical strength to mask our own inner search for ritual and meaning. We outwardly laugh off anxiety to conceal our own overwhelming sense of focus. Everything becomes a joke. Everything gets laughed at. Aren't all of our fathers comedians?

All I asked for is a frickin' rotating chair.

On certain rare occasions my father and I try to speak without joking. Times of learning about sex at twelve, or tying a fish hook at seven, or stumbling home drunk off my ass at sixteen. We try to talk through these coming-of-age rites without laughter, and without much success. This is serious and we know it. But left to ourselves we have no idea how to proceed. Both of us keep waiting for the other to start. It's like we're in the middle of a game called Father/Son and we don't know the rules. We have no playbook, no manual, no troubleshooting guide at the back. There's no 800 number for technical support. On television I watch Mr. Brady talk to Peter about his voice changing. Mr. C consoles

Richie after missing a free throw. But they always do it with laugh tracks and a live studio audience. It's almost too easy.

My father and I work without benefit of script or direction. I wait for my talks on sex, on fighting, on falling in love, marriage, and idealism. I wait to ask questions and I wait to hear answers. I want to find out the secret to unhooking a bra. I want to know how to kill a man with one blow. I want to know when I'm allowed to cry. I want to know why watching fireworks on the 4th of July is so lonely. I want to find out whether I can or cannot change the world, and if it's worth trying either way. But there are no answers from my father and no questions from me. He only knows how to show, and I only know how to imitate. Conduct, demeanor, and bearing are taught by his example and learned by my impersonation. Behavior is demonstrated like some wrestling move on rubber mats, then quickly mastered and mimicked for a lifetime. Take down, guillotine, soufflé, grapevine.

Here, hold out your hand.

Now hold the racket like you're shaking hands.

No, like this.

Is this how you shake hands? Are you going to shake my hand like that?

I learn to go through the motions proudly, and with self-respect. At my father's urging I learn to watch, play, and love sports. Some I'm good at, some I'm not. I could never get that shaking-hands bit or hitting a baseball. At ten, I am given the choice of which sport to compete in, but not the choice of whether or not to compete. Dad tells me I have to start either competitive tennis or competitive swimming. *It's your decision, son. Which one is it going to be?* To me, the decision is either funny white shorts or Speedos. And I don't want to do either. I just want to play dodge ball at school and Marco Polo at home. I just want to draw pictures indoors by myself, and play games outdoors by myself. That's what I want. That's my decision.

Speedos win out. I join Covina Aquatics against my will. It's just the lesser of two evils, like picking the coast guard over the marines. We work out at a shallow high-school pool next to livestock pens and a football field. I go to my first day and hate it. Everyone's looking at me. I don't have any goggles, I don't have a warm-up bag, and I can't do a flip turn. I get in lane five and swim straight down the lane, bumping heads with a dozen other kids until the coach laughs and tells me I'm supposed to swim on the right side of the lane. Circle pattern. *Get it?* How am I supposed to know that? Twenty thousand more workouts to go and I want to quit. My shoulders hurt and my eyes burn. Afterwards Ma takes me to Chick's Sporting Goods and buys me my first pair of goggles. They're sold out of blue lenses, so I get the smoke ones. I don't want to go back the next day, but Dad says I have to. I go back to workout #2 on Tuesday. The next day I go back to workout #3. Then #4. Then #5, and so on. I swim through junior high, through high school, and through college. Along the way there are other sports that come and go, but swimming stays my real home. I never really think about whether I like it or hate it. I just do it.

I learn about competition and intimidation and fear, realizing first and foremost that you can't beat someone else if you can't beat yourself first. Swimming, water polo, basketball, volleyball. Numbers become measures of success early in life and continue into adulthood. 20.89, 4 goals, 8 assists, .572. I learn to take my confidence from athletic accomplishment, and my father learns to take pride in the various ceremonies invented to let him feel pride in his son. Both of us rely on these foundations. No matter where I go, deep down I know I can swim faster than the kid teasing me, than the relatives not accepting me, than the girl laughing at me when I try to talk to her and her friends. I can swim the 50, shoot upper corner, run a three-man weave, hit outside. How can a father not be proud of an MVP?

What a build you've got, son. I never had a build like that.

The 50 is the premier spectator event in swimming. People don't like to admit it, but it is. I mean, who wants to waste twenty minutes watching some guy swim a mile? How many times can you yell *"Go-o-o-o-o!"*? In the 50, two laps take about twenty seconds and even the smallest mistake costs you the race. All the training staples of yardage, weights, speedwork, and diet go by the wayside, until all you have left is an eight-man poker game. Every good race gets won and lost in your head, and everyone around you knows it. Bluff and call. You start trying to psych each other out from the beginning of the meet, way before the race. It's like some made-up chess game where you're both pieces. You each have your own set of rules and you're trying to get the other guy to play by them. You see each other. Sometimes you say hi and shake hands. Usually you just ignore each other. You always know where the other person is and what he's doing—when he's eating, when he's flirting, when he's warming up. You know how many heats before the race he goes behind the blocks to prepare, and you know how he prepares. Before a race some guys sit rocking out with their Walkmans. Some guys swing their arms and jump around like spazzes. I just sit alone behind my block with a towel over my shoulders and my goggles on. I can sing to myself. No Walkman. No jumping. Check.

Tension comes to a head quickly, and swim-meet audiences become dead silent for the start of the 50. Everyone is focused. Everyone is watching. It's the shortest race in competitive swimming, and the only one that even comes close to all out 0–60 speed. There should be something shorter, something comparable to the 100 in track that takes ten seconds or less. Then we'd be talking real speed and perfect races. Then we'd be talking a real test of reaction time and pure acceleration. I could never top out like some of these extra tall guys with 36″ inseams and arms down to their knees. They're like Ferraris—once they get going you can't touch their top speed, but with a good first gear you can usually take them off the line. The 50 is a too-long drag race. And I've got a great start and no second gear. I just take off and hope the race is over before the other guys catch up. At nationals one year I took Matt Biondi for 45 meters, until he passed me inside the flags. The kind of small detail that ruins an otherwise good story. *Almost* beating a gold-medalist doesn't have that same kind of ring to it. It's an almost claim to fame.

Sprinters are funny. Maybe it's because the race is so short or that there's no room for mistakes, but everything has to be just right. You're jittery and excited and nervous and superstitious. You walk around meets like a serial killer with a happy face. Before a race, everyone is your enemy. And deep down, everyone knows you're psycho.

When I'm a-walkin', I strut my stuff, yeah, I'm so strung out.

Even as a kid everything is methodical and systematic. Just before the race, you go through the final routines of your pre-race ritual. Some guys splash themselves silly. Some guys cross themselves or spit in the water. I'm not sure what I do, but I know I do it and I know when I do it. As I get older my pre-race rituals become more and more elaborate and more and more necessary.

I get on my block at any random meet where the next race is the most important thing in my life. It always is. I look down the pool and see a bunch of friends standing at the end of my lane cheering and screaming something. Maybe it's my name. I don't hear them. I barely see them. I know who's next to me, what his qualifying time was, whether he's shaved, and what kind of meet he's having. I know who's on my other side and I know he's got a tendency to choke in finals. I breathe deeply two times, three times, and then quickly start to hyperventilate. Someone somewhere is yelling something. Someone somewhere is calling my name. I hear a whistle and the starting official saying something about two lengths of the pool freestyle and calling us "gentlemen." I shake my arms and slap my legs. Everything everywhere is tingling. Quiet for the start, please.

My father hates swim meets. Says they're too loud. Says they're like a bunch of people yelling and screaming inside a goldfish bowl. He doesn't understand why it has to be so loud. What are they yelling about? Plus you can't smoke on the pool deck and the snack bar only serves burgers, hot dogs, candy, and soda. It's hot and humid at indoor meets, hot and sunny at outdoor ones, and my father is wearing a sport-coat and tie among the million other fathers in shorts and T-shirts. Always the professor. Sometimes he brings student papers in manila folders to grade with a red felt-tip pen. Other times he brings a news-paper. I've swum 1,000 races in my lifetime and won 75 percent of them. Of those my father has watched maybe twenty. In those twenty races he has never yelled and never cheered. He's never stood at the end of my lane and never called my name out on the block. But in every single race he wants me to win more badly than any father on that pool deck. That I know. That I hear.

Once the starting beep goes off, people scream their hearts out for the race. That's funny, because as a competitor the only time you hear anything is the one second you're in the air just before you hit the water. Once you're in the water, you don't hear anything. But it doesn't matter. It's the thought that counts. Once you're in the water, everything is automatic. I breathe once at the flags, hit the turn, streamline under the wake, breathe again three strokes out of the turn, and bring it home. I swim the 50 more than any other race. Some meets I swim it and nothing else. At twelve, I'm going 26.4. At fourteen, I'm going 23.6. At fifteen, I'm going 21.5, which ranks me sixth in the country. My mother tells every Chinese American in Southern California that I'm going to the Olympics while my father just enjoys my success quietly and places my trophies over the fireplace. Sometimes watching, sometimes not. Then one day I stop growing. It just happens. There's no fadeout and no epilogue. The newspaper articles slowly start to trickle away and Chinese Americans start to focus on pre-pubescent figure skaters and violinists again. I'm still fast in the water, but no one really talks about the Olympics anymore.

Five

"Don't get into trouble."

On a twelve-year-old Saturday morning, my father wakes me up, tosses me a small paper bag, and says these four words. Okay, Dad. I won't.

I open the bag. Inside is a box of Sheik condoms from Thrifty Drug with the receipt still in the bag. $1.99. Lubricated. Reservoir end. Spermicide. "For the ultimate in satisfaction." I have no idea what they are and my father has left the room. There are football games waiting for him and cartoons for me. This is my talk on sex.

Weekday afternoons I watch Japanese cartoons on channel 52. *Kimba the White Lion* plays at 4:00. It's about a white lion cub and his adventures in the jungle with all the other animals and all the evil hunters. All kids love animals, but human beings are pretty bad, I guess. It's an all right show, but not the kind of show you can admit to watching in front of your friends. *Ultraman* comes on next, which is a step cooler but not totally cool—basically a bunch of Japanese guys wearing robot outfits and rubber monster suits, fighting each other and stomping toy houses and shooting sparklers from their fingers. What I'm really waiting for is *Speed Racer,* which comes on at 5:00. Now this is a great show. It's about Speed and his older brother Rex Racer, who unknown to Speed is actually the mysterious Racer X. Speed races the Mach 5 and gets in adventures and battles bad guys and evil empires. Every episode gets its fair share of fistfights, gunfire, explosions, and drivers careering their cars off cliffs to their blazing deaths.

The Mach 5 is a twelve-year-old's pre-pubescent boner dream car. It blows Ferraris, Corvettes, Lamborghinis and every other testosterone sandwich out of the water. Button A springs the Mach 5 into the air to jump over other cars. Button B turns on the super-grip tires that can get across any surface on the planet. Button C brings out the buzz saws to go through forests or break your way out of buildings for daring escapes. You can go underwater, put up a periscope with an in-cockpit monitor, and fly a remote-control bird that shoots out of the hood. You never have to get gas, pay insurance, or go to the dry cleaners. You never have to take piano lessons. Plus the bad guys die by the dozens while you just get knocked unconscious every other episode or so. What more can you ask for? *Go, Speed Racer, go-o-o-o-o-o!*

The show is so cool Dad forbids me to watch it. Too violent or something. Ma probably won't let me watch it either. I mean, she yanked me out of the theater during *Taxi Driver*. But Dad's never home at 5:00 anyway, and Ma can't tell the difference between *Speed Buggy, Speed Racer,* and Race Bannon from *Johnny Quest* (I mean, Ma gets "Colgate" and "Gatorade" mixed up). And why shouldn't I watch it? I know you're not supposed to shoot anybody. I know you're not supposed to run people off the road. I don't write my R's backwards like Toys Я Us and I think Ronald McDonald is retarded. Why is it adults think kids are so stupid? Like when I can drive I'm gonna plow my car over the cliff because of some cartoon? Like I'm gonna find out my brother really is Racer X? Gimme some credit. Besides, Speed's dad always forbids him to race, but Speed does it anyway and it always works out. It's like as long as the end counts, it doesn't really matter how you get there. Bad guys die or go to jail—Speed, Trixi, Sprille, and Chim-Chim end up on top. That's the way it is. That's the way it works out. It only pays to win races because hearing, "Well, you did your best, son" gets old really fast. Sooner or later you're going to stop growing and races are going to get harder to win. That's the way it is. That's the way it works out. It's just a TV show and I like it. *Okay?*

Saturday mornings are for American cartoons—*Super Friends, Fat Albert,* and *Scooby Doo*. Saturday mornings are for eating Lucky Charms, Trix, and Tony the Tiger in front of the TV. Every Saturday I eat my cereal out of porcelain rice bowls with multi-colored Chinese soup spoons, the kind with the long handles you can sip out of. Like any kid, I prefer my ice cream stirred and my cereal soggy. Pour the milk in, sink the cereal, turn on the TV and wait for it to soften and taste good. Squish it between your teeth. I watch *Fat Albert* without realizing all the characters are black until my sister asks me why they all talk so funny, and why they play in a junkyard. I don't know. I'm just waiting for my cereal to mush. I don't care why cartoon kids are black or white or why they play in a junkyard. What's it got to do with me?

I eat the cereal until I get to the sugar sludge and pink milk at the bottom of the bowl. It's thick and warm and sweet like some cross between oatmeal, Kool-Aid, and pancake syrup. Ma says to eat everything. She says there are children starving in China. I don't care about kids in China—I'm not eating pink Kool-Aid sugar sludge. And what's China got to do with me anyway? What's with all the questions? It's Saturday morning. It's kid time. Just let me watch my cartoons, eat my cereal, and read my condom instructions.

Put the condom over the head of the erect penis. Leave about 1/2" space at the end. Some condoms include receptacle ends which provide the required space to collect semen. Squeeze the end slightly to release air and avoid air pockets.

Fat Albert goes to commercial. It's one of those *Schoolhouse Rock* things that I hate. They have them for multiplication tables, science, grammar, and American history and government. They all have stupid songs that get stuck in your head that you can never get out. That's how we learned times tables in fourth grade. Every single person knew every single song. "Three Is a Magic Number." "Lucky Seven Sampson." "Hey Little Twelve Toes." Whenever we'd have multiplication tests, all you'd hear is everyone humming *Schoolhouse Rock* songs. It's like some weird elementary-school test-taking chorus.

We went to the 4-legged zoo,
To visit our 4-footed friends.
Lions and tigers, cats and dogs,
A goat and a cow and a couple o' hogs.
And 8 antelope have 32 legs cause 8 x 4 is 32.

I put down my porcelain rice bowl of uneaten Kool-Aid, pancake syrup, sugar sludge and I open up one of the foil packages. Inside is a slimy rubber ring with white stuff all over it. I put it to my nose and smell it. Smells funny. I look back at the directions.

Do not use oil-based lubricants, such as those made with petroleum jelly, mineral oil, vegetable oil, or cold cream.

I stick my finger into it and it starts to unravel. It gets long, like those wiener-dog balloons you see clowns use at lame birthday parties. I mean, why can't we just go play miniature golf or something? Does *any* kid like clowns? On TV the commercials are over and we're back to *Fat Albert*. It's the end of some episode where Russell's been getting beat up by some bullies or something and they're about to get to the moral of the show. It'll be something cheery like "Don't Fight" or "Have a Little Understanding." There's always some kind of lesson in every episode. Then the Junkyard Band plays a song about it and the show's over. Fine. Trouble is, the morals and songs don't work in real life. Because in real life the only kids who watch *Fat Albert* are the kids who get beat up. Bullies don't watch *Fat Albert*. Bullies don't listen to the songs. They're busy extorting lunch money and putting kids in trash-cans and rolling them down the stairs so Ma can take you to Kaiser Pediatrics and ask you over and over again how you can manage to get so hurt playing kickball. So what, now after *Fat Albert* all the kids getting beat up can sing the "Don't Fight" song? That's just going to get you more beat up. How are you supposed to sing in a trashcan?

Rough handling, jewelry, or fingernails can lead to damage and reduced effectiveness.

31

At twelve, I know all about getting beat up. It's old hat and I'm a veteran. From kindergarten through second grade it's part of my morning bus-stop routine, part of my public school education. It's how I learned I wasn't quite American. Five white boys in fourth or fifth grade taught me that bit of information in kindergarten on day one. At the bus stop they rip my Superman backpack and stuff my head in a mailbox, telling me there's no room for me at Mesa School. I should go back to China with Michael Loo, the other Asian kid at Mesa. *Hey maybe you and Michael Loo are fags! Maybe you guys like to suck each other's rice dicks! Do you? Huh? Do you?*

I learned all the things you're supposed to learn as a new Asian kid in a white school, and I learned them fast. Sing the "Ching Chong Chinaman" song. Sing the "Dirty Knees" song. Chinamen fight like pussies. Chinamen have little dicks. *How come you can't fight like Bruce Lee, huh? I'll tell you why. 'Cause he's a fake!* It sounds rough, but as a kid it's not that big a deal. You have nothing else to compare it to. For all I know, every kid in the world starts out half-Chinese and beaten up at the bus stop every morning. You just get used to the routine. You don't have a choice about going to school or not, and the bus stop is how you get to school. That's the way it is. That's the way it works out. I just got used to hiding my lunch money. I just learned to never answer questions, and to never let them see me cry. And I learned to never, ever hang out with Michael Loo. He's a fag.

The withdrawal should be done as quickly as possible so that the penis is still somewhat erect.

I don't get this Sheik thing and my hands are getting all sticky. Ma is yelling from the kitchen about eating my Kool-Aid sugar sludge. She's going on and on about eating all of my food and I'm so spoiled and blah blah blah blah. *In China we would be so lucky to have any kind of food. We would be so happy to eat anything at all. We would just eat it. You don't know hungry. You just eat McDonald's! You think we have McDonald's in China? When the Japanese invading we eat anything we could find and it would taste so good. Those damn Japanese! We eat bark. We eat insects. We eat flowers. And they taste so good. When you're hungry everything tastes good.*

I put the condom to my mouth and start to blow it up. It tastes bad. Must be the spermicide. I don't care how hungry I am or how much the Japanese are invading, this is never going to taste good and I'm never going to eat it.

On TV, *Scooby Doo* has just started. Fred, Daphne, Velma and the gang are cruising through some swamp in the Mystery Mobile. *Scooby Doo* means it's almost time to leave for piano lessons and I'm still in my pajamas. I haven't practiced all week and I'm supposed to be able to play "Ode to Joy" without the music today. Ma's gonna be pissed. My sugar sludge hasn't gone anywhere and it's not going to. Ma is still in the kitchen washing dishes and going off about starving children in China and those damn Japanese. Not coincidentally, there are no Japanese products in our house. We have an RCA television, a Magnavox stereo, and a Cadillac and Dodge in our garage. No Sony, no Toshiba, no Sanyo, and no teriyaki sauce. The only Japanese stuff that comes near our house is a coffee table we got as a gift from Uncle Jimmy and our weekly visits from Mr. Okada, the gardener. He's from Hawai'i. Ma says that's okay.

Dad is off in his study watching some random sports event and grading papers with another one of his red felt-tip pens. I wonder if he'll ever wonder what happened to the Sheiks or if that's just it. I wonder if he thinks I might really need these for anything other than water balloons and spermicide lip gloss. The sun is blazing down and it's already hot at 10:05 even with all the windows open. Soon Ma will realize we're late for my 10:30 piano lesson in San Dimas, and she'll throw me in the car and run red lights trying to get me there on time again. We'll be late. We always are. I'll suck at "Ode to Joy." Miss Johnson will yell at me about curving my fingers and counting aloud and practicing more. She'll tell me I'm playing the same as last week and where's the improvement? Ma will squirm with embarrassment and try to pinch me on the drive home.

David was so good. David always practiced. Why don't you practice? All day you're just daydreaming and doodling. And you watch too much TV! Come here so I can pinch you!

Nothing's worse than Ma's pinches. It's a Chinese thing, I think, at least in our family. Absolute. Corporal. Punishment. We all have horror stories about Ma's iron fingers pinching and pulling and twisting the skin at the back of our arms. It's way worse than a Dad spanking. That only hurts for a while. Ma's got a system. She pinches first. Then she pulls. Then she twists. Then she snaps. You'll have a welt for a week. Especially when she's been embarrassed like today. Then she goes extra hard. Why couldn't Miss Johnson just tell her I played the song good? Is that too much to ask? Tell her it's a new interpretation. Tell her it's a remake. I mean, do you have any idea whatsoever about the consequences here? Do you have any idea Ma's Chinese?

You think I like to drive you here so you can play bad? You think I'm a taxi driver for you not to practice? Come here so I can pinch you!

Good thing I have to sit in the back of the Cadillac for safety. It makes it hard for Ma to reach me when she's driving. It's a deep back seat and Ma's got short arms. She's got to try to watch the road, keep one hand on the wheel, and come after me in the back seat with the other. The car's going all over the place while she's trying to drive and catch me and pinch me at the same time. Ma's got her hair up and she's wearing this pearl necklace that keeps click click clicking as she flips her attention back and forth. Road. Me. Road. Me. Road. Me. Her right hand's like this cobra striking out of the front seat at me again and again while I'm sneaking and slinking and skulking, trying to avoid it. The car's drifting all over the lane and Ma doesn't even care—I didn't practice. Period. Pinch time. Who cares about traffic?

We're gonna get in an accident. I can feel it. Some cop's gonna see us and we're gonna get pulled over for reckless driving. I'm gonna freeze in the back seat while the cop walks up to her window and asks her for license, registration, and proof of insurance. I'm not moving. I'm not even breathing. What's she gonna say?

I'm trying to pinch my son. He can't play "Ode to Joy."

What is she *thinking?* The cop's gonna look at her for a second, then lean forward and stick his head in the window. He's looking back at me. I'm not moving. I'm not even breathing. Ostrich Defense. Ostrich Defense. Don't move don't move don't move don't move. The cop lifts his mirrored sunglasses and they slowly come up over his eyes and they're looking right at me. His eyes are small and his eyes are black and his eyes are . . . *he's Chinese?*

SHIT! THE COP IS CHINESE! THE COP IS CHINESE!

Don't move don't move don't move don't move—Ostrich Defense! Ostrich Defense! Head in the hole NOW NOW NOW!

It's too late and I know it. I'm just going through the motions. I'm just struggling. I watch the cop slowly bring his sunglasses down over his little eyes and I see myself reflected in the silver lenses again. I'm a little kid in a Cadillac with a seat belt on and I am *screwed.* The Chinese cop smiles at me slightly without showing any teeth and I notice for the first time the little Buddhist traffic safety thing hanging off his rearview mirror. I notice for the first time this big hairy mole on his chin and the Tag Heuer watch and all these other telltale signs. How could I not have seen? What was I *thinking?* His cop car's a slammed white Integra with tinted windows and Momo rims and a huge bored-out HKS exhaust. The windows are cracked and you can hear old-school New Order playing from his Rockford Fosgate amp at 200 watts per channel. His cop uniform is completely Tommy Hilfiger. His sunglasses are Guess! You know damn well this guy can play "Ode to Joy" with his eyes closed along with "Für Elise" and a whole slew of Chopin études, and he can do it without missing a page or messing his fade. There's a whole new penal code working now and I know exactly what he's thinking. It's all over. I'm screwed.

He leans back and smiles at my ma.

You go right ahead and pinch, ma'am. I'll clear the road ahead.

We're drifting back into our lane again and I'm still ditching Ma's hand like a bandit. There's no cop and everyone else is just clearing out of our way. I don't blame them. Ma's going off. She's snapping like a snapping turtle and I'm dodging like a rabbit in the alligator pit.

And no more TV for you! And more practice! Every day!

Oh no. Brake lights ahead. The car's slowing down. Red lights are the worst because then Ma can throw it in park and get fully turned around on me. And she doesn't fall for the "Green Light! Green Light!" trick anymore. *Got to get mobile.* The car slows down and comes to a hard, jerking stop. She throws it in park. I undo my seat-belt. Need mobility. Need looseness. I feel the need for speed. C'mon, green light. She turns herself around and SNAP! her hand's zinging out at me like some high-speed crab claw—and now she's got extended range. Feet, don't fail me now. She's on premium. She's on high octane

SNAP! SNAP! SNAP! SNAP!

and I'm all over the back seat dodging this thing like David Carradine on *Kung Fu*—I'm up against the back window. I'm back against the far door. I'm down in the floormats. She's 0 for 5 and *I am in the zone!* Come on, green light. Snatch the pebble from my hand and then you may leave. *Yeahhh baby!* C'mon, grasshopper! You can't hit what you can't see. You can't pinch what you can't catch. HEY BATTER BATTER!

SNAP!

AIRRR BALLLL . . .

C'mon, Shaolin monks! C'mon, *Jeet Kune Do!* Darts, knives, spears, bullets, what else you got? 0 for 6. *C'MONNN . . . SEVEN! Baby needs a new pair of shoes!* Is that all you got? Is that it?

You talkin' to me?

You talkin' to *me?*

You talkin' to *me?*

Well, then, who the hell else are you talkin' to—you talkin' to *me?*

Well, I'm the only one here . . .

Who do you think *you're* talking to?

Oh *yeah?*

OH YEAH?

I rule this back-seat universe. I'm Kwai Chang Caine, Mannix, and Spider Man all rolled into one. I can dodge anything. I'm catch-proof, pinch-proof, waterproof, and bulletproof, backseat piloting the Millennium Falcon straight out of the Death Star with my eyes closed and using The Force. Past red lights and piano teachers and Chinese cops in stormtrooper uniforms—sing a *Schoolhouse Rock* song to that one. No one catches me, I practice when I want to, and I don't have to eat my sugar sludge if I don't feel like it. Ship it to the starving kids in China. C.O.D. What can I say? It's my world and everyone else just lives in it.

This is kid time. This is Saturday morning. Green light.

Come here so I can pinch you!
SNAP!
(dodge) (0 for 7)

Come. Here. So. I. Can. PINCH. YOU!

ペ

You can bet horses at Del Mar all day. But no matter how good you are, no matter how fast you are—if you play anything long enough you're gonna lose. The world's got it stacked. You only get so many aces in blackjack. Cats only get so many trips across a busy street. I only get so many dodges. Next thing you know, Balboa is coming to rough you up, your credit's called, and Adrian's nowhere to be found. Probably at the pet shop.

I wanna know how come.
"You don't wanna know!"
Yeah, I wanna know how come!
"You wanna know?"
I WANNA KNOW HOW!
"Okay, I'm gonna tell ya! 'Cause you had the talent to become a good fighter, and instead you became a leg-breaker to some cheap, second-rate loan shark!"

. . .
It's a livin'.
"It's a waste 'a life!"

It's clockwork. I get home, get out of the car, walk straight to our baby-grand Baldwin, sit down, and start practicing—the welt on my arm still fresh. Over and over and over. I practice week after week, occasionally getting pinched from time to time until I can finally play whichever stupid song I'm playing flawlessly. I still hate "Ode to Joy," "Minuet in G," and "The Happy Farmer." But, like tying my shoes, I can play them with my eyes closed—even though to this day I never touch a piano. There are just too many detours involved. Too many Miss Johnsons leaning over my left shoulder when I can't remember a passage or can't find my fingering. Too much apprehension at hearing the shrill of her voice or the quiet exhale of her frustration. Too many dinner parties playing for my parents' guests and colleagues while they eat prime rib, tell three-part jokes, and chime their glasses around a Sam Maloof dining table with matching chairs. Every piece joined and sealed in black walnut. Always black walnut.

See, no matter how perfectly I could play a song or interpret a movement or move my audience, playing piano was never something I enjoyed.

What do you mean, you don't play? Of course you play.

Maybe I was looking for that kind of permission to come from someone outside

Oh, don't fool me. I remember you playing when you were this big! You were wonderful!

and maybe I was waiting for it within myself. Either way it was never received. There was never any passion or drive in my playing because I never fully believed in the truthfulness of what I was doing.

Now come on, just play some for Auntie! I love that one you play with the doo-dee-doo-dee-doo-dee-doo part. It's so beautiful. Please?

I always felt like some kind of classical robot. A good robot, sure, but still a robot.

He says he doesn't want to.

I knew Beethoven was tortured, Schumann went mad, and Liszt knocked them wild.

I don't know . . . he just says he doesn't.

I knew there was something in there somewhere, because I saw other people feeling it when they played.

You know your Auntie has to leave soon.

I saw it in their bodies and I heard the love for it in their voices. I just couldn't see it myself. I couldn't smell it. I couldn't get to the gingerbread house and all I heard was good things. It's like I had the arpeggios, the fingered octaves, and the bread crumbs, but somehow I got cast in the wrong fairy tale. I didn't want to say my lines and I didn't want to wear my costume because inside I was always a counterfeiter. My lines were supposed to be "Let down your hair" and "The better to see you with, my dear." I was born ready to say them. I was born practiced.

I wanted to stamp my foot to the downbeat. I wanted to allow my body to rock. I wanted to *groove*. I wanted to feel the music surge through me from my core, through my arms, down my hands and out my fingers like Ray Charles or Professor Longhair or Keith Jarrett or Thelonious Monk. But that wasn't part of the program. Miss Johnson didn't teach that kind of music. They were black artists. They played black music. They were more "expressive" in their interpretation. More "spiritual." To play piano properly I had to play Bach, Haydn, Mozart, Beethoven, Schumann, Chopin, Liszt. To learn a sport properly, I had to learn swimming and tennis instead of baseball and football. To learn a language properly, I had to learn French instead of Spanish—even though we lived in Southern California. It doesn't matter what makes sense and it doesn't matter what you love. Line up my 1,000 SoCal Chinese cousins shoulder to shoulder and they can all serve confidently at love–30, but they can't recognize a nickel defense. They all speak beginning French, but none of them can understand their Mexican maids. Put them behind $20,000 Steinways and they all sit down with their backs straight and their heads poised and their feet flat on the floor. Slide their benches in and they can all play the same dozen songs, and they can all play them in exactly the same way. Flawlessly. But drop them off in the middle of an urban blues bar and they're fucked. *That* I love.

J'entre dans la classe.
J'ouvre le livre de français.
Je cherche la leçon.
Je trouve la page.
J'étudie la leçon.
Je ferme le livre.

Like anything else in my life, playing well was just something I had to do. Piano was never something I liked. I certainly didn't like practicing. What kid does? But in a too-real-to-be-made-up gesture of my childhood, I still knew I had to be good at it, and I knew to be good at it you had to practice. There wasn't any other option. I think that's one of the hardest things to explain to people who haven't grown up in overachieving Asian families. It's not as simple as some *Time* magazine "Those Asian Whiz Kids" article, and it's not as complex as some genetic predisposition towards logic and sciences and classical music. It wasn't a question of whether I *wanted* to play piano well or win Junior Olympics or be valedictorian. It's just something you have to do. Perfectionism is a way of life. A way of interacting. A way of expressing and showing love and respect and gratitude. Mothers correspond with each other by talking about which son is practicing medicine and how well each niece is figure skating. Happiness is measured in degrees and patents and square footage and Advanced Placement credits. Perfectionism is above all, our family religion. And, like any religion, if you believe in it enough, it will make you content.

I never quite understood how to believe. I never understood how to close my eyes to so many other things I thought were important. As a kid I did what I was told because what other choice do you have? As an adolescent I rebelled and questioned because that's what teenagers are supposed to do. As an adult I just look back in disbelief. Things haven't changed at all in our extended family. I'm still the rebel, still the clown, still the artist, still the dreamer. I'm just more acceptable because I wear a professor's moniker and no one has to worry about me starving anymore. Or at least not as much. No one understood my need to act with abandon then and no one understands it now. No one understands touch. No one understands the joy of kissing a stranger on New Year's Eve or following the Grateful Dead or drumming on plastic buckets or surfing at daybreak. My father is the only one who even comes close to understanding giving $20 to a migrant worker or staying up until dawn, because he's the only one who's ever done it. More than that, he's the only one who's ever *wanted* to.

I work on my brother-in-law's strained back muscle for a while and he marvels at my hands. "Where did you learn to do that?" he asks. "Did you take a massage class or something?" I sing in the gospel choir in college and my relatives laugh—sarcastically mimicking some scene from a Whoopi Goldberg movie and doing their best version of sassy black-on-black Ebonics (which isn't very good, if you hadn't guessed). I drive my dog out in the country to let him fuck his heart out with every bitch in sight because we have to put him to sleep the next day. *Come on, he's just a dog.* No one understands, because everything around us gets measured only in quantifiable terms. No, I didn't take massage lessons. Yes, we really do sway with the music and clap our hands. Yes, he is just a dog. It's as if value is only understood if it's something you have to pay to learn, or something you have to charge to do. Nothing else makes sense. When my brother-in-law asks me how I learned massage, I respond by asking him how he can live his life *without* learning massage.

"I'm serious," he says.

"So am I."

Special-order me a piano teacher who starts me on hearing and improvisation instead of memorizing which dead Euro-composer belonged to the Baroque or Romantic period. Erase every nursery-room phrase that helps me remember music theory—theory that still leaves me impotent at a piano, unable to improvise a simple progression or even play along with a four-chord pop song. Grant me the confidence to remain silent after hearing the don't-you-miss-its and give me the guts to follow my own sense of smell. I smell cookies baking in here somewhere. It's just a matter of time till I find them. I mean, I'm glad Yo-Yo Ma gets off on what he does. I really am. But I'm somewhere else in the forest. The porridge isn't too hot or too cold anymore, and you can't reach me by phone. I want to be in the gingerbread house, holding a surf-green Stratocaster and playing to a Buddy Guy 12-bar, as natural as sipping water or walking across the floor. I'm watching the sweat of my left hand stain its maple neck, and snapping an endless supply of Ernie Ball high E strings. I want my pick guard scratched, my pitch perfect, and my bridge in constant need of readjustment. I want the porridge, the bread crumbs, and the Power Bars to be *juuuuust* right.

Through all those years I never understood music without the lessons and the pressure and the perfection. It was all part of the same package and I was just another worker bee in the Asian-kid-playing-classical-music factory. Practice, pollinate, make honey, and serve the Queen. Repeat. It's like I had to take kindergarten all over again. I had to relearn that there's nothing wrong with being natural, that taking naps and eating paste were okay and non-toxic. I had to discover you could do things like make music and relax and celebrate, and it was all right to do them all at the same time. What a concept. I had to figure out I could love playing music as much as making art or spoken word, and that they're all part of the same drive. And that's a good thing to find out at any time. I know I'm no Albert Collins or Albert King, but I've been out of school for a while. I'm a re-entry student. I just started today and I'm a little late. Better late than never.

violet

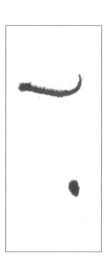

Six

My father married a Chinese woman, but he doesn't like Chinese food. Doesn't even eat rice. Picks up a menu in any random Chinese restaurant and orders the same thing every time. Fried shrimp. Steamed clams. Custard tarts. On Sunday mornings, we drive separate cars to *dim sum* because he always wants to leave early. Chinese restaurants are too noisy, he says. Like a bunch of people banging pots and pans together. I think he's right for the most part, but I kind of like the noise of pots and pans. Sounds like summers with my cousins fighting over who gets the wings off a whole chicken and who gets stuck with the head. It's all part of the experience, part of the atmosphere.

Twenty minutes on the 10 West gets us into L.A. Chinatown. I'm not a big fan, but at least my cousins and I can go off on all the trinket stores full of Bruce Lee books, plastic swords, and candy cigarettes. The plastic swords come apart at the hilts after a couple good smacks, and we end up tossing them before we even get back to the car. As far as I can tell, there is no Cantonese word for "refund." You just kiss your 99¢ goodbye and wait till next weekend. The candy cigarettes taste like some kind of milky, chalky, wannabe peppermint, but they look pretty damn cool dangling from your lips. We make sure to cut off the pink ends, because red dye #5 causes cancer. Ma read that in *Reader's Digest.*

Alan and Bobby (A and B) are always older than me. If I'm seven, they're ten and eleven. If I'm ten, they're thirteen and fourteen. It makes them always stronger than me, smarter than me, and better at everything than me. They decide where to go and what to do while I just tag along. Right now they're into the whole Chinatown gang thing. They're into looking around back alleys trying to find all the stuff we see on TV and in the movies—ninjas, *nunchaku,* silencers, protection rings. We're looking for tongs here. Secret societies. Full triad stuff. We're looking for the crime bosses with dark suits, sunglasses, and dragon tattoos. We're looking for the *cheung sam* ladies with long cigarette holders and pistols in their purses. Beats hanging around with our parents waiting for a table.

We never find any, but it's still fun to look. We cruise down side streets filled with cardboard boxes, milk crates, caged chickens and ducks. We cruise by F.O.B. dishwashers squatting on the wet pavement, smoking Marlboros on their breaks. Once in a while we'll get to see one of them actually kill one of the birds. He grabs it by the wings with one hand and slits its throat with a razor blade with his other. The bird body starts fluttering around and he tosses it into a basket so it can flutter around without getting away. Flutter flutter flutter. Flutter flutter flutter. Alan, Bobby, and me are standing around wide-mouthed while the F.O.B. guy looks over at us and gives us a smile. His mouth is cigarette-stained and every-other-toothed. He's looking right at us. Let's go.

Come here, boy. I'm not gonna hurt you.

LET'S GO!

We scamper by nervously, trying to catch a glimpse of his knuckles on the way past. Gotta check for calluses. You never know which one of these guys is actually a secret gung fu master just masquerading as a kitchen boy. It's the perfect disguise. Who would suspect? You never know which ones are good guys and which ones are bad guys. This guy could be Iron Fist or he could be Count Dante, master of "The Death Touch." You never know. Chinatown kitchen boys are all nameless and interchangeable. None of them have good teeth. They all smoke. They all squat. Permanently sweating faces. Permanently soiled aprons.

The real criminal element isn't nearly as glamorous or interesting. My cousin Denny Wong is *Wah Ching,* and he doesn't wear any cool outfits or even know gung fu. Mostly Levi's and an army jacket the few times I've seen him. Since he got older, he stopped coming to Thanksgiving and Christmas celebrations. And after word got out that Denny brought a sub-machine gun to some Chinatown thing, Ma forbade us to talk about him anymore. That's what happens in our family. People just get erased from conversations. Their names disappear and they just start doing their own thing. Pretty soon no one ever talks about the drug addict cousins. No one ever talks about the uncles in jail. No one ever talks about the suicides, the homosexuals, the divorcees, or the B+ students. Our oral history becomes an extended Chinese family tree of lawyers, businessmen, engineers, valedictorians, and doctors, doctors, doctors. You're either in the tree or you're not. And if you're not, you don't exist.

We're not supposed to mention Denny's name anymore. Ma says so. He's out. We can't even talk about a Denny's Restaurant without Ma cutting us a death glance like Count Dante. So what's the big deal? It's not like he *fired* the sub-machine gun or anything. I mean, it wasn't as if he *killed* someone. But Ma's rules are Ma's rules, and some things aren't worth questioning. Pinch, pull, twist, snap.

Time to eat. Uncle whistles for us from 200 yards across Broadway and then ducks back inside the restaurant. He's got one of those really recognizable, old-man whistles. One quick, high chirp that cuts through your central nervous system. The kind of whistle that destroys dog brains. You're running towards it before you can even think.

This is your brain. This is your brain on drugs. Any questions?

We get to the crosswalk and push the I-want-to-cross-now button. It's already been pressed, but we make sure we each push it anyway because the more you push it, the faster it goes. I push it until the light turns green, the cars stop, and we run across the street. There's a crowd of people outside the main doors waiting for tables, but our family is already seated. Somewhere in one of the three huge banquet rooms our family is starting to eat. We go in and look across a sea of black-haired Chinese people banging pots and pans together and eating potstickers off of carts. We all look for my dad because he's the easiest one to spot. If you can spot him, you can spot the family, and the sooner you do that, the sooner you eat. Dad's the only one wearing a suit. He's the only one speaking English, and he's the only one ordering white wine from one of the waiters. Chinatown waiters are all nameless and interchangeable. They all wear red. They're all rude. And they all pretend not to understand you. Looking around we spot Dad pretty easily and head over to our tables. He's the only white guy in the banquet room. Me and him together make it 1.5, but as a kid I look pretty full-blooded Chinese. Especially when I'm hanging around ABCD.

We go through *dim sum* restaurants like toilet paper. Thousands of them. I watch the Chinese population gradually spread eastward from L.A. towards Covina, with different *dim sum* restaurants getting more or less popular. Our weekend drives get shorter. First it's Golden Dragon and Empress Pavilion in Chinatown, then Deerfield and NBC in Monterey Park, then finally House of Louie and Sam Woo out by us. Ma forbids us to eat *dim sum* at restaurants that aren't outrageously busy, so we always go to whichever one is most packed and popular. She says the fast turn-around means the food is good and fresh and hot. You can't eat it cold, she says. You just can't. I can't tell if the food is any better or not, but the shorter drives are cool.

These busy restaurants are exactly the kind of restaurant Dad hates. Direct correlation. Put together a parking lot full of double-parked Mercedes, a hundred hungry Chinese pushing against one another at the door, and some girl in pasty makeup screaming Cantonese over a crackly loudspeaker and you've got your basic Dad hell. No decorum, no English, no wine list, and no quiet. Over the years Dad starts avoiding the *dim sum* runs altogether. By the time I'm in high school he's staying home and asking us just to bring him back something. I'm surprised it took this long. We bring him some custard tarts, a few *har gow's,* and a couple *siu mai's* and call it a weekend. He says thanks and eats them in front of the TV. Sometimes cold, sometimes warm. Never hot.

Weekend sports carry certain priorities with Dad. USC football holds top bill—Dad's a Trojan. Then NFL football. Then pro boxing. Then amateur boxing. Then Channel 34 Mexican boxing. Dad doesn't do basketball, baseball, or any kind of Olympic individual sport. Too much high scoring, too damn slow, or just not interested.

Dad would rather spend his down time in a quiet restaurant, or stay at home. There are always new football games starting, each one circled in the *TV Guide* several days before. If we're in the restaurant you can tell the game's about to start, because Dad gets really antsy. Sometimes he'll even go out to wait in the car and listen to kickoff on the radio. Rams vs. Patriots. Giants at Dallas. Raiders at Denver. It's funny because besides USC he doesn't really like any special team. He's not a diehard fan of any particular one. I mean, he'll root for a local team if it's in the Super Bowl or Rose Bowl or something, but basically he just likes football. He just likes the game. He'll grade his student papers with the game on. He'll read the newspaper with the game on. He'll eat cold, soggy shrimp balls with the game on. Whatever.

Once in a while Dad will put his foot down and take me and Ma to a Charley Brown's or a Hungry Tiger on a Saturday night. Something not Chinese. Places neither of us really wants to go, to eat food neither of us really wants to eat. Dad-style restaurants are quiet. They're dimly lit. They've got candles burning in these red domes with criss-crossing mesh around the glass like hair nets. They've got heavily padded chairs and extensive wine lists. Most of all, they've got their own sense of time. Chinese restaurants may bang pots and pans around, but at least stuff gets done—people move in and out, food gets served, food gets eaten, goodbye. Here everything just seems to sit around like a PBS pledge drive. It's *Close Encounters of the Third Kind.* Seriously, how can a dinner take two and a half hours?

The dinner menus are broken into sections—"Steaks," "Seafood," and "From the Broiler." Wine is served by the glass, half-carafe, carafe, and bottle. Wine stewards pour small amounts to taste before serving. By the time I'm fifteen, I've watched the ritual over and over. I've got it memorized. The wine steward sets the tasting glass on the table. Dad picks it up. He looks at the glass, then swirls the taste around a few times in the candlelight. Swirl swirl swirl. Swirl swirl swirl. Swirl swirl swirl.

This is stupid.

He brings the glass to his nose and sniffs it. Sniff sniff.

I want Taco Bell.

He puts it to his lips, slowly tilting the glass so just the tiniest amount of wine—just a touch—enters his mouth. He squishes it around with his tongue.

Two Burrito Supremes and a Taco Bell Grande. To go.

Dad stops squishing and pauses for one second. Two seconds. Then he swallows. He smacks his lips almost inaudibly a few times.

Like anyone ever sends it back anyway.

He puts the glass down on the table, turns to the wine steward and nods. The wine steward disappears into the darkness and is instantly replaced by an incredibly buxom waitress named Brandy or Carol. She's in one of these low-cut, high-skirted chambermaid outfits. Her white stockings have little black lines that go up the back. Score one point for the Dad restaurant. Buxom waitress Brandy or Carol asks how we're doing tonight. *I don't know how "we're" doing. I'd like to get out of here and go to Taco Bell. Want to come with me?*

"Fine, thanks."

Dad orders prime rib rare. Ma orders a seafood salad. I order red snapper. Entrees come with baked potato, rice pilaf, or french fries. I order a baked potato. Buxom waitress Brandy or Carol looks at me twice when I order it dry.

I'm serious. Come home with me. And leave the waitress outfit on.

"And will anyone else be needing a wine glass?" she asks.

Yes, I know it's a stretch, but he really can drink that whole thing himself.

"No, thanks," I tell her.

"And what would you like to drink?"

You in a bathtub with your waitress outfit, soaped up. I'm serious.

"Hot water."

"You mean hot tea?"

What, do I stutter? Hot water. Like in the bathtub. Soap up, already.

"No."

"Just . . . hot *water?*"

This is stupid. That thing about the point for the Dad restaurant? Cancel it.

"Just hot water."

Dinner goes as slow as the dinosaurs. We get warm bread in a basket wrapped with a red napkin. Butter comes chilled in little individually wrapped gold rectangles with cartoon cows on the side. We get salads with oil and vinegar served in two separate little pitchers. Buxom Brandy occasionally comes by as punctuation, giving us a couple more how-are-we-doings and anything-I-can-get-yous to pass the time. It keeps me paying attention, anyway. She always seems to come right when you put food in your mouth and can't respond, right when you stuff the whole salad leaf in or gnaw off a chunk of sourdough. She's probably doing it on purpose. Maybe she's been watching me eat from out of the darkness this whole time and just timing it right. I mean, has anyone seen where she and her chambermaid outfit really disappear to?

None of us is talking much. For the most part we're just chomp chomp chomping on bread and munch munch munching on salad. I mean, we live together, you know? We're a family. What's there to talk about? We know how each other's day was. We know what we've been up to. We know how work was, how school was, and how whatever hobby we're into has been going. The only thing we don't know about is the food in front of us. And bread and salad doesn't go very far conversationally. I hate butter. You know I hate butter. Don't offer it to me.

"Bread is good."

"Mmm hmm."

My salad is totally soggy and gross, but nobody asks about it. Whoever thought up the separate pitchers for oil and vinegar is an idiot. You can't tell how much to put on, so you always put on too much. I mean, you tip the pitcher and the whole thing gushes out. This stuff is *oil*. It makes little rain puddles all over your greens and it never comes off, even if you shake the leaf all over your plate and your lap and the table and the restaurant. It's shiny and slippery and reflecting rainbow prisms off a dozen red candles and bread baskets. My whole salad is a psychedelic acid trip. I might as well set it on fire. I want to dab it up with my napkin, but last time I did that I got in trouble with Dad. I'm supposed to keep my napkin on my lap, my knees off my chair, and my elbows off the table.

Hold the fork in your left hand. Now hold the knife in your right.
Cut off one bite. Not too big. Don't cut off more than one bite at a time.
Put the knife down, and switch the fork to your right hand.
Go ahead and eat it. Chew slowly. There's no hurry.
Now dab your mouth with your napkin. There you go.
Remember, there's no rush.

During the main course Buxom Brandy comes back again asking how things are going. I nod my agreement to her in between bites of over-buttered red snapper and soggy green beans. I haven't even started Mr. Dry Potato yet. Dad tells her the food is excellent and she singsongs "Goooood" and walks off with a smile. Of course the food's excellent—her big tits are held together by a tiny chambermaid outfit.

What are you supposed to say? Dad and I watch her black-lined stock-ings walking off, without saying a word to each other. We don't meet eyes or wink or anything. We don't even nudge each other under the table. You don't do things like that in a restaurant like this.

"How's the snapper?"

"It's all right."

Dad is enjoying his wine and his beef and his restaurant. His enjoy-ment isn't really visible—I mean, it's not like he's laughing or anything. But he's definitely enjoying himself. Ma and her seafood salad seem more resigned to the whole experience, just going through the motions of eating and being eaten. I'm through with my butter fish and starting in on Mr. Potatohead. I peel open the foil and start to cut into it, but the skin is too overcooked and hard and crusty to eat. Like, what, I'm supposed to eat the inside?

The PBS pledge drive is entering the red zone. *If you value your right to view quality public programming, we need your support now. It's viewers like you who keep public television available and help ensure a future of superior programs. We have open phone lines, and for a $100 membership you can be enrolled in the "Friends of PBS" club, which includes a monthly issue of . . .* I tune out and start listening to other conversations in other red booths. Some balding businessman behind me is talking about going to Tahiti or some-where. Some blonde woman in a red dress is laughing really loud at everything the nimrod across from her is saying. Jesus, even eavesdrop-ping is boring. They might as well be talking about their food. Why don't you ask her if she wants to come back to your place and try out your snapper? See if she laughs at that one, funny boy. I mean, where do they get these people in here? Do they advertise? Do they take out ads in the paper offering free food for people with nothing else to do with their lives? I mean, who comes to a restaurant to talk? How long have we been in here anyway?

Dessert carts start shooting by like ice-cream men or crack deal-ers, asking if we'd like some chocolate mousse or cheesecake or eclairs. *Pssst. Hey, kid. C'mere.* Dad eyes one of the carts and asks me if I want any. Are you serious? I don't like sweets. You know I don't like sweets.

"No, thanks."

Dad's left most of his prime rib uneaten but has almost finished his bottle of wine. He's got about half a glass left. We can never leave until his glass is completely empty, so I figure I've got a while. He always slows down towards the end. Maybe I should get some dessert. Buxom Brandy appears out of nowhere and starts to clear my plate.

"Would you like me to wrap this up for you?"

I look at my watch and the hands are spinning backwards. I must be in some kind of time warp or something. A dimension not only of sight and sound but of mind. They don't teach you this stuff in school. Everything's moving too slow or too fast. It's like my jumping jacks are a half-step out of sync. I'm looking around and all the waitresses are overweight and naked. This I don't want to see. They're serving early-bird specials of medium-rare mastodon with baked potatoes the size of basketballs. Dr. McCoy's gone insane and fallen in love with a pre-face-lift Joan Collins. Spock's wearing a beanie. Captain Kirk has hair again. He's ordered two early-bird specials. How much can this guy eat? Dad's got half a glass left in front of him and each sip is taking him six months. A swallow takes a year. I'm sitting like Rip Van Winkle watching trees grow, getting old by the second with a crumpled cloth napkin in my hands. The napkin's decomposing in front of me like some H. G. Wells time machine gig—going frayed, then torn, then tattered, then dust. I'm just sitting watching the colors change. I'm counting one second. Two seconds. *Energize* . . .

Red . . .

orange . . .

yellow . . .

green . . .

blue . . .

indigo . . .

violet . . .

Somewhere in the bar across the restaurant three go-nowhere musicians start warming up. I recognize the sax player. He's an asshole. He treats his girlfriend like shit and she keeps coming back for more. What else is new? Six months pass and Dad takes another sip. Nothing's changed. In front of me Buxom Brandy has cleared my plate without my knowing it and brought back the check. The crack-dealing dessert vendors have scuttled off into their individual cubbyholes. They're nowhere to be found. Dad's MasterCard gets picked up, processed, and returned to him for total and signature. Dad writes "INC." after tax before penciling in the gratuity, because you're not supposed to tip on tax. He totals the receipt and signs it. The receipt gets picked up and the musicians start playing the usual standards. Another six months. Leaves change and fall from the trees. Days get shorter.

The crack-dealing dessert pimps have returned with their carts for the next round. Dad says I can still get something if I want to. We'll just start another bill. It's no problem.

"You sure you don't want any? Have anything you like."

"Go on . . . have anything you like."

Seven

My father married a Chinese woman and I was determined not to do the same thing myself. Actually, "determined" isn't a good way to describe it—that suggests some kind of purposeful action. I wouldn't even call it a decision, really. A decision implies some kind of actual thought and deliberation, and there was nothing remotely close to that here. As a kid, it wasn't that I didn't personally find Asian women attractive; it was more like I didn't even know they could *be* attractive. Asian women just weren't on my radar, period. From kindergarten on, I love and desire. But this love and desire is an exclusive club. Whites only, and I'm looking for membership.

Look . . . see?

My last name's Fulbeck.

It's Welsh.

As in . . .Wales?

As in ENGLAND?

It's not so easy. As a kid I'm cursed with having dark skin and slanted eyes in a sea of white sea-bass schoolmates. It's a decade before these same slanted eyes and dark skin turn into exotic turn-ons for jaded white women searching for something different, and a decade before you start noticing countless Asian women looking at you as just possibly the perfect mix. Just Asian enough for their parents. Just white enough for them. Chinese girls are usually the worst.

You're mixed, aren't you? I can always tell.

There are dragging glances along sidewalks and shopping aisles, blatant stares in restaurants and elevators. It's something you never get past, and something you never really come to terms with. You just get used to it. You get used to seeing the warning signs and you get used to fielding amazingly personal questions from complete strangers. You learn to ridicule job applications and check-one-box-only forms as party-conversation staples. You see waiters in Chinese restaurants completely ignore you while greeting your mother and father over and over again. You watch interracial couples come up to you and scrutinize your face, trying to get an idea of how their hypothetical kid might look, and you learn to smile politely when they explain why they're doing it. Asian weddings turn into gauntlet after gauntlet of smiling Asian women and stand-offish Asian men, where your every move, glance, conversation, and smile gets analyzed and interpreted by an increasingly fascinated yellow peanut gallery. At certain times in your life you learn how to instantly spot, and instantly ignore, other Hapas, while at other times you learn the importance of seeking out your own. It all depends on where you are, what you're doing, and what you're looking for.

As an adult I slowly realize an odd phenomenon. The darker my skin gets, the more some white women show interest in me. Blondes in particular. This is a huge change from when I was a kid, where the darker my skin got, the more white girls seemed to run away. Maybe it's just a different time, a different place, and different people. Or maybe all those conversations that veer towards Russell Wong, Keanu Reeves, Brandon Lee, and Dean Caine represent more than a passing interest in current events and the entertainment industry. Maybe we've all got something deeper to work out, something more than just deciding how much time to lie out in the sun, or speculating how interestingly your genes might combine with someone else's. Maybe there's more to the whole picture than your own personal versions of affirmative action when it comes to dating.

"I've always preferred . . ."
"I've just always tended to date . . ."
"I seem to get along better with . . ."
"You know, I've never really been attracted to . . ."

I hope you don't mind me asking, but is she Asian? Asian American or Asian Asian? Full blood or Hapa? Part Chinese? Which half? Does she speak? Cantonese, Mandarin, or Taiwanese? Did she go on the Love Boat? Filipina? Malaysian? J.A.? What generation? Were her parents in camp? Does she play volleyball? Cambodian? Vietnamese? Ethnic or Chinese from Vietnam? Thai? Indian? Indian like Tomahawk or Indian like 7-Eleven? White girl? Black girl? Mexican? European? Does she shave her armpits? Doesn't that bother you? What is it you're really looking for? Do you have some kind of geisha fantasy going with your Japanese girlfriend? Just how much of you is stuck in this whole traditional Asian woman thing like any other random white guy? Do you try to speak Japanese with her? How about in bed? Do you "come" and "go"? How do you date a Korean girl without having to deal with Korean guys? When you say you prefer to date Hapas, isn't that just more of this exotification bullshit? So when you date a white girl, do you identify as white yourself? Is that a choice you're making, or are you just another Asian guy trying to prove he can get a blonde woman? What do you think of white girls who only date colored men? What do you think of Hapa men being exotic to Asian women? So was her last boyfriend Hapa? Does that bother you, or do you just figure it's just . . . coincidence?

As a kid, and even up through high school, it's so much simpler. I don't notice the questions any more than I notice who I surround myself with, or who I distance myself from. There is no curse of awareness yet. I haven't had to think about all the issues that accompany racial consciousness in this country. I haven't had to think about the possibility of choosing my own identity instead of having someone else do it for me. I haven't had to think about who I date being a political decision, and I haven't had to engage in debate based on any of my own personal actions or non-actions. It's just where I am, what I'm doing, and what I'm looking for. There's no question about *why*. It's like that Latin phrase Dad's always throwing at me—*De gustibus non disputandum est,* which is either "There's no disputing taste" or "The bus is out of gas." Life is like *Cliffs Notes* instead of the real thing. As a kid, everything's so much simpler and straightforward. I just like white girls.

Elementary school is all about simple games. Capture the Flag, Team Ball, SPUD. And simple games get rigged as easily as a Don King prizefight. Maybe easier. I mean, who hasn't cheated at Heads Up Seven Up? And the it's-only-a-game thing doesn't apply to me here. My games have stakes. My games have issues. Maybe I'm the only boy who actually likes girls or maybe I'm the only boy who admits it, but there are other things in my life besides seeing who can say "not it" the fastest. I mean, is there any point to Red Rover besides trying to get next to a girl so you can hold hands?

Here, see? If you interlace your fingers it makes it harder for them to get through.

I know what I like and I know what I want, but this simple game called elementary school is rigged. I'm convinced there's a fix. Every year I'm playing a grammar school romance slot machine, and every year a different girl's name pops up between my emotional bells, bars, and cherries. Six years running and I haven't had a payoff. I'm dropping coins like crazy. I mean, sooner or later you're supposed to win *something,* right?

Third grade. *Pull*

. . .

Bell.

Bell.

Chrissy Snyder.

Insert coin.

Fourth grade. *Pull*

. . .

Bell.
Cherry.
Lori Klink.
Insert coin.

Fifth grade. *Pull*

. . .

Bell.
Bar.
Trisha Nichols.
Insert coin.

Sixth grade. *Pull*

. . .

Bell.
Cherry.

Now let's meet our bachelorettes! A sixth-grade student from Covina, California, with pale brown eyes, Ditto jeans, and sandy-brown hair down to her butt. She's a girl on the go with no room for shy boys! Let's have a warm Dating Game welcome for Renée MacDonald!

(applause)

Slow motion. We're in the cafeteria. The first bars of Rod Stewart's "Tonight's the Night" are drifting in over the cafeteria speakers. No room for shy boys. No room for shy boys. Left foot . . . Right foot . . .

Stay away . . . from my window

I walk up to Renée and she's in the middle of a huddle of girls. The light is drifting in from the side windows and falling gently on her cheek. No room for shy boys. No room for shy boys. The huddle reacts to me like Cape buffalo, turning their heads in unison at the intruder.

"You want me to *what?*" she says.

Laura Louie is the third, and final, Chinese kid in our school. Second and a half, if you really want to be anal about it.

Kip and Laura, sitting in a tree,
K-I-S-S-I-N-G.
First comes love, then comes marriage.
Then comes baby in a baby carriage!

It gets old fast. Kids ask if we're brother and sister. Sometimes they get a little more original, saying the two of us are gonna squeeze out some rice babies or Siamese twins. Even teachers get in on the act occasionally, asking us if we want to talk to the class about Chinese New Year, or casting us as Pocahontas and Geronimo for the Thanksgiving Play. People ask me now if that sort of thing bothered me at the time, but it didn't really. I mean, it's not like the teachers knew any better. I got to wear a cool headdress and carry a tomahawk. And besides, what did you expect us to do? Be *pilgrims?*

Me and Laura are friends, but she's got it different here. Most of the kids like her pretty well. Some of the boys even have crushes on her from time to time. And she's pretty good-looking. For a Chinese and all. But the main difference is she's a *girl,* and girls don't have to take the kind of shit Michael or I do at Mesa. They just don't.

Basically, it goes like this. Even if you make it through the new-Asian-kid thing, you still get to relive a little bit of it everytime anything "Oriental" pops up. If *Kung Fu's* on TV, I take shit. If the cafeteria is serving egg rolls, I take shit. If we study WWII in class or take a field trip to Chinatown, I take shit. If any word even remotely sounding like *woo, wang, ching, chang, ding, dang,* or *dong* gets uttered, I take shit. You just learn to deal with it. And by sixth grade, I have it down.

I've finally worked most of the bugs out. I've established myself as a decent if not great dodge ball player. My hair is bleached to a lighter brown from all the chlorine, and my music collection is cruising along comfortably with a dozen Stevie Wonder, ABBA, and Steve Miller Band 45s on tap, including "Dancing Queen" and "Fly Like An Eagle." Plus I've taken care of Michael Loo the fag—he knows his place and he stays in it. The situation may not be perfect, but it's workable. And as a kid, you don't know any better anyway. If I have to take the occasional slap on December 7th or egg roll day, so what? That I can deal with. Then, one day in the middle of sixth grade, Brendan Yang moves into town.

Brendan Yang is the quintessential Asian geek. He's full-on F.O.B.—I mean, he's been here three years or something and his English is still broken. *Three years.* His family just moved out from downtown L.A. and they've taken over Kung Pao Kitchen on Grand Avenue, a take-out MSG-overload place that's always going through different owners while keeping the same menu. We used to get take-out from there, but Ma got overcharged one time and, well, you know how that goes. Brendan Yang walks into our sixth-grade class for the first time with his mom. She sees him to the door and looks inside at us. Mrs. McMullen stops talking and we all turn around to stare at the new kid. Brendan's mom gives him a kiss in front of all of us and says, "Be good boy, Brendan," leaving him standing in the doorway with his backpack. Only she's got this heavy Cantonese accent that makes his name sound more like *Blen-DAN*. Talk about setting the guy up for abuse. We're cracking up and he hasn't even walked in the door.

Blen-DAN walks into the class with his head down and goes up to Mrs. McMullen. He hands her his papers and starts to turn away, but he doesn't have anywhere to go. Doesn't even have a seat yet. So he just kind of turns back around and stands next to her while she reads over his transfer note. What a geek. Everybody's looking at this guy. He's got it all. Brand new Taiwan backpack. Stick-up hair. Leather belt. Hush Puppies. The works. The teacher's reading the note while Brendan Yang shifts his weight around nervously and adjusts his glasses. 20/7000. Mrs. McMullen is scanning over his transfer note and nodding to herself. Steve Hellmueller sitting next to me nudges me in the arm and whispers, "Hey, you know this guy?"

"I don't know him. How should I know him?"

"Chinks all know each other. You're probably related to him. Him and Michael Loo."

(Shit.)

Class, this is Brendan. Brendan Yang.

Jesus, gimme a break. This guy's sporting a full stick-up bowl cut and his Hong Kong shirt is buttoned all the way to the top Hong Kong button! Like what, I want to go through this shit all over again? I just got done with all this crap! And now Steve Hellmueller and all his Led-Zeppelin-pot-plant-in-the-closet-future-Camaro-driving flunkies are gonna start putting me and this F.O.B. together?

Brendan's new to our school today. Where do you come from, Brendan?

Brendan Yang looks up and doesn't say anything. Sheepishly, he starts glancing around the room from beneath his glasses. He spots me and makes eye contact for a second and . . .

All right.

Maybe it's an accident.

Maybe it's nerves. Maybe I'm just a familiar-looking face in a class full of white kids, but did I just see Brendan Yang nervously *smile at me* for a second?

"I told you you guys know each other!" Steve Hellmueller laughs.

All right, hold on a second.

Listen carefully.

DON'T EVEN THINK ABOUT IT. I just got done with this, okay? You're gonna have to learn something here, Mr. *Blen-DAN* Yang, and you're gonna have to learn it fast, so pay attention. I want you to keep your stupid little Coke bottle glasses, and I want you to keep your stupid little Sears Toughskin floods, and I

Everyone be sure to make friends with Brendan today.

want you to keep your stupid brand-spanking-new Hush Puppies the hell away from me, all right? You get it? Keep the hell away from me. Stop looking at me. Stop smiling. And keep the hell away from me. Understand? Get it? *Nay ming ming?*

Two days later, me and the boys have got the whole scenario constructed. I lead. I mean, I'm not planning on ever driving a Camaro myself, but whose side you gonna be on? In two days it's all legend. Brendan Yang's mom parts his hair *way* on the side and greases it down with Vaseline at night. They all work in the Chinese restaurant and when they're out of chicken broth they pee in the soup and serve it to customers. You can get food poisoning and die if you eat there because American doctors don't know how to fight Oriental diseases. They capture neighborhood dogs and fatten them up to eat them, but none of them are fat enough yet. That's why he's so skinny and pasty. Can't you tell?

Brendan Yang tried playing dodge ball with us for a while, but after a couple games of us head-hunting him he stopped. No one explained the rules to him, so he always got caught on the wrong side of the square at the wrong time. Usually right next to the guy with the ball. One time I face-pegged him so hard I knocked his glasses off, leaving two red welts on his face where the nose piece got pushed in. I got a round of high-fives for that one. Now at recesses Brendan Yang just sits off by himself under the tree. He plays with bugs in the dirt or something with his Hush Puppies and Sears Toughskins and his backpack. Maybe he just beats off. Whatever. Serves him right.

We walk by him on the way back in.

Hey, Chinaman! What's your name? "Cum Suck Yu?"

Brendan Yang never really makes it out of the hole. He spends his recesses under the tree for the rest of the school year; he spends his lunches at his own private bench, eating leftover chop suey out of a recycled take-out box. The next year he transfers out and we barely notice. Probably to another school, another MSG-overloaded Chinese restaurant, and a brand new set of class bullies. He probably gets into computers or some kind of technology when he grows up, and he's probably making a hell of a lot more money than I am right now. Maybe he's gotten a new wardrobe and a better haircut and laser corrective eye surgery. But probably not. The weak ones don't survive in nature. What's the big difference here? I mean, sure, I felt a little bad about it from time to time during that year, and sometimes I feel a little bad about it now. But overall I figured it was just his turn. I mean, I had to go through it, so what do you expect me to do? If you can make it out—great. If you can't—don't come running to me. It's not *my* fault.

㇏

"You want me to *what?*"
Stay away . . . from my back door, too
"Dance," I say, feigning irritation. "You wanna dance or not?"
Renée MacDonald doesn't say anything. Not a "maybe later." Not even a "no, thanks." Just disappears like magic into the herd of Cape buffalo wearing tank tops and designer jeans. They're all huddled together staring at me. I've been here five seconds and it's done. No— see, that's not fair. My games have stakes here. My games have issues.
"Go ask Laura!" one of the larger buffalo screams over the music. She's a big cow. Probably the alpha. She's got a puka shell necklace and a gap between her front teeth big enough to drive a Land Cruiser through. Game always get cocky when they're out of season. No matter what firepower you're packing, they sense when you're harmless. The herd turns from me in unison and starts grazing and gossiping again, heads down in the grass. Fine. I walk off with my hands in the front pockets of my white OP corduroys. Velcro wallet, comb in pocket. The spinning silver-ball thing is casting colored tracer bullets across the cafeteria. Left foot . . . Right foot . . .
I go down past another line of girls towards the safety of the punch-bowl. Every other girl looks like she's trying out for a sixth-grade *Charlie's Angels*. Feathered hair. Macrame shoes. If they had breasts, they'd be in tube tops. No matter where you go, it's all the same. In the eighties they'll be *Breakfast Club*. In the nineties they'll be *Friends*. The punchbowl is surrounded by the same guys who are always around it. The kinds of guys who'll stand around this thing the entire two hours

of a school dance. Longer if they could. It doesn't matter what age they are or what's going on around them. We could be at our 25th reunion and these guys would still be punchbowling. These are the guys spending way too much time online. These are the guys standing in line for adult film-star autographs. These are the guys going to *Star Trek* conventions in their forties. Vulcan ears. Phasers. Everything.

Can you make it out to "John," please?

Laura and I are each other's "safe" date. Nothing more. Nothing less. It's understood. We're marked. We're wearing arm bands and security badges. Everyone stays real still and no one gets hurt. Everything's gonna be okay. Sure, maybe we'd both rather be dancing with someone else, but dancing with another Chinese is still better than standing around the punchbowl talking baseball cards and Romulan. Sometimes you have to just take what you can get, and we're both pretty far down the food chain. It's like taking your cousin to homecoming. It's fun. It's safe. But at the end of the night the person across from you is still your cousin. It's like fishing for stockers in some city park pond, and we both know this cafeteria's an ocean in comparison. I look around me and a hundred sixth-grade anglers are throwing iron all around me and getting hit. Tady 45's, U.F.O.'S, and Krocodiles. Everyone's on. Diamonds, candy bars, and spoons stream by me through the cafeteria on 12-lb test and strobe lights, and I don't even have a line in the water. Everything around me is spinning and flashing and shiny and glistening. Everything around me is reflective. All I see is me.

Badges? We ain't got no badges. We don't need no badges. I don't have to show you any stinkin' badges!

Clinch knot.

Pass the line through the jig eye.

Double back. Make five turns around the line.

Pass the end through the first loop, then through the large loop.

Slide coils down.

Cast and retrieve. Left foot . . . Right foot . . .

Now, when you go up there, I don't want you to be the PG-13 guy where everybody really hopes he makes it happen. I want you to be the Rated-R guy. The guy that you're not too sure where he's coming from. The guy you don't really know if you like or not. Now, get over there! You're a bad man! You're a bad man! You're a bad man!

I walk up to Susie Levy—a Jewish girl with dark, kinky hair, big eyes like a sparrow, and a nice personality. She's sitting with a friend, sipping watered-down fruit punch.

"You wanna dance, Susan?"

"Okay."

You are so money. You don't even know how money you are.

Susie Levy and I dance the magically awkward slow dances that only sixth graders can do. My arms are on Susie's waist, touching her shirt. Tight but not too tight, and nowhere below the beltline. School rules. Her arms are at my shoulders, touching but not too heavy. Like any other couple out there, we're barely contacting each other, trying to think of something to say as we rock from side and side, each step turning clockwise like wind-up plastic robots. Left . . . right . . . turn. Left . . . right . . . turn. Usually I'm pretty busy just trying to stay off the girl's feet and keep my hands from sweating through her shirt. But this time I've got more important business going on. I want all the Cape buffalo in all their tanktops and designer jeans seeing us having a good time out here. A really good time.

"You like this song, Susie?"

"It's okay."

"Yeah."

Okay. That topic's used up and the song's not even half over. They're just getting to the bridge and if I can't pull off having a great time and entertaining Susie Levy, it's over. I'm done for. I might as well slink back to the punchbowl, put on my Vulcan ears, and call it a life. I might as well join Thespians or some Japanese animation club and officially declare myself a loser. Come on, man, think. I want this girl having fun. And, most important, I want this girl *looking* jazzed. Pull it together. Don't step on her feet, don't sweat through her shirt, and think of something to say. Something funny. Something surprising. Something sophisticated. Left . . . right . . . turn. Left . . . right . . . turn. Left . . . right . . . turn.

"My brother knows Rod Stewart."

So it's a lie. These are battle conditions. Sue me.

"Really?" she pipes up.

Susie pulls her head back to let her big sparrow eyes see me, but her hands stay on my shoulders. Nice. I think her hands may even be pressing a little harder, actually. She's saying something about Rod Stewart being so cool and what a cool accent he has and what a cool voice he's got and I love his hairdo and blah blah blah blah blah. All I see is her head tilted back and her smile. It's pure Kodak moment. Frame it and put it on the mantel.

I keep talking Rod Stewart and Susie keeps looking up, smiling her orthodontically correct smile and asking your typical Rod Stewart questions. How tall is he? Do you ever get to see him? What's he really like? I'm just keeping us smiling. I cheat glances over Susie's dark, kinky, Jewish hair and spot the pretty-girl Cape buffalo posse still giggling and talking with one another against the wall. Susie's pretty short, so it's easy to see over her. The top of her head only comes to my shoulders. With all the lights flashing around, I can't quite make out their faces. I *think* they're looking over. I mean, they could be . . .

"Can he get me an autograph?"

"Autograph? Sure."

"Cool!"

The conversation continues like you'd expect. I dig holes and try to bury them. Susie smiles away. The song hits its repeated chorus and Rod's gravelly voice belts out each word like it's his last. We throw together a few final slow-motion clockwise spins during the extended fade out, and I use each to look over more carefully, hoping to catch Renée MacDonald's eye or maybe even that stupid alpha female with the puka shells and front-tooth gap. But I don't see them. I don't see anything. It's like the top of Susie's head is the water line and my eyes are just clearing it. I'm kicking frantically just trying to stay up in here. What's underneath me anyway? What's holding me up? Susie's smile and sparrow eyes are lit up somewhere beneath my field of vision, talking about autographs and posters and maybe even concert tickets if only her dad would let her go. All I'm saying is yeah yeah yeah yeah and all I'm hearing is cool cool cool cool. The spinning ball cascades colored squares around the room while a hundred sixth-grade anglers are still tossing iron all around me like there's no limit. Greens, blues, golds, silvers. Everything's flashing and shiny, but I'm just not interested anymore. Maybe the water's too cold or there's a full moon. Maybe I'm too tired or too full. Maybe I've already got my hands full.

The song ends and Susie's hands come off my shoulders. Twenty-five sixth-grade girls say "thanks" in unison and run off to the punch-bowl together like grunion. The *Star Trek* boys get ready to offer twenty-five cups of punch that will all get politely refused. Susie prances off to her friends and starts telling her latest Rod Stewart gossip. Boom boom boom boom boom. Each friend tells each of their friends. And so on . . . and so on . . . and so on . . . It's a Clairol Herbal Essence commercial. Next to me, Laura is saying thanks to Danny Baxter the future punk rocker and eventual heroin addict. I never even saw her next to me on the dance floor. I'm sure she never saw me either.

Eight

Asian girls hit my conscious radar not long afterwards, and they hit it hard. Like Zeros on December 7th, I discover the enemy too late. I get caught flat-footed. By the time I hear the motors, by the time I see the flames, it's all over. I run around limbless, confused, and ready for retaliation without an enemy in sight. I can't even find my glasses. I just punch air. Before I know it, all I've got left around me are ruins to pick through and a long, long process of rebuilding.

It happened during an age-old ritual. My schoolmates and I had snuck into our treehouse to look at dirty magazines on a hot summer afternoon. Every boy in America owns pornography. So do most men. We keep the magazines under our mattresses and way, way back in our closets. We hide them in chests of drawers and comic book collections and clubhouses as if no one has ever thought of that before, and no one could ever discover them. We don't keep anything really skanky in our treehouse—no liquor store *Hustler* or *Swank* or *Gent*-type beaver-hunt stuff that could gross out even the most horny American male. We have more of the "acceptable" adult material. The stuff a guy could argue he was buying for the articles or the sports commentary or the fashion advice and actually almost be able to pull it off. The stuff that won't give your mom an instant heart attack when she finds it. We're out of elementary school and about to enter junior high in the fall. It's any random weekday. No school, no job, and no piano lessons. Swim practice is over and it stays light until 8:30.

Let's do it.

The stash in our Holt Avenue treehouse is mostly just old *Playboys* we'd get out of the garbage dump or score through the ultimate boyhood scam, the Cub Scouts recycling drive. Didn't you ever wonder why we always volunteered? Together we had issues going back ten years or more, tattered and torn. High clout went to the occasional *Penthouse*, which always included some kind of soft-core sex spread— sometimes even girl-on-girl. That never did much for me, but all the other guys seemed to go crazy for it. I think they just didn't like having to see naked men in the hetero spreads.

"Sick! I don't want to look at some guy's butt!"

Sitting in Mike Grabowski's treehouse with four, maybe five other white boys, we go through the ritual. Mike deals us each an issue off his collection like poker cards. It's an instant feeding frenzy. The air is high and your fingers are tingling. As soon you get one in your hands you're flipping through it like gangbusters looking for the pictures. Mike flings me an ancient, tattered April '67 and I'm off to the races. I know by touch how to bypass the articles and advertisements and editorials. *Playboy* never changes. You just feel for the centerfold crease, back your fingers up a few pages, open up and go. It's like a Christmas present. Ribbons, bows, wrapping. What's it gonna be?

I pop it open and pull out the centerfold. I look down at my new toy, and the woman's Chinese.

What a rip-off.

I mean, this is a joke, right?

"Anyone wanna trade?" I ask. But no one answers. The other guys are too immersed in naked girls and their own mini-corduroy boners to respond.

"Come on, I've seen this one before," I lie. "Someone trade with me . . . Mitch! Lemme see that one!"

"No," he says without lifting his eyes.

"Come on! Lemme see it! I'll give you this one!"

"No!"

I don't have time for this. I pull Mitch's July '72 issue out of his hands and toss him April '67 before he can react. It's like switching bones with an angry dog. Do it fast enough and they never know what hit 'em. The issue flies open and lands on his lap with the Chinese-girl centerfold sticking out.

Jesus, now I had to see it again.

Mitch looks down at Miss Chinatown and forgets his argument. He picks up his new doggy chew and almost instantly returns to his mini-corduroy boner mode—eyes locked in and glazed over, face completely relaxed, mouth slightly agape and chomping away. Whatever. To each his own. I got enough of a glimpse to get sick the first time. She had brown nipples. *Brown nipples!* You're gonna chomp on brown nipples? Gross. She's got that flat Chinese nose and black hair and yellow skin. Even her pose is full John Robert Powers you-too-can-be-a-model crap and she's wearing pearls. *My ma wears pearls.* Enough already. I don't need to see this. I don't want to see this. I don't have to see this. I might as well be hanging out with Michael Loo or Brendan Yang and playing with our little rice dicks in the backyard. Toss me a scrap once in a while. I might as well be wearing Hong Kong polyester pants and ordering roast duck and almond gelatin in the same red-chaired Chinese restaurant every day. I mean, why don't you just make fun of me for the rest of my life while I can't get a date? Why don't you just beat me up right here and now?

Throw me a frickin' bone here.

Nobody's paying attention. Nobody's looking. Everyone is chomping and chewing and gazing and flipping pages. I look into my hands at July '72 and I suddenly feel a little better. Back on autopilot and I'm back in the game. The feeding frenzy is on and I've been missing out. Time to catch up. I'm feeling for the centerfold crease again, backing my fingers up a few pages, opening it up and going. Haven't lost a step. I look down at my second chance and Miss July is Carol O'Neal.

Merry Christmas.

She's gorgeous. She's everything my twelve-year-old mind wants in a woman—big hair, big eyes, big breasts with pink nipples. White. My mini-corduroy boner has its direction set for the next decade and I'm comfortable with it. Issue? There's no issue here. The only issue I know is a five-year-old copy of July '72 and I got it in my hand. It's under control. It's just where I am, what I'm doing, and what I'm looking for. I know my enemies and I know my friends. I know about feeding frenzies, war games, surprise attacks, double agents, and dogfight maneuvers. Radar on, I'm choosing sides. I do it because I have to. And I do it because I can.

Asian girls?

I'm not attracted to them.

They're . . . I don't know, too much like my sister. Or my mom.

Words are cheap. I never say Asian girls are too much like me, or too much like part of me. Sometimes it's too hard to ask yourself questions. Sometimes it's easier to just go on. What is it that makes you immediately turn away from your own reflection? Why is it I wanted to immerse myself in milk? Pouring a vanilla veneer over every aspect of my life all the way into adulthood—from my clothes to my speech to my tastes? Up to and including whoever and whatever I wanted to put my tongue, finger, or cock inside. Where is the Peking-duck taste on a woman's skin and what makes me so sure it'll be there? I've never tasted or even smelled it myself. I just know it's there. I hear things.

As a kid I spend hour after hour in mirror after mirror—trying to pinch my nose together to make it less wide, or pulling it forward to make it less flat. All it does is swell up even bigger. Stupid, my sister says. What does she know? In junior high I listen to Cheap Trick and Foreigner while every other guy with blond hair gets a perm. My own once-almost-blond hair has given way to its Cantonese genes and turned dark brown, making me resort to monthly doses of Sun-In like a million Japanese tourists with orange hair and bad teeth. At home I watch my nephew use Scotch tape to make himself a pair of double eyelids, and I see him looking over in envy at my own. I don't blame him. I don't even blame the Japanese tourists. It's like we've all been to the same place and we've all bought the same shirt and worn it on the same day. We want to pretend we didn't, but everyone can tell. We're part of the same team, part of the same unit. Just different ranks. My Chinese American nephew outranks the Japanese tourist with orange hair. I outrank them both.

It's too easy to blame childhood fights or a lack of positive media roles. It's too easy to get angry and write letters to the editor. Everybody was the only Asian at their school. Everybody got beat up. Everybody had to choose sides. Pop-psychology soundbites, like assimilation and projection and aggressor identification and displacement, only get you so far. It's too easy to claim some Asian American Studies course or *The Joy Luck Club* as your wake-up call to identity. It's not that simple. I mean, where were you before your awakening?

I hope you don't mind me asking, but what did you do to lighten your hair? Doesn't that damage it? Did you get your nose done, too? How about your eyelids? How much did it cost? Did it hurt? Have you ever considered colored contacts, like Kristi Yamaguchi? How exactly do you identify yourself anyway? How do you answer the question "What are you?" When someone calls you "exotic" do you consider it a compliment or an insult? Do you notice when another Asian walks in the room? Do you gravitate towards them or do you move away? When you pass another Hapa on the street do you make eye contact? Or do you just study the intricacies of your shoes? By the way, how are your shoes now? Any scuffs? Who's the first person you see when you wake up in the morning? And who's the first person you want to see? What's the first thing you taste? What's the first thing you want to do? If she asks you to stay in bed instead of surfing, what's your call? Do you rush Charlie's Point anyway? Do you do it because you can? Or because it allows you to go both ways?

Answer any way you like. Use all the words you want. They're always available. You can get them cheap, sometimes even second hand. Half the time they're on sale at outlet malls in random go-nowhere towns. They're in there somewhere between all the other stores you've never considered walking into—Bugle Boy and American Tourister and

The Leather Loft. Walk in proudly. Use your rank and take big steps. Walk in playing Wagner and lay waste every Peking duck in sight with Ching Chong 00 buck and 20mm cannon. Leave your calling card on the bodies so they'll know what hit 'em. Leave it on their single eyelids and their backpacks and their Hush Puppy outlet bags. Leave it for the tide coming up in six hours, and leave it for you to look back upon when you wonder how it was you ever became who you are. Read the cards. For twenty years running I chose sides—dropping cards, smiles, and phone numbers without even the slightest thought of touching an Asian girl. Twelve years later I can finally write about what it was like, and maybe about what I learned. It's almost too easy. As an adult we're allowed to use cheap words. I can say I went through stages. I can say I matured. I can say I grew up. I can say rank never really mattered. If you listen closely enough, you can almost believe the air.

I love the smell of white girls in the morning.
Smells like . . . victory.

daffodil

Nine

A lot of people talk about their first love with a sense of nostalgia or reminiscence. They say "My first love?" and smile inwardly, drifting back to some nervous delivery of hand-picked wildflowers or an innocent kiss behind the bleachers or a Spin-the-Bottle game. Older people fill with warmth thinking about it, and sometimes a tiny bit of sadness, as if this first love carried with it some kind of precious natural charm that spoiled with age and maturity. A charm you can never find again. Kind of like sea life you pick up along the rocks and surfline. The ones that catch your eye and draw you to them with their movement or their shape or their sound or their color. Sandcrabs, limpets, urchins, seastars. Some are beautiful and full of life in your hands, but when you take them home they die. Others immediately sting your touch. A few follow you home and slowly poison you. You never know. I guess that's why nature has warning signs. Black and yellow on wasps, rattles on rattlesnakes, raised tails on stingrays and scorpions. If you pay attention, you'll be fine. If you don't, whose fault is it?

I don't talk about my first love with a sense of nostalgia. I talk about it as something that just happens, something you learn from. Her name is Carly. We meet at some Friday night high-school football game. South Hills vs. Northview at District Field. She's visibly stunning. Kind of a Brooke Shields look, but bigger hair, bigger eyes, and bigger breasts. Just what I, like any red-blooded sixteen-year-old American guy, am looking for. At sixteen you have no other idea. She has a huge smile, the kind that makes older men feel like much older men. She's fourteen going on twenty-eight. I'm sixteen going on sixteen.

I'm feeling quite in control of myself. Starting out my junior year, I'm doing well in school, swimming, and dating. What else is there to life? I have a nice car and a good circle of friends, though we spend too much time demeaning others for our own enjoyment. We stand around at break, waiting to make fun of the next person walking by.

Check out his pants. I swear that guy's gay.

It's open season on anyone and anything around us, and we've all got hunting licenses. We've lettered and we're college bound. What else are we supposed to do all day in high school? Be nice? Make friends?

Sometimes when there's a shortage of prey we become bored, turning cannibalistic and picking on our own. Anything's game—

clothes, behavior, body posture, whatever. You know what they say. All work and no play makes Jack a dull boy. Living in constant fear that we might be embarrassed by one another, we learn to dress the same, stand the same, talk the same, and listen to the same music. Complete herd mentality. Strength in numbers. Strength in anonymity. We're zebras in 501s and Nikes.

It's the second quarter and South Hills is up 3-0 and about to attempt another field goal. They're running a wishbone offense as usual. Option left. Option right. Option right again. *Borrrring.* I turn around and see Carly sitting a couple rows behind me in the stands.

Oh my God.

She's beautiful. Long, brown, wavy hair put up high in a pony tail and tied with a red ribbon. Huge green eyes. *Green eyes.* Tight jeans, a white oxford shirt, and a pale-yellow cardigan. It's 1981, remember? Everyone's got their own copy of *The Official Preppy Handbook.*

The kick goes up and it's good. 6-0 now. Ask me if I care. Everyone jumps to their feet and starts cheering like crazy. Jesus, now I can't see. *Sit down!* The cheerleaders start up the "We got spirit" thing. C'mon, everybody!

We got spirit! Yes we do!

We got spirit! How about you?

Everyone's into it. Gimme a break, it's a stupid field goal. What do you expect running the wishbone? Touchdowns? I stand up, still turned around, and spot Carly again.

We got spirit! We got pride!

We got it all on—our side!

I'm locked in and silent. I notice the way she moves and dances and cheers. I notice the shape of her body, the sound of her voice yelling, the color of her eyes and skin. She sees me staring and we smile at each other across the football bleachers. We try to yell some insignificant conversation, but the cheerleaders are we-got-spiriting so loud we can't hear.

We got spirit! We got cheer!

All our spirit is—right here!

Finally I wave her over. Carly climbs down the five rows between us. 5 . . . 4 . . . 3 . . . 2 . . . each step she looks better than the next. Nice. I feel every other male in the bleachers watching her come to me and it feels good. On the last step, she puts her hand on my shoulder for balance, and our bodies rub against each other as she squeezes in. Excellent. She's smiling big. I notice the swell of her breasts beneath her pale-yellow sweater, her cascading hair past the middle of her back, her full lips, and tight 501s. I'm smiling bigger. I realize she is much more beautiful than I first noticed and feel my cock rise with its head rubbing against the roughness of my own jeans. Shift-and-adjust time. There we go.

We sit laughing and touching shoulders throughout the game. We go through some meaningless conversation to get to the essentials.

Name

Year in school

No boyfriend

Occasionally her hand grabs my arm in a mock display of audience excitement that's really an excuse to touch me. I like it. Almost involuntarily, I instantly tighten my arm upon her touch. Not so tight as to be obviously flexing, but tight enough for some pubescent display of masculinity and physical prowess. I work on my arms a lot. Can you tell? Touch me again.

Touch me again.

ት

The night progresses like any John Hughes high-school film fantasy. I don't know if we won the game or not. Probably did. Does it matter? Carly and I meet up at the after-game dance in the school cafeteria. It's decorated with green and gold streamers and crepe paper bells. School colors. I get it. After talking for a while, we make up individual excuses to go outside and meet up again at my locker. I tell the Dean of Boys it's too hot in here and I want to put my letterman's jacket away. I'll be right back, okay? He nods. I don't know what Carly says to the Dean of Girls, but I see her leaving through the other door. Bingo. This message will self-destruct in five seconds. Good luck, Jim.

Red touch yellow, kill a fellow.

We meet up again at my locker, alone this time, and have our first kiss. It's good. Really good. Too good. What's wrong with this picture? She's fourteen with the body of an eighteen-year-old. Everything's big where it's supposed to be. Everything's small where it's supposed to be. I'm young and healthy with my arms around this beautiful girl. I just kissed her and I'm gonna kiss her again. We're leaning against my locker on a warm, windless Covina night, with her head buried into my chest and my hands resting on the pockets of her faded jeans. I don't think it gets any better than this. I mean, I'm waiting for the first bars of "Good Vibrations" to come wafting out of the darkness. I'm waiting for Ed McMahon to come ring my doorbell with a giant check in his hands. I'm waiting for Ma to wake me up and tell me I'm late for school.

Ah . . . I love the colorful clothes she wears,
And the way the sunlight plays upon her hair.

We go back into the cafeteria and rejoin the dance, holding hands. The Dean of Boys sees us walking back in together and smiles at me. He knows what's up. He was young once. Maybe he still kinda is. Maybe he's sporting a full boner, like I am right now, and its wedged underneath his plaid polyester pants. I doubt it. Actually, if he were, that would be a little scary.

Inside it's full '80s night. Oingo Boingo, Flock of Seagulls, Devo, the works. None of us can dance, but none of us knows any better so we have a blast. I mean, it's not as if someone can pogo any better than anyone else anyway. We all look equally stupid. Carly's breasts bounce when she pogos. Her hair flies up and down. She's got a great ass, and from what I can tell from two minutes' worth, the girl knows how to kiss. I keep thinking to myself "What's wrong with this picture?" and I can't think of anything. So I just keep dancing and watching her and smiling.

We keep going until they close the dance at 11:00. The DJ's packing up. We walk outside, soaked with sweat.

"You need a ride home?" I ask.

"Yeah," she smiles.

We get in my Volkswagen Scirocco and I drive her home. She lives out of the school district, across the railroad tracks. She says her mom lies about their address so she can attend South Hills. It's a better school than the one around her neighborhood. That's for sure. Her parents are divorced and she lives with her mom. Mom works in some gift shop at a local hospital selling flowers and stuffed animals and cheesy cards. Stuff like Garfield and Paddington and Ziggy. Stuff I hate. Carly doesn't know where her dad is. Hasn't seen him since she was a baby. We get back to her block and no one's home at her house. It's 11:30.

"My mom must be out."

Warning. You are too close to the vehicle. Step back.

I drive down the block and park behind a 7-Eleven that gets robbed every other week. There's always some story about it sandwiched in the local paper between city politics and drought warnings. I put the car in first gear and put the handbrake down. Carly and I lean across the Recaro seats and make out. The girl's got no inhibitions whatsoever about kissing. Full tongue extension—sucking, biting, everything. Most important, she does it with her eyes closed. Okay, big deal, so I checked. I had to. Every time I opened my eyes with my last girlfriend (who incidentally was my first girlfriend), she was either staring right back at me or looking straight up at the ceiling like *Night of the Living Dead.* That's just too weird.

Carly's eyes are closed and she's way into it without a warmup. She's sucking my tongue and rolling hers around it like a popsicle. Go ahead. One of her hands is pressed into my back. The other is tucked under my inner thigh and squeezing slightly, six inches to Broadway and I can walk there from here. My hands are as far as they're allowed to be and I'm pushing at the borders. The guards are nervous. Her sweater pulls off her shoulders and I can see the tops of her tits pushing through the third button of her shirt. Jesus. Everything's falling into place, so what's wrong with this picture? I can't think of anything and I don't want to think of anything. I'm just waiting for the Beach Boys to cue up again. Everything is fine. Everything is just fine. Leave me alone and let me listen to my music.

At this point, as with any new woman, it is a time of amazing discovery. It's a time of complete eagerness and anticipation—of their movements, their intimates, their tastes. You wonder how she moves, what her panties are like, how she sweats, how she moans. But, more important, this is a time of potential. You wonder about other things. A little voice pops up in your head out of nowhere. You can't stop it. You can't restrain it. You can't ignore it. You've got no control over it whatsoever. The little voice is jumping up and down like a kid in the candy store, yelling *This is it! This is it! This is it!* while you're trying to act cool and nonchalant and just keep your head on straight. You try to shut your ears, but it's already inside. I mean, this thing's got the sub-woofer cranked to eleven and it's shaking the walls of your brain. *This is it! This is it! This is it!*

Shhhhhh!

All right, just relax.

Might be. Might not be. Probably isn't. I mean, the odds are

(This is it! This is it! This is it!)

Relax.

Think about something else. Bio paper due Monday. 10 percent of your grade. Venomous reptiles and marine life.

The highly venomous coral snake is distinguished from its more harmless relatives by its color pattern, which consists of red and black bands separated by yellow stripes

Stay cool. Don't rush her.

Take it slow.

as opposed to the non-venomous king snake, which displays red and yellow bands separated by black stripes.

Carly's mouth moves to my neck. Then my

(ear?)

. . .

. . .

. . .

She's beautiful.

Try not to think about it.

" . . . it tickles . . ."

Shhhhhh.

While both snakes appear quite similar, you can avoid confusion and possible injury

Just relax.

by remembering a

Relax.

simple rhyme.

Relax . . .

There you go.

Isn't that better?

(You like that?)

Red touch yellow, kill a fellow.
Red touch black, venom lack.

ᠵ

Carly's lips and tongue move back to my neck. My ear feels her leave and wants to chase after her like a puppy. *When are you coming back? You're coming back, aren't you?* She nestles her head above my collarbone with her hair falling on both sides of my right shoulder like a blanket. I feel some of it touching me under the collar of my shirt. I can feel her hand tucked under my inner thigh against my jeans. Carly's mouth is sucking my neck hard, but not too hard. She's running that fine balance of getting right to the point of a hickey without leaving a trace. I feel her lips suctioning and pulling, and her tongue caressing me between them. Everything about me feels alive. Her lips are completely confident and in control. No questions asked. No prisoners. I feel my blood vessels trampling over each other trying to get to the surface and meet them like crazy girls at a Beatles concert. They're speeding on the freeways and ignoring one-way streets trying to get to the surface and breathe. All I want to do is breathe. *John! Paul! George! Ringo!*

Deal with it.

Open your eyes. You're sixteen. You just met her at a high-school football game, all right? You had a couple dances and now you're parked outside a 7-Eleven making out. She's fourteen. *Fourteen.* Yes, she's phenomenal-looking. Yes, she knows how to kiss. Yes, she's

Stingray poison is protein-based toxin, with victims often describing the pain as burning rather than stinging. Immediately immerse the wound in hot water. The temperature should be as hot as the victim can tolerate without scalding. To avoid stingray encounters, always keep both feet firmly planted in the sand.

(Burning rather than stinging . . .)
I've got it.

"Can I see your purse?" I ask.
Carly's eyes open and she comes off my neck. "What?"
"Your purse. Lemme see it."
"What for?"
"Just let me see it."

Carly hands over her little purse and I open it. I know what's wrong with this picture. This girl is too good-looking and too sexy and too phenomenal to not be totally screwed up somewhere. She's got to smoke. I'm sure of it.

I open up her purse while Carly just sits there silent with her hands between her legs. Maybe she's upset. I don't know. I don't care. I'm waiting to find the Marlboros or the Camels or the Winstons. It's just a matter of time now. She knows it and I know it. I'm gonna find cigarettes in here. Then I'm gonna drive her back down the block to her house, pull into her driveway, say goodnight, and say goodbye. That's it. Get out early before the market crashes. You know what they say. Bears make money. Bulls make money. Pigs get slaughtered. If she's smoking at fourteen, she's got to be about insecurity and fitting in and white trash. I got better things to do with my life. Protect what you've got and get out while you can. My fingers enter her purse and I start pilfering through it in the dim 7-Eleven backyard security lighting.

Lip gloss . . . gum . . . makeup . . . wallet . . .
There's nothing here.
(She doesn't smoke?)
(What's wrong with this picture?)

"What are you looking for?" Carly asks.

I pull my fingers out quickly.

Upon hearing a rattle, immediately stop all movement. Locate the snake and slowly back away. Remember, do not run.

"Uh . . . I was looking for cigarettes," I say confused. "I was seeing if you smoke . . ."

If no help is available, make two small incisions over each puncture wound and attempt to suck the venom out. Be careful not to ingest any of the poison. Rattlesnake venom is considered extremely lethal. Seek medical attention immediately.

Carly's just sitting there looking at me. I'm waiting for a reaction, but there isn't any. No swelling. No redness. Nothing. She's just sitting there beautiful. I don't get it. I've checked and double-checked my figures. Everything adds up, but nothing makes sense. Somehow the multiplication tables don't work anymore. What's wrong with this picture? I'm punching in facts and figures on my calculator, but everything's coming up gibberish. The keys are all goldfish instead of numbers. How are you supposed to use this thing anyway? It's like we're in the middle of some crazy Soviet plot for world supremacy or something. All those *Schoolhouse Rock* songs I memorized? Wrong lyrics. We've been sitting around singing 8 x 4 = 48 like little math nazis and no one suspects a thing. No one questions anymore. Everyone has just adapted to things being crazy. They're so used to it they think it's normal. A drunk driver offers you a ride and all you do is smile and get in. Your bedroom window gets broken and all you do is make coffee. A man opens himself up to you and all you do is make believe. What is going on?

Carly isn't yelling. She's not angry and she's not leaving.

I don't get it.

(She doesn't smoke?)

I look over at her. She's beautiful. Somehow her lips are glistening with lip gloss. I look down and the purse is no longer in my hands. Carly's got it. She's looking through it and asking me if I want a piece of gum. Trident Cinnamon. *Four out of five dentists surveyed prefer Trident for their patients who chew gum.* I don't know how the purse got in her hands or how the lip gloss got on her lips. I don't know and I don't care. How did you know my favorite gum? What flavor are your lips? How long can we stay here?

I'm back in the market and letting it ride. Carly leans forward and kisses me again, but this time her lips are wet and glossy and flavored. Lip Smackers Strawberry. Some of it stays behind on me. I run my

tongue along my lips and taste it a second time. By the third time it's
gone entirely. Carly is backlit and smiling at me, her hair illuminated at
the edges like a Pantene commercial. All I see are her eyes and her smile
coming at me out of the dark. Three white specks. The little voice in my
head is back again having a field day. I can't shut it up and I can't think
of any more biology questions. That's all right. I'll study later.

"So you want a piece or not?" she asks.

(This is it!)

". . . a piece?"

"Of gum."

"No, thanks."

Sixteen years later I'm talking to a counselor, and I realize I can't
remember a thing about Carly. There's nothing here. I can't feel her
touch on me anywhere. I don't feel her inside me and I don't cringe at
her name anymore. What's there to talk about?

"I don't really remember much," I tell the counselor.

"So what is it you do remember?" he asks.

"I don't know . . . just little stuff. Stupid things."

"Like what?"

"You really want to hear?" I ask, getting more and more conscious
of my $2.50 a minute ticking away. "It was high school, you know?
Everything's stupid in high school."

"Tell me about stupid, then," he says, sitting back.

I talk about silly things. I talk about buying her a Polo shirt for
Christmas and not being able to afford it—how I steal my mom's credit card and lie about it when the statement comes through. I talk about
Carly going down on me in the back seat with my mom driving the 60
eastbound, and how I still don't know to this day if she saw us or not.
I talk about crying in the corner of a room while Carly, her mother,
and her little brother and sister laugh at me and call me a baby. I talk
about how for years afterward I imagined elaborate ways to kill her
without getting caught. And I talk about how I learned to tell amazingly painful stories about her without accessing any emotion whatsoever. What's the point? It's just a bunch of silly things I remember
about growing up.

The counselor looks at me with a concerned face.

"That sounds terrible."

I shrug my shoulders and smile slightly. "You get through it."

We talk some more, and it goes pretty easy for me. It always does. It's almost like college. *Go to lecture. Take notes. Do your reading. Take your mid-terms. Write a final paper. Get a grade.* Because when I talk about this stuff, it's not like I'm really talking about myself. It doesn't even sound like me. Everything is removed and conceptual. It's nowhere near the me that I know, and I don't even remember who this girl is. I can't feel her touch on me anywhere. So when the same questions come up again and again, from every close friend and every therapist—I don't know how to respond. It's like the system breaks down. Education doesn't work anymore. Grades are worthless. *Your money's no good here, Mr. Torrance.*

(If she was so bad, why did you stay with her?)

"What were you looking for?" the counselor asks.

I glance at my watch. Twenty minutes left and we're still talking about high school. I'm out $75 and counting.

"I don't know if I was looking for anything," I respond. "I mean, I was sixteen. She was just a beautiful girl . . ."

"Is that all?"

"No, I mean, I know she had problems. I mean, she pulled some really evil shit on me. Stuff you wouldn't believe. I mean, I told you . . ."

"But you stayed with her," he interrupts.

What he's getting at? I've been through enough therapy to second-guess these guys half the time. I should be taking odds with Jimmy the Greek. Maybe I should open my own practice and sit in the chair that makes money instead of pays money. I know the routine. Look for mood, anxiety, or depression symptomatics. Treat the client with unconditional positive regard. Consistently gauge comfort and trust level. Be mindful of your own countertransference. Note avoidant behaviors. Avoid triggering an empathic failure. Stay removed. Don't get sucked into behavioral baits. Look for habits and lapses of directed attention. Body language. Eye contact. Offer support without encouraging dependence. When they tell you "Nobody cares about me," respond with "Why do you say that?" When they tell you "It's just high school," encourage them to continue.

Any client is on stage performing, and I'm on stage twenty-four hours a day. Every single person in the room is looking me over from head to toe. Hair. Shirt. Pants. Shoes. Accessories. Sometimes every single person in the room is 500 people in a lecture hall. Sometimes every single person in the room is just a psychotherapist. Sometimes every single person in the room is only me. I'm aware of every movement from the inside out like a Power Ranger. I'm aware of its motion, its read, and how it changes my body line. Some things are more obvious—crossing your arms, touching your face, shifting your weight. Others are more subtle. What is it you want to talk about?

"So you stayed with her?" he asks.
"Yeah."
"For how long?"
"I don't know . . . nine months maybe."
"And it was bad the whole time?"
"Pretty much," I say, "except for the beginning."
"But you stayed with her."
"Yeah."
The counselor leans back in his chair and folds his hands behind his head.
"Why?"

Look, if I knew the answer to that I wouldn't be here, and you'd be out $125. Why don't we switch chairs and let me ask you the questions? I know the routine. I can do it and I can use the money. She was beautiful, okay? I was sixteen. She was a beautiful fourteen-year-old Brooke Shields look-alike with bigger hair, bigger eyes, and bigger breasts. What else do you want to know? We've got ten minutes left in the session. What else is there to say?

Ten

My relationship with Carly moves fast. Within a week we're boyfriend/girlfriend. In three weeks I tell her I love her for the first time, and I experience fellatio for the first time. I don't know if there's a relationship between the two or not. I hope there isn't, but I kind of think there might be. After she finishes, she tells me my cum tastes like chlorine. I don't know what to say to that, so I just pull up my pants while she rinses her mouth out over the sink.

Carly runs the show physically. She's got experience. Her last boyfriend was nineteen. Before that, she was thirteen and her boyfriend was twenty-one. She's done everything, everywhere, while I've had sex one time watching *Enter the Dragon* with my pants pulled down to my knees. I mean, I've never had a tongue in my ear before, and you expect me to know what to do with my mouth when it gets next to a pussy? Where am I supposed to have learned that?

It's after school and both my parents are out. Carly and I are messing around in my mother's bed. It's completely bright in here with all the curtains open and we're both completely naked. She's beautiful. Carly spreads her legs and starts to push my head between them for the first time. Before I know it, I'm going past her tits and her ribs and her stomach like I'm freefalling. She's pushing fast. She's never been one for hesitation, but this is a new one for me. This is fresh. All of a sudden I'm buzzing in over her pubic hair forest and I don't have any landing gear. Incoming! My head is saying whoa whoa whoa whoa gimme a second, but my mouth is frozen. I'm not saying a thing and I'm not resisting. Tractor beam. *The captain has requested that we prepare the cabin for landing. Please check to see that your seatbelts are securely fastened. At this time please pass all service items to the center aisle for pickup. Bring your seat backs forward and place your tray tables in their upright and locked position. Make sure all carry-on items are once again stowed beneath the seat in front of you.* The ground is approaching at Mach 2 and Carly's hands are still pushing my head down into her crotch. I'm six inches away and closing. I look around me and

Yikes! There's all sorts of stuff down here.

5 inches . . .

4 . . .

I mean, that part I know. But what is *that*? No one told me about *that* part.

3 . . .
2 . . .
1 . . .
I close my eyes, open my mouth, and dive in.
. . .
Okay. I got no idea here. I'm drowning.
I've fallen and I can't get up.
Call 911. I'm serious.

I fumble around kissing and licking as best I can while Carly comes to my rescue. I'm just trying not to run away. I mean, I'm in living, breathing quicksand here and I'm sinking fast. Nobody told me anything about the quicksand, all right? Nobody told me anything about anything. I feel her hands start to direct me in the darkness, nudging me in the right direction, and trying to clue me in on pressure and tempo and rhythm. Thank God. Occasionally she even feeds me a couple courtesy moans for my ego. I know it's a courtesy clap, but I need all the help I can get in here. I have no idea what I'm doing. All I can remember is Bruce Lee saying, "Always keep your eye on your opponent," and I'm way past that now. I don't know when to start or when to finish. I don't know how slow or fast I'm supposed to be going, or if I'm supposed to be using my lips or tongue or what. They never taught us this stuff in Sex Ed. It's like walking into a gym for the first time and getting put in the advanced aerobics class. Kiss kiss. Lick lick. Tongue tongue. *Repeat.* Kiss kiss. Lick lick. Tongue tongue. *Again.* Kiss kiss. Lick lick. Tongue tongue. *Push it now!*

Carly knows exactly what she wants. She knows when she wants it, she knows how she wants it, and she knows when she's through. I keep going through the motions for about five minutes until I feel her hands gently nudging my head up and off her. Time to wake up. I come up out of the depths, my hair wet on my face. I let my tongue relax and allow my eyes to adjust to the light again. Carly lies back on my mother's bed and slowly brings her legs together. Okay. What do I do now? I'm just sitting here. Hello?

My face is dripping with her. She's starting to dry on my lips and cheeks. I run my tongue along my lips and taste her again. I look up over her pubic hair. My vision comes up over her stomach, over her ribs, over her breasts, over her neck, over her mouth and lips and eyes. She's beautiful. At sixteen I'll do anything for a beautiful woman. Who wouldn't? I mean, it's not like you have a choice. Your body is a mixture of testosterone and erections and fantasy, while your heart and experience are convinced you've stumbled upon your soulmate. This *is* your lifetime goal. Kiss reasoning and boundaries goodbye. There should be a band playing. They should be popping imported champagne and throwing streamers and making toasts. Where's my parade?

Carly's eyes are closed as if she's sleeping. Her hands are splayed out on the bed and relaxed now. I guess we're done. Do I ask her if she liked it? Do I ask her if it was good? Do I ask her for technical advice, or should I just keep strong and silent and not risk anything? I don't know. I don't know if I should move. I don't know if I should lie down beside her or pretend it's no big deal to me. I don't even know when my parents are coming home. I don't know anything. I sit there for a second, tell her a feeble "I love you," and start putting my clothes on.

I love you.
I love you.
I love you.
I love you.

The third time I lick my lips I can still taste her. The fourth time too. I look over at her and she's lying on the bed with her eyes closed. I put my pants on slowly. Then my belt and collared shirt. There is no sound here, not even outside through the windows. There is no movement. Only the rustling of my clothes. Carly takes a deep breath as if she's about to say something. I stand there listening and waiting, but nothing comes out. She just exhales into more silence.

I'm sitting on the bed pulling up my socks when she stirs. I look over again. Her eyes open, but she doesn't look back at me. She rolls over and sits up on the other edge of the bed, naked with her knees together. She leans on her hands with her elbows locked and stays motionless for a few seconds. Then she reaches down and pulls her panties on. They're beige and laced. Nordstrom Intimates. She doesn't look over or say anything. She stands up, puts a t-shirt on, and walks to the bathroom. Her tan legs walking away are beautiful. I want to tell her my parents might come home and maybe she should put on her jeans. I want to ask her if everything's okay. I want to tell her it's okay not to talk as long as we're here together. I mean, nothing matters as long as we're together, right? I want her to come back and hold me, and I don't want to ask. I want a lot of things. She walks into the bathroom and closes the door partially, almost all the way. I hear her start running the water in the sink.

"I love you."

For the most part, we get along. More changes happen and I adapt to them. All my decisions become influenced. I learn to deal with occasional silences and frequent requests. I make myself more available, more accommodating, more accidentally in the area. I have to.

"Hi, love. You need a ride?"

"Yeah."

I do Carly's math homework for her because she has trouble. She can't do fractions or even some basic division. It starts out with my trying to help her do her own homework, but somewhere along the line we always end up messing around instead. Which would you rather do? By the time we finish, it's too late and we're too tired to go through the stupid math problems, so I end up offering to do them for her at home. Carly smiles big and kisses me.

"Thanks, babe!"

I learn to mimic her printing and the way she double-bubbles her 8's, and Ma likes seeing me at my desk working on "my" homework so much. Pretty soon it's just habit. I work late at night. I give Carly her homework in the morning. She turns it in and starts to get A's in math.

This is how David got to be a doctor. He always studied.

I am blind to every warning sign and I embellish Carly's every quality. I rationalize her behavior, her provocative dress, her communication as just part of her neighborhood and upbringing. The girl didn't have a family to depend on. She didn't have a shelter she could always come home to. She's moved from guy to guy to guy with no one ever really caring about who she really is, and she's done so without the benefit of having strong female friends who can help lift her out of the muck. Her girlfriends are more concerned with raising their own stock through association—complete pack-of-pretty-girls mentality. Big hair, big boobs, ripped sweatshirts, and Jordache jeans. Everyone looks like *Flashdance*. It's the curse of the beautiful woman and it's hit early. Later in life it turns into Donna Karan and Donatella Versace and Karl Lagerfeld and seeing who's more anorexic. It's all about who can stop a room. It's all about male attraction and my complete inability to get around it. I still like the clothes and I still like being captivated. Yes, I know I'm being taken. Your point is . . . ?

Carly gets attention everywhere she goes. Gas stations, restaurants, shopping malls, football games. Men fawn over her. They see her, then nudge their friends and look back at her again. Top to bottom. I look at her and realize that every single day of her life men will ask her out. I look at her and realize that every single day of her life men will want something from her. High-school boys will tell her to sneak out at night and meet them in the neighborhood park. College boys will offer to buy her drinks and take her to concerts. Older men will talk to her about modeling and acting and recording deals and diamond earrings. And she'll never, ever have to ask for a ride home.

I don't know what she's gonna say or how she's gonna handle it. Maybe she'll see that it's all just an excuse to fuck her, and that fucking her is all just an attempt to possess her. Maybe she'll see male attention as both constant and temporary, and realize the only time most men are ever really satisfied is the moment after they've come inside you. For about thirty seconds they relax. Then they wonder what you're doing the rest of the day and who you're doing it with and what time you'll be home. Everything is temporary. Maybe she'll get to the point of laughing at the Mariah Careys and Sharon Stones and Anna Nicole Smiths with the rest of us, instead of admiring their dresses and engagement rings and divorce settlements. I hope so anyway.

It happens again and again throughout my lifetime. But I don't know where the lesson is or where the experience comes in. Where's the part about learning from mistakes? Somehow it all becomes interchangeable—like Legos or Lincoln Logs or Tinkertoys. All we can do is play with our own erector sets over and over again. So she got drunk with her friend at a party and had guys chasing after her all night. Guys are idiots. She can't help what they do, and it's not like she does this stuff all the time anyway. Who cares what people say? So you can see through her sundress sometimes. It's not as if she's walking around naked or something. And maybe it's not my place to say anything about it to begin with. Who cares what people think? So she saw a movie with her ex-boyfriend and didn't tell me. I mean, not telling me isn't really *lying,* is it?

I hold on to certain things instead. I hold on to the wonderful moments of laughter and passion we've had together. I hold on to watching her baby-sit, and seeing the beautiful nurturing and caring qualities within her. I hold on to the way I feel when I see her come to the door or hear her voice answering the phone. This is more than just husband number twelve for Liz Taylor, or the next episode of *Friday the 13th.* I'm different and she's different. I'm offering her more and she's responding to it. How can she not? I imagine a *Brady Bunch* kiss in the doorway and waking up to each other in the morning. It's all potential and it's all within reach. At home I put away my brother's *Beach Boys Greatest Hits* album and start listening to *Pet Sounds.* I mean, it's the early '80s. What do you expect me to listen to? Styx? Night Ranger? The Romantics? Brian Wilson knows what it's about.

Wouldn't it be nice if we were older?
Then we wouldn't have to wait so long.

Eleven

Carly sucks my cock at every opportunity. I can't be alone with her any-where. I can't get in a car without her going down on me. It's supposed to be a sixteen-year-old's ultimate fantasy, but I'm just scared about getting in an accident. Can't we wait and park somewhere? Can't we just talk or something? How am I supposed to drive? After a while our every argument starts to end with a blow job. Actually, our arguments don't really "end." It's more like whenever Carly's had enough, she just gets that look in her eye and starts doing her thing. I've tried to stop it and I can't. Come on, I want to talk about this, okay? This is important to me. I mean, have you ever tried talking about your girlfriend flirting or partying or wearing see-through dresses while she's got your cock in her mouth? Here's basically how it pans out. Whenever she's down on me, the answer to every question is "yes."

Carly even follows me into a locker room during swim practice. She walks me into a stall, closes the door, and bolts it. I'm dripping wet in my Speedo and goggles. Come on, I just got out to pee. Coach is gonna kill me.

"Not now . . ."

"We have time," she says before dropping to her knees and grabbing my hips. One hand starts to untie my suit. I try to stop her.

"Come on, Carly . . ."

She reaches under my legs and grabs my balls. She pulls them towards her underhand. I try and push her head off me and her hands just grip me tighter. I try to keep my suit on, but she's already untied the bow and she's massaging my cock. Don't get hard now. Come on, think about something else. I try to tell her to stop again, but how much can you say without sounding like a pussy?

You want to stop her? What's wrong with you, man?

My cock pops up out of my suit. Dammit. I'm semi-hard now and I can't hold it much longer. Think about something else.

"Please, babe . . . I got to get back . . ."

I feel her lips take me into my mouth.

Oh my God.

I try not to get hard. I try not to . . .

. . .

Outside my coach yells at me for taking so long. *How long can it take to take a goddam piss? You want to win* CIF *or not? You think Jackson and Eslinger and Vargas aren't training right now? Huh? Do you?* I jump back in the water and start back into the workout. We're repeating 100s on the 1:10 and I can't make my splits. I can't even see straight. How many more do we have to do? Coach is leaning on the block above my lane shaking his head. He stops me and tells me to move down into a slower lane. I move into lane 5. They're repeating on the 1:20.

What the hell's wrong with you today?

Carly and I are parked in the back seat of my mother's Oldsmobile Cutlass Supreme, somewhere in the hills overlooking the San Gabriel Valley. Through the smog we can see the lights of Christmas decorations at Eastland Shopping Center downtown. KROQ is playing the usual Duran Duran and Billy Idol crap in between commercials for Perkins Palace concerts and car insurance. We're stripped and ready to go down on each other. We've got a whole system worked out now. Shoes in front. Jeans folded. Shirts and sweatshirt within reach in case of headlights or cops. The only questions are what radio station to listen to and who goes first. I've gotten a lot better at this whole thing. I don't grimace anymore and my tongue isn't as tensed up. That's what Carly tells me anyway. Tonight she tells me she also wants to make love.

". . . Are you sure?"
"Yes."

I tell her I don't have any protection. She tells me she does. I tell her our first time together should be special. She tells me she knows that already. Duh. I don't know what else to say except I'm not ready, and I don't know how to tell her that without sounding like I'm gay. We've been together three months. I dated my *Enter the Dragon* girl for a week and tried to get in her pants every night, succeeding once with our pants pulled down around our knees. Somehow this is different. I want to tell Carly it's different now. I want to tell her we should wait or something. I mean, shouldn't we? I want to talk about being comfortable with each other and trusting each other and feeling like she's there. I just want to talk about talking, if that makes any sense, and I have no idea how to get any of this across to her. How do I tell her any of this? We're parked under the pine trees on a cold December Saturday night. I'm naked, nervous, and my cock is soft. I guess that'll probably tell her enough on its own.

Carly's ready. She grabs my cock and realizes I'm half-mast. She lets out a quick breath through her nose.

. . .

(Was that a laugh?)
(Was it a snicker?)
(Should I ask?)

Carly looks at me in the dark. All I can see are the three white circles of her eyes and teeth. She's smiling.

"Well, if you don't want to . . ."

"I want to!" I interrupt.

"Are you sure?"

"Yes."

Carly brings a trio of condoms out of her purse like soldiers. I can't tell if they're Sheiks or not. She rips a pack open with her teeth, puts the condom in her hand, and puts my soft cock in her mouth. On the radio they're playing The Clash's "Train in Vain" off *London Calling*. Outside the Eastland Christmas lights turn off, leaving just the skeletal lights of the giant tree shining. It must be 10:00. Time for *Loveline*.

ᕮ

Over time, like any man with a beautiful woman, I begin to experience the fear of losing her. It starts slowly and innocuously. Before I realize, it begins to envelop my everyday experience like nothing else. More than school. More than swimming. More than friends. More than family. Like an after-image from a bright light or a camera flash, I find her inside my eyelids and realize I can never again feel this type of drive with anyone else. Everything becomes temporary and nothing is satisfying. Our physical intimacies work like morphine, temporarily dulling the desire, but hours or even minutes afterwards I impel again towards some vague and unattainable goal. I find myself like any of the men I ridicule—men marrying the Mariah Careys or Sharon Stones or Anna Nicole Smiths. So I'm a few inches taller, a few million dollars poorer, and thirty years away from the hair implants. We're still in the same boat, casting our love at beautiful women and hoping for something there beneath all the smiles and red ribbons. There are no rituals and no promises to offer shelter for any of us. Boyfriend, fiancé, and husband status offer only surface-level security. And though you use these words in introductions and references to bring some sense of stability and permanence to your passion, when you wake in the morning you are still where you are. The world has closed in around her, enveloped her, and asked you to protect her for all the stakes in the universe. How can you say no? At sixteen it's excusable. At thirty-two you should be able to read the signs.

ત્ર

It starts simply enough.
"I smoke."
"What?"
"I smoke."

Too late. You're already in the market and if you sell now, you just lose. We had a contract. You signed.

I try to talk to her about it. I go through the usual why-didn't-you-tell-me's and how-could-you-lie-to-me's. She gives me the I-never-lied-to-you and I-was-afraid-to-tell-you excuses. I want to go into more but I can't. I'm not there yet. I don't know how. I want to tell her about my father smoking cigars in the car with the windows rolled up and the heater on. I want to tell her about swimming competitively for fifteen years and missing Olympic trials by two-tenths of a second, and about trying to fall asleep afterwards with an electronic clock ticking away inside your eyelids. I want to tell her about asthma and Ventolin and Theodore and Prednisone and Beclamethasone diproprionate, about doctor visits and having to leave an inhaler next to my lane just to get through practice. I want to tell her about what it's like to try to make your makeshift lungs work normally while watching everyone else around you poison their perfectly healthy ones. I want to talk about what's fair in life, and what parts of my body I'd trade. But I don't know how to talk about these things yet. And I haven't learned that nothing's fair.

It moves faster than I can take it in. Within a week I go from ultimatums of you-quit-or-we-break-up to okay-but-only-when-I'm-not-around. You're already in love. You've taken the bait and the metal claw has clamped around your leg. Now it's either gnaw off your foot or sit there and make the best of it. What would you do? If I don't see it or smell it, there's not really any difference, right?

I'm driving Carly home from a Haircut 100 concert at Irvine Meadows. It was terrible. The band was good, but I was so busy trying to keep guys away from her I couldn't think straight. Throughout the whole concert she just danced and bounced and smiled back at any guy in a Polo shirt with muscles and short hair. All I could do was hold on to her waist from behind and pretend to be dancing and having fun myself. I could barely watch the band. A couple times Carly even shook my hands off and ran into the crowd. I'd spot her jumping up and down in the front with a crew of guys dancing around her. Even one of the band members was smiling at her. Worst of all, whenever she'd come back, she'd make a point of giving me a huge public kiss.

Remember this and don't even think about telling me what to do.

It satisfies me until our lips part. Everything is temporary. Then she's bouncing and dancing and running around and smiling again, and I can't say a thing. If I did, she'd accuse me of not letting her have fun. If I did, she'd accuse me of getting mad at little things. If I did, she'd roll her eyes at me.

"Isn't this fun, babe?"

I know what boys like . . . I know what guys want . . .

We're in the car on the 57 northbound and I want to talk to her about it. I don't like this. *I* took you to the concert. You went with *me.* What am I supposed to be doing while you're off running around with these guys? Is it too much to ask to have you

Carly's hand is on my cock. Jesus, not now.

"Carly, I . . ."

Her hands pop open the buttons of my 501s like she's opening a birthday present. Her head buries into my lap and I can feel her fingers slipping under my boxers. I start to get hard. I don't have much time.

"Come on, Carly, listen. I want to talk about something."

I can feel her breath through my boxers. She starts to pull them down and runs her tongue along the top of my shaft at its base. I'm getting harder and harder while she's slowly pulling my underwear down against me. I'm cranked down like a fishing pole, held by the elastic of my boxers and the tension of her fingers.

"I'm serious! I want to talk about tonight!"

The slingshot reaches its breaking point. The elastic band slips off me. My cock bucks away while the boxers slip down my thighs. Carly's lips immediately move to my head. She's gonna swallow me. I have to move now.

"*Stop it!*" I tell her, pulling her head up and off me.

Carly jerks her head up with her eyes narrowed. She's incensed.

"WHAT'S YOUR PROBLEM?" she snaps.

I'm stuck for a second.

". . . *My* problem? I want to talk about . . ."

"Forget it!" she spits. She slaps my boxers back up on me. Then she reaches down with the other hand and yanks my jeans up angrily, hard enough to shift my hips in the seat. The jeans bunch up around my ass. She shoves me hard in the thigh with both hands and moves back over to her side of the car.

"Forget it!"

Carly sits back up in her seat without putting her belt on. She knows I hate that. Come on, that's not safe. What if we get in an accident? What if we get hit? She crosses her arms and looks out the window. We're crossing the exit for Imperial Highway. We still got a half-hour to go. What am I supposed to do? Drive?

We sit in mutual silence for a minute or so, the only sound the murmur of the radio. It's a block party weekend. Both my hands are on the wheel and I'm watching traffic. There are a lot of trucks on the 57. Have to be careful. My pants are still unbuttoned and bunched around my ass. I want to pull them up, but I don't want to move. My cock has shrunk away to nothing. I want to talk to her. Or change the station. Or open the window. Or *something.* I just want to do something besides replaying this scene over and over in my head. I mean, I don't think I'm being out of line, am I? I look over at Carly and she's still sitting with her arms crossed and looking away. I want to talk to her, but I know she won't respond. I know this already. If I try, she'll ignore me. If I touch her, she'll pull away.

My crying starts quietly in the dark, too quiet for her to hear. I feel the tears start coming down. They start slow at first like a midnight grunion run. A few scouts. Then the tears suddenly turn into two solid streams pouring down my face, finally falling in drops off my chin and landing in my lap. Some of the drops land on bare skin exposed where my pants are open. Some land on my boxers and my pubic hair and my disappearing cock. The drops and tears are silent. All I hear is 3,500 revolutions per minute. All I hear is tire hum.

Boys don't cry.

I cry through the Lambert and Tonner Canyon exits into L.A. County. I try to focus on lane lines and exit signs and license plates and bumper stickers. I don't look over, but through my peripheral vision I can see the back of Carly's head as she looks out the window with her arms crossed. She hasn't even glanced at me. We pass the Diamond Bar Boulevard exit and I sniff my nose once. Loud enough to hear. I think Carly hears me, but she doesn't respond. She doesn't even move. A car flies by on our right-hand side and I watch its red lights disappear into the darkness. Please come to me, love. I'm sorry, okay?

No response. Passing Grand Avenue I sniffle again, louder. Then again. The 57 is splitting off into the 60 and I have to switch lanes. Carly still hasn't turned her head or even moved. How can she not hear me? I look over my left shoulder, but my eyes are teared and I can't see that well. No car headlights. I signal to change lanes, and start drifting the car over slowly, like Mr. MacDonald taught me in Driver's Ed. Hands at 10:00 and 2:00. I wish Carly would put on her seat belt. What if we get in an accident and she's not wearing it? What if some truck doesn't have its lights on and I can't see because of the tears? What if it slams into us from behind and Carly goes flying through the windshield while I'm buckled in. What if she dies and I survive? How can I live with that?

I try to undo my own belt, but it's too late. The car flies into the center divider and flips over and over and over. I see Carly explode out of the windshield into the darkness. I'm reaching for her, but I'm buckled in and the belt has locked down absolutely. Everything is flying in circles like pudding. The car flips a final time and comes to a stop. Without looking down, I know I'm completely unscathed. Pristine, virginal, I open my eyes and look around me. Carly's lying twenty yards up the road, splayed out in a pool of blood and oil and broken safety glass and hazard flashers. Live electric wires are sparking everywhere and undulating like a million living eels. I unbuckle myself and climb out of the wreckage through the shattered window and corrugated metal. I run to her in slow motion through the eel forest, dropping to my knees on the asphalt and the blood and the safety glass. I cradle her in my arms.

I'm sorry, love. I'm sorry, love. I'm sorry.

Carly's eyes open slowly to me, but she's dead to the world. Her face is pasty white and her gaze is like glass. Somewhere a car radio is playing Haircut 100. Her green eyes are looking straight up at me, but she doesn't see me. I'm not even here. I'm not even close.

A hundred muscular firefighters show up in blue Polo shirts and suspenders. They see her body, then nudge each other and look at her again. Top to bottom. Left to right.

What are you looking at?
What are you looking at?

⌐
Ⴟ

KROQ has started a block of The Smiths. Morrissey fills the car. My pants are still below my waist. My face muscles are sore from crying.

Take me out tonight,
Where there's music and there's people who are young and alive.

Carly hasn't moved an inch and she hasn't put on her belt. She hasn't turned around or even shifted her weight. She hasn't heard me, or at least she's pretended not to. I start to cry audibly now. Slow and soft at first, then a gradual stuttering moan that gets louder as we go. I don't care anymore. Please come to me, love. Come to me and hold me and tell me it's okay. Don't make me cry louder. Don't make me ask.

Carly moves her head.

"Shut up."

(What?)

I stutter my breath for a second the way crying babies do when they're surprised. We're at the 10 freeway intersection and I'm taking the Los Angeles transition. What? What do you mean? What are you doing? What's going on? I feel more tears welling up under my eyes and I see headlights cascading all around me. I'm sniffling with my mouth partway open and my tongue relaxed. Carly turns around and faces me. Her eyes are narrowed into little green cat slits and her hair is tossed around her shoulders like a mane. She's beautiful.

"Shut up!" she spits.

I'm stunned into silence again. No breathing. I look over at her. My face is covered with dried snot and tears. My pants are pulled around my ass and I'm trying to keep us on the road. *I'm fucking sixteen years old, what are you doing to me?*

". . . Babe, I . . ."

"Don't call me that! Just shut up, you baby!"

I'm merging into the traffic on the 10 westbound and heading up the hill towards Forest Lawn Mortuary. I take my right hand off the wheel and reach over to Carly's leg. Look, babe, I'm open. I'm unarmed. I'm on my back and my throat is up. I got nothing here, okay? I got nothing here.

"Get your fucking hands off me!"

No—see, you don't get it. *I got nothing here.* I love you. I'll do anything for you. I got nowhere else to go. I got nowhere else to go.

"Please, babe . . . I . . ."

"I SAID GET YOUR FUCKING HANDS OFF ME!"

I start crying more now, uncontrollably. All I want is for you to come to me. That's all I want, okay? That's all I want. It's like I'm stuck in some crazy surrogate-monkey experiment and there's no placebo. There's no control group. We already know the results, but we have to go through the motions anyway to keep our funding going. I don't care if you're made of carpet or full of spikes. I don't care if you blow cold air at me. I don't care if you're electrified. I don't care if scientists are watching and taking notes and publishing findings. Just come to me.

I have no idea where to go from here. Carly has sat back and crossed her arms again. She's looking straight ahead out the windshield, chewing gum, and shaking her head slightly with each jaw motion. I'm just trying to see straight and drive safely. I reach my hand over to her leg again and touch her. She lets out a quick breath of air through her nose and shoves my hand back over.

"*Jesus!* I need a smoke. Pull over."

". . . What?"

"Pull over!"

I get off the exit at Via Verde and stop the car next to a field. Carly unlocks her door and starts to get out. I try to touch her arm, but she rips it away from my hand. She opens the car door and storms out into the field. It's dark and there are no streetlights, but I can see her walking away. She's wearing faded jeans and a tight red and white striped shirt that hugs her every curve. After about twenty yards she stops. Carly reaches into her purse and pulls out a pack of Marlboros. She goes through smoking ritual 101, packing the box down on her palm over and over and over. I don't know if I should be getting out of the car or not. I'm just looking out the open door into the field.

Carly starts feeling her pants pockets for matches and doesn't find any, so she walks back towards the car. At the door she leans in.

"Push the lighter . . . *Oh Jesus,*" she says, looking down at my crotch and rolling her eyes.

She stands back up, turns around and shakes her head with her arms crossed. Her cigarette is tucked in her ear and the pack is bulging out of her back pocket. Is she laughing? I look down and see my pants are still around my thighs. Embarrassed, I tuck my cock in and pull up my boxers quickly. I lift my hips off the seat and pull up my 501s and button each button. I turn the ignition key to "battery." The radio comes on and the door-open alert starts beeping. I push the cigarette lighter button in.

Sweetness . . . Sweetness, I was only joking when I said I'd like to smash every tooth in your head . . .

Carly still hasn't turned around. I check myself in the mirror. I'm a fucking mess. I start wiping my face and fixing my hair until the lighter pops back out.

pop

Carly hears it and is immediately back in the door reaching for it. I'm faster. I grab it and pull it out to give to her. It's burning a bright orange.

"Give it to me!" she says, snatching it out of my hands before I have a chance to.

The wind is still, and Carly's smoke sifts all around the area. She stays close to the car on purpose, dragging on her cigarette and blowing her smoke in the air. We had rules once, but I'm not saying a thing. I got nowhere else to go. I'm just watching. Her smoke comes in the door and sees me. It smiles slightly, then slowly seeps deep into the vents and the seats and the upholstery. Nice place you have here. Don't mind if I do. It comes into the neighborhood and lives on my hair and my skin and my clothes and my mouth. I taste it. I smell it. I feel it. It buys some new furniture, fills out a change-of-address form, and orders newspaper delivery. It gets used to the rhythm and the tempo of the people and the cars and the animals. After a while, it's just like home.

Carly takes her last drag, then flicks the butt into the field. It flies off end over end, rotating its tiny ember in little circles like an insect. It's probably gonna start a brush fire. I don't care. She gets back in the car and I've stopped crying. Driving side streets, I somehow get her back to her house. She gets out of the car and goes in the side door without looking at me or saying a thing. I don't even get a chance to turn off the engine. I drive home, and the smoke follows me. We get into bed together and turn out the light. The night ends. The next day begins.

Over the next few weeks Carly increasingly ups the ante. She's cleaning me out and I can't do a thing about it. From smoking pit-stops, she shifts into smoking in my car. From after-school breaks, she shifts into smoking in my room. The physical boundaries shift till I taste smoke and ash on her lips and tongue and skin. Each time, we argue. Each time, I cry. Each time, we print up new instructions, make new pieces, and create a new playing board that's only good for the next week or so. No one even knows what game it is anymore. We just do what she feels like doing. The world is still cradling her and watching me to see what I do. We had a deal here. Remember?

"Now *you're* gonna buy *me* cigarettes."

Go on. Do it.

We drive to a gas station where some nameless Middle Eastern man works behind bulletproof glass. I get out of the car, walk up to him, and read his shirt. The man has a name. It's Hakim.

"Can I help you?" he says.

Go on. Do it.

"Marlboro Redbox."

"$1.75."

ᘯ
ᘰ

A thousand cigarettes later, Carly and I break up. I don't remember how it happens exactly. Sometimes at sixteen or seventeen everything is just a blur. Sometimes everything happens so fast you can't keep up. All of a sudden you're just there. You look around. The deal is off and everyone's just going about business as usual. Where you been?

It's early summer before my senior year. Early summer is the best time to break up because you escape seeing each other for a few months. Even better, you escape seeing her friends. School is out and we set up our own separate territories with no intersecting areas. Carly spends the summer hanging around her neighborhood sucking cocks and doing coke. Across town my friends and I have all just gotten our first jobs. Raging Waters Water Park has just opened up and we're making $6.00 an hour as lifeguards. I put on red shorts for the first time and begin a lifetime of watching people in the water. It's where I should have been in the first place. And it's where I'm gonna stay. The only thing I hate about the job is they play Beach Boys all day long.

ᘯ
ᘰ

You look for things to say afterwards. You search for morals and lessons and silver linings. You try to get to that point where you can actually grasp why it is you are the person you are, why it is you feel the things you do. I'm waiting for senior status. I'm waiting for wisdom. I'm waiting to put a first love, a first sex, and a first white-woman fantasy to bed. But I don't know where to go with it besides some strange sense of pride in having lived through the experience. I don't have any lessons or advice to share. I don't even know how it happened. All I have around me is a tangible sense of accomplishment in having survived. Like a firing squad or an attack on Godzilla—after all the smoke clears and the toy tanks drive away, I'm still standing. I don't know how and I can't explain why. I just am. I walked out of the burning vehicle without assistance, but no one was there to catch it on videotape. How do you prove it happened? Looking in the mirror, I have no physical evidence. No bullet holes, no blood. I may have shot the sheriff, but the deputy wasn't even nearby. Maybe you shot him. Maybe you didn't.

Re-check your ammunition and shoot again if you want. Come closer, and place your guns against my head, heart, and crotch. Call in Rodan and King Ghidra, and turn them loose on me when I'm not expecting it. All the wind and three-headed electrical bolts you can throw at me won't do you any good. I know deep down, they're just guys in rubber suits. I know the guns are shooting blanks, and all the bombs being dropped on Monster Island are coming from toy planes. It's like we've been watching one long film with really bad voice-overs and a stand-in that doesn't even look like me. I've seen the real thing and I'm still here. I got no time for imitators. Standing at the video rack, I'm looking at tape after tape of Bruce Lee impostors named Bruce Li and Bruce Lei and wondering if this deserves some kind of discount for false advertising. I'm trying to sort all the Jackie Chan tapes and DVDs into separate pre–eyelid surgery and post–eyelid surgery piles, while all the clerks are looking at me like I'm crazy. I don't have any idea what to rent and I hate Blockbuster.

Sometimes there's nothing else to say. I may not be able to remember a thing, and there may be no touch on me anywhere now. But I know how far I can go without going down. I see the limits to what I will never go through again. And these are good things to see. I know throughout my life there will be other girls to negotiate, and other issues to work out. Some things you can just count on. I know Blockbuster employees will swarm around me every time I walk in the store, peddling Red Vines and Kit Kats and microwave popcorn. I know they'll offer me their viewing suggestions, as if working at a video store somehow makes you worth listening to. I also know, from this time onward, Monster Island will never be the same. Not even close. It will always be surrounded by water, just where it's supposed to be.

"How about *Trading Places*? Do you like Eddie Murphy? It's really funny."

(Because I'm a karate man! Okay? Karate men bruise on the inside!)

"Seen it."

carnation

Twelve

At eighteen I come of age. Suddenly, I can vote, go to jail, and die for my country. Whoopee. I fill out my Selective Service form and the day continues like any other. We have no other coming-of-age rites in this country. No other transitions into manhood. Besides candles and presents, a birthday is like any other day in your life. You wake up the same. You fall asleep the same. We look to our fathers for guidance, but their aging bodies and our own measures of value have betrayed them. None of us sees what's really important anymore. We measure strength only by the most childish of means—who can most control his world, who can most control his emotions. Our fathers pass on to us what they can, but the world has changed without them. Like honeybee drones, we watch cycles of love and sex repeat again and again, while we desperately search about for our own meanings and rituals. It's kind of like kindergarten. Sometimes we just want to be told what we're supposed to be doing.

On an early Saturday morning my father tells me he wants to talk. We sit down together at the kitchen table with coffee and orange juice, and he gives me my first and only ultimatum. Either I go ROTC or he doesn't pay for my college education. Period.

"What is that you've got written on your helmet?"

"Born to Kill," Sir!

Stunned for a second, but filled with the cockiness of a high-school senior, I tell him I'm not going to be part of some U.S. war machine. I swallow hard and maintain eye contact. Don't blink.

"You write 'Born to Kill' on your helmet and you wear a peace button. What's that supposed to be, some kind of sick joke?"

No, Sir!

"Now answer my question or you'll be standing tall before the man!"

I think I was trying to suggest something about the duality of man, Sir!

"The what?"

His coffee cools and my orange juice ferments, but there is no more discussion and no more decisions. Two stubborn men, too much like each other for their own good, sit back in their chairs and watch the summer go by in silence. Pick up the paper. Go to swim practice.

Eat dinner. How was your day? Folger's Crystals burn a ring into the white porcelain, and the pulp settles to the bottom of my glass. Both of us know we're right. Both of us wish the other understood. By the time school comes around, it's become as routine as shaving. September ends. My father quietly writes a check to the U.C. Regents and I go to school a civilian. We don't say a thing about it.

It's more than youthful politics, though. And it's more than my father's expression of tough love. Because he honestly wants me to experience what he experienced. He wants me to go through the bonding of strangers and the fear of death. He wants me to know the joys of discovery and the overcoming of personal limitations. I know this. The war was his ritual, and it was a good one for him. But he can't lead me back there because there's no place for it anymore. There are no more wars like his. No more heroes. No more parades. No more *Life* magazine photos of VJ Day and sailors kissing nurses. Just dead men, torture, rape, and guilt. No one loves a soldier today. Maybe in my father's day the best and brightest enlisted. Too often now it's the most lost and impressionable. How many losers did I go to high school with who gave up and joined the army? How many guys see *Top Gun* and enlist, thinking they'll meet themselves a Kelly McGillis? How much is a navy recruiter like a used-car salesman? They both wear uniforms. They both smile and shake your hand and call you by your first name. And they both want something from you. I figure everyone does, sooner or later.

Towards the end of the year, my father and I fly down to Cabo San Lucas. It is my turn to catch a marlin. It is my ritual, my ceremony. It is what my father did on one of the many days he came of age. I agree to go only if we can release the magnificent fish, and my father books a catch-and-release boat for the following day. They guarantee it. No harm to the fish. Sure, Hemingway might have scoffed. But Hemingway blew his brains out. I place a seasickness patch behind my ear in preparedness for the next morning, but all it does is knock me out completely. I don't remember the fish. I don't remember the struggle. I don't even remember leaving the dock. I might as well have gone to the moon. Waking up in the hotel eight hours later, groggy and marlin-less, I tell my father I've had enough fishing for this trip. And for 300 bucks an outing, I'd rather spend the rest of the vacation hanging around the pool eating guacamole. That, Hemingway would have laughed at.

The hotel is posh. It's got one of those ritzy swim-up-to-the-bar pools, big fluffy towels, fruity drinks with the little plastic swords and umbrellas. All the patrons are rich and white and old, while all the workers are young and brown and wearing linen. Everything is palm fronds and banana leaves. It's like *Fantasy Island* without Mr. Rorque and Tattoo.

The plane! The plane!

Dad and I hang out by the pool like vanilla and chocolate. He carefully reapplies SPF 45 across his body on the hour, while I fall asleep in the sun with natural melanin like a giant solar cell. Dad drinks white wine by the bottle. I drink Evian by the glass.

You guys! Vicki just game up with something . . . something wonderful! 'Evian' is 'Naive' spelled backwards!

The clientele around us are mostly rich Californian types. Most over fifty. Some families. An occasional blonde movie star with her Latin lover. I've come to terms with the fact that I'm not going to get laid here. Fine. It's still my sun and my water. I notice some older folks giving Dad and me quizzical looks now and then, but I figure we're just getting the new guest treatment. Maybe we're sitting in someone's special lounge chair or something. Or maybe we're not wearing the proper colors for the day. Maybe we're not rich enough and everyone can tell. Or maybe they just think my Speedo looks funny. I mean, it's not like Speedos ever look normal anyway, but at least in a swim team context you're expecting it. I decide to ignore them and fall back asleep again. I get to do things like that. It's my vacation.

Lying under my Oakleys, my light suddenly dims. I open my eyes and I'm looking up at some mid-fifties white woman. She's scampered up to me in a flowered bathing suit with matching shoes, and cottage-cheese thighs. Kraft or Knudsen or Lady Lee. I see the outline of her sun hat silhouetted in the day sky. I see her enormous earrings, and her long, red nails gripping her black purse.

"Hi there," she says from behind her Jackie-O glasses. "I've *got* to know something . . ."

(I've got to know something?)

Instantly I'm on the defensive. From a lifetime of training, I'm immediately assessing what it is she wants from me. Sooner or later, everybody wants something. I'm trying to gauge her threat and motive, and I'm trying to decide how rude I'll have to be to get her to go away. But I can't figure it out. She's not Amway and I'm not wearing a watch to tell her what time it is. I don't speak Spanish and she's too old to be a prostitute. Or at least to make any money at it. I'm out of references. I've got nothing to interpret with here. In California I know when someone approaches and says "Hi there," they want one of three things. They want my money. They want my sex. Or they want me to go to Bible study. And I know that responding with "I'm broke," "I'm straight," or "I'm the Devil" will end the conversation and get them to leave me alone. But here in Mexico I don't know what she wants from me. I don't know what to say. So I just take the bait.

"What do you want to know?" I ask, without lifting my sunglasses.

"You two," she says pointing to my father, then back to me. "What's up with you two? I've *got* to know."

(What's up with us?)

"Oh, I'm Jack Fulbeck," my father says, extending his hand and smiling. "This is my son, Kip."

"Oh, your *son?*" she says, surprised. She glances at me, and for a moment I catch her eyes underneath her Jackie-O glasses. They're big, with dark purple makeup caked into the creases. And I suddenly realize what this woman was thinking all along. Old white man. Young Asian guy. In Speedo. Hanging out together by the pool in Cabo, "vacationing." Suddenly I realize what she was looking for and what she wanted to know. How could I fall for this? How could I not have seen? I just took the bait without thinking. I heard the doorbell and I just opened the door. I might as well have signed up for the motivational tapes or become a Mormon. Jesus. Get your mind out of the gutter, lady. Cut your red nails off, wipe that shit off your eyes, and leave us alone. And don't look so heartbroken.

Dad is waiting for her to extend her hand in return. But she's so caught up in her gossip-world-tabloid-paparazzi disappointment, she doesn't even see him anymore.

"Well," she says, turning to walk away, "you're obviously not from the same gene pool."

I write the woman off. There's no shortage of stupid people in this world, and I'm not looking to buy. I look over at my father who is caught somewhere, gazing forward with the same slight smile on his face. He brings his hand home and puts it to his wine glass again. I smile when something embarrasses me. I smile when something hits too close to home. Dad leans back in his Mexican lounge chair and raises the white wine to his lips again. We sit together in silence, save for the occasional quiet tick of his glass. What is there left to say? He and I have argued about a lot of things on this trip already. The internment camps. Hiroshima and Nagasaki. The color of my skin. The color of his. The night before I walk out of a dinner, unable to come to terms with my father telling me I don't confront racism as a mixed-blood. It's all in how you look at things, he tells me. It's all in your attitude, and I'm just looking for it. I walk away when I could smile instead. It hits too close to home.

"The what?"

The duality of man. The Jungian thing, Sir!

"Whose side are you on, son?"

Our side, Sir!

Dad sips his alcohol at 10:30 in the morning. I lie under the sun in my Speedo and Oakleys. The Jackie-O lady, now disappointed in her rice-queen theory proving false, is walking away to gossip about someone else. Everything slowly goes back to normal again. My father and I are left alone by the water, like any other two men in the world, wondering about the life in our hands and the life out of our reach. I wonder if he regrets his decision to choose my mother, in turn choosing me? Did he freely sacrifice his Irish Catholic heritage to the overwhelming power of a Chinese family, or was he naive enough to imagine some sort of happy medium? Did he ever think, in his initial passion, about what it would feel like to have some stranger not recognize his son as his own, or to have this same son question his own legacy and selfhood? Did he imagine our father/son arguments and miscommunications, or was it just dreams of cigar clubs, Saturday afternoon chess matches, and unabashed pride? There are hard things to think about.

A linen-clad waiter comes by, offering refills.

"*Sí, por favor,*" my father says.

I remove my sunglasses, roll off the lounge chair, and slip underwater. Sounds disappear and I am embraced again.

Thirteen

The day after Thanksgiving, I visit my parents for the annual missed-holiday guilt slinging and early morning shopping spree. Covina is still desolate, still smoggy, and still east of L.A. Maybe at one time it used to be about oranges and oranges and oranges. Now it's more about paintball guns and Target stores and marijuana. No more oranges and no more horses. Just looking and looking for parking spaces. You might as well keep the car running.

Four hours of outlet-mall shopping and next-year-I'll-be-there promises later, I decide I need a massage. I flip through the yellow pages until I come across Fumiko's Acupressure. Licensed. Professional. It's out in Upland—another town even more east of L.A., where car dealerships line both sides of the 10 freeway to watch the traffic not move. I call up and a *Nihon-jin* woman answers. She tells me they charge forty bucks an hour.

"Is there someone special you'd like to see?" she asks.

I figure that's a decent price, so I tell her to schedule me with the next available person ASAP. Ten minutes later, I'm driving out to Upland for a 4:00 with Connie. It takes forty-five minutes to get there, because everywhere takes forty-five minutes to get to. Nobody walks in L.A.

Red flag. My car's parked and I'm standing outside this massage place, considering whether to actually go in. Because all my warning bells are sounding. It's all here. Mirrored windows, blinking ORIENTAL MASSAGE Vegas lights, and a parking lot full of full-sized American pickup trucks parked every other space like men at urinals. Hint hint. Nudge nudge.

Suddenly I'm face to face with this whole idea—this whole stigma—ORIENTAL MASSAGE. I'm at the tip of the iceberg. The edge of the black hole. I'm next to the all-powerful Sarlacc, and Boba Fett has already been pulled in. And once you're pulled in, there's no turning back. You get digested for the next hundred years. Once inside, it's dark, and "massage" is just a code word for prostitution. Add on the term "Oriental," and Asian women ooze out of the walls to slowly devour you like enzymes. Shy and mysterious on the outside, unbridled sex vixens on the inside. You get slanted-slit vaginas and mysteriously forbidden sexual techniques. You get women whose ultimate pleasure is to serve you. It's the whole James Clavell *Shōgun* syndrome, with a million middle-aged white men lined up to buy books and movie tickets and overpriced trips on Singapore Airlines. Because there's never a shortage of middle-aged white men in this country, ready and willing to try to cash in on some kind of instant social status and feed their ethnic fetish at the same time. Two birds with one Oliver Stone. And every Asian woman in this country deals with the residue.

Do you speak English?
Konnichi-wa.
My last girlfriend was Korean. Do you play the violin?
You know, I was stationed in the Philippines.
Are you a lesbian?

Here I am. Standing outside this place and I have no idea what to do. Because I'm not completely sure it's a whorehouse. I really wouldn't know how to be sure anyway. I mean, how are you supposed to know what one looks like? I can recognize a hooker on Kalakaua as fast as the next guy, but this isn't Waikiki. There's no Guido hanging around with a fur coat and a pink Cadillac. There's no Eddie Murphy saying, "I'm Velvet Jones. Be a Ho." I don't see any girls walking around with lime-green body suits and glazed expressions. So who knows? Maybe it's just the way they advertise. Maybe these guys are just the clientele of the area. I mean, I *am* in Upland. And I've driven all the way out here anyway, so I decide to just go through with it. For the novelty if nothing else. I figure it's like skydiving. All you have to do is take that first step. And sometimes you just gotta do things to make life interesting. I open the door and enter, the almighty Sarlacc. Begin countdown. Ninety-nine years, 364 days to go.

Inside, I'm feeling a bit better. There's a waiting room with magazines and a sign-in clipboard like any random dentist's office. Fine. Ten minutes of *Sports Illustrated* and *Cosmo* and *People* go by, until this woman calls from inside for me to come on back. I go through this door and she points to another. She tells me to shower first, then come out in a towel carrying my clothes and shoes. And that's a bit odd. I've never done that to get a massage before. But then I've never had "acupressure" before. And from what I can tell, this woman seems fairly normal looking. So I shower. The hot water sprays off my face and body. It feels good. I start to relax. I'm reminded of China Airlines and getting hot towels before meals and all these other Asian cleanliness customs I've grown up with. The kinds of customs that Americans take for granted, and that turn prospective girlfriends into noncontenders. After they ask

104

me *why* I want them to take off their shoes in my apartment. Hint hint. Nudge nudge.

I turn off the water, step out of the shower, and towel off. I walk out of the room and see this woman—Connie. Southeast Asian immigrant—Vietnamese at a guess. Mid 30-something. Permed hair. Pock marks. She tells me to go into Room #3, and I feel myself slowly starting to wig out. I'm hanging on to the edge and I can feel the tongue wrapped around my leg and pulling. Because this woman's wearing a miniskirt and pumps. I rub my eyes, blink a few times, and look again. She's still wearing them. And I've been to a lot of massage centers and none of them has ever included miniskirts. But at this point, it's like you just don't want to admit to yourself that you're in this situation. So you pretend you're not. You pretend it's just common everyday interaction and this stuff doesn't happen to you.

I go into this room to get a massage, just a massage—and the room's got one door, no window, one lamp, and one futon. On the floor.

From the doorway, I catch a glimpse of another Southeast Asian immigrant woman in a black teddy. Don't ask how I know. She's shorter, with straight hair and thinner ankles. I catch a glimpse before I close the door and I see her putting wrinkly bedsheets in the washing machine. I think of washing machines and black pumps and wet plastic and teddies. I think of permed hair and pock marks. I don't feel so good inside anymore.

Outside I'm clean. I took a shower.

I stack my clothes in the corner and lie on the futon. Face down. The door opens, but I don't want to look and see miniskirt or pumps or permed hair or pock marks because this stuff doesn't happen to me. I'm not here. If I hold my breath, no one will see me. She puts a towel over the lampshade. The already dim room darkens even more. I feel the futon shift as she sits down next to me (oh God) and says in broken English,

"What you want me to do?"

And I'm getting really scared, because all I want is a massage. No, really. All I want is a massage. No, really.

"Just a massage."

パ

She moves closer behind me, and I realize I don't like that white man I passed at the entrance. Him going out, me going in. I don't like that white man I passed at the entrance without meeting eyes. We pass without meeting eyes. But I saw you, man. I know why you're here. I got you down—balding, late thirties, heavy. I saw your car. Don't think for a minute I couldn't pick you out of a police lineup. One-way mirror or not, I'm gonna pick you out. Don't think for a minute I can't peg you. Or won't peg you. I will.

Outside in the parking lot it's a four-wheelers' convention. Big, swap-meet-type white guys with mustaches, who stop talking and look at you as you walk by. This stuff doesn't happen to me. Keep your sunglasses on and keep walking. Walk with a purpose. I'm face down on a futon and it's not that far away. It's not that far for this guy at the entrance door—him going out, me coming in—that he wants *me* here. Face down. Yellow. Submissive. A man/boy. Handcuffs. My hair in a ponytail. Him behind me with his thick hairy hands gripped around my waist, screaming, "DON'T MOVE! DON'T EVEN FUCKING LOOK AT ME!" His rice-queen redneck cock up my ass. Bleeding and no rubber. A slanted-slit asshole and a mysteriously forbidden sexual technique. I know it's not that far a reach. You understand what I'm saying? I know it's not that far a reach. I know. And don't think I won't peg you out of a police lineup, man. Don't think I can't do it. Don't think I won't do it.

But I don't need to. Because things like this don't happen to me.

ト

She puts a towel over the lampshade and the room goes dark. I feel the futon shift as she sits down next to me (oh God) and says in broken English,

"What you want me to do?"

And I'm thinking—I'm here. I've got to go through with this now. I mean, I can't just run out and leave, wearing a towel. And all I want is a massage. No, really. All I want is a massage. No, really.

"Just a massage."

Silence. She moves behind me and touches me. My back tightens instinctually. And somewhere inside I experience realization, or insight, or epiphany. I reach and turn off fluorescent lights, televisions, and computers. All the humming stops. It becomes amazingly quiet. All I hear is my heart, my breath, and my blood. I take chemistries off my skin and refined sugar out of *e. coli*–polluted sewage systems flowing into the ocean. (I'm clean outside. I took a shower). Eyes closed now, I see black pumps in a rice-paddy washing machine. Blinking Vegas lights. Truck-driving, redneck rice-chasers. I feel the touch of fingers on my back and suddenly realize this is where I am. Zoom in. Rack focus. It's like the locator map in the shopping mall. I realize this is where I am, and I realize this is for real. And the thing that tips me off is *she can't massage for shit.*

This woman couldn't massage to save her life. She doesn't even know how to touch. Barely pushes on my traps. Her touch all light and scratchy and weenie. Why am I paying for this? Is this it? Are you *serious?*

So I'm thinking, okay, either she's never ever done this before, or she just sucks at massage. And if you really suck at something, you don't do it for a living. Usually.

"Why don't you take off towel?" she asks from above.
". . . What?"
"Take off towel."

My hands go to my waist and I start to loosen the towel. I mean, I can't just let her know I'm completely sicked out by her. How's that gonna make her feel? And why am I worrying about her self-esteem? I undo it a little, and her hands jump right to my butt. Scritch scratch. Scritch scratch. Scritch scratch. All light and scratchy and weenie.

丬

I'm waiting for my cousin to see *The Fugitive* at the Waikiki 3. Same Bat time. Same Bat channel. But parking is always impossible during high tourist time, and it's always high tourist time. He drops me off at the entrance to get tickets and cruises off to look for a parking space. No matter where you go. There you are.

Cruising around, I'm standing on the sidewalk between all these Polo-wearing Japanese and crowds of local hip-hop kids. It's like try-outs for the dork convention. I see blistering, blonde, fat people with neon hats and Gecko T-shirts. I meet eyes with Chinese girls from California and mustached men in polyester aloha shirts. I see a local kid packing his cigarette box. I see a dippy white guy with a beautiful local girl. I look to my right and there's this haole guy sitting on a bench, smiling at me. Smiling at me like he knows me.

I figure this guy's gotta be a tourist. Because no one in Hawai'i wears a wool blazer. Nobody. Maybe he's here to try out for the convention, too. I give him a look of feigned recognition and start internally scanning for where I know him from. I don't have much time. The last thing I need is to get stuck in that awkward moment where someone calls you by name and you have to resort to *"Heyyyyyyyyyy . . ."*

A moment later it's here. This guy who knows me comes up and says, "How's it going?" Which spares me by not using my name. But also changes the entire scenario, as I realize this guy doesn't know me at all. Not yet anyway. He's just some gay tourist looking to pick up on a brown-skinned local boy. And here I am. How do you figure while I'm waiting for my cousin I somehow look like I'm waiting to get picked up on? Especially by gay white tourist men in wool blazers. Am I missing something? Does he have any idea how hot it is out here? Which 7 Days/6 Nights Waikiki package is this guy on? How many times has he seen *North Shore*?

"My name's Joel," he says. "Are you gonna see *The Fugitive?*"

I tell him yes.

"I love Harrison Ford."

And I'm ready to bail. But you can't just up and run away. How's that gonna make him feel? And why am I worried about his self-esteem? So I figure I'll just talk to this guy, at least until my cousin Kenny shows up. Because sometimes you just have to do things like this.

Joel is working frantically at finding something in common between us, but the conversation is going nowhere. He's standing with his hands in his front pockets, slightly looking away and nodding his head while he thinks of something to say. Something smart. Something funny. Something cool. I'm suddenly embarrassed for all the stupid things I've said to beautiful women in my life. Is it really this bad? Are we really this pathetic?

"So . . . you surf?" he asks.

How do you plan to spend the prize money, Rick?

I'm going to Hawai'i to surf the big waves of the North Shore!

I tell him yes.

And he tells me in his wool blazer, "Yeah, been pretty good out here lately . . ."

And I've had enough. But I still keep talking to the guy so as not to hurt his feelings. I see Kenny come around the corner and spot us. He instantly assesses the situation and heads straight into the theater, laughing to himself. Which is a pretty funny move, I have to admit—leaving me stuck outside with a horny wool-blazer tourist. So I tell Joel it was nice meeting him, shake his hand, and go running in the theater after Kenny. Thinking maybe Joel will figure I'm with him, and not feel bad about having to readjust his gaydar.

In counseling I tell another random therapist—this time a J.A. woman—that my whole life is about helping other people. As an artist. As a teacher. As an activist, a lifeguard, or a friend. And that I've been thinking for the first time about some things in life I might actually want for myself. Because although I've gone through cars and stereos and a quiver of surfboards, I'd still like somebody completely radical to eat dinner with. Someone able to surprise me. Someone to travel with. And see movies with. And dance with. And fuck.

She tells me this is actually a very common Asian trait that shows up in Asian Americans. (Fortunately, she's not one of these people who consider Hapas not "really" Asian American.) She refers to this with the J.A. term *en ryo*—to see your life in terms of helping others. Sacrificing yourself always. Putting others first. Never being able to say no. And that makes a bit of sense to me. I can't even let friends pay for dinner unless I really trust them. I've never really been comfortable not paying. But it doesn't explain my relationships with women or my love of individuals or my anger towards men. It doesn't explain black teddies, oranges, bananas, guns, or targets. It doesn't explain why I am here. And I'm waiting for her to ask, like all my other therapists have,

"Have you been sexually abused?"

And for me to say no.

And for her to say, "Are you sure?"

But she doesn't ask. And she hasn't asked. Yet.

So she's grabbing my butt cheeks and squeezing really firm—the massage prostitute, not the therapist. That would be a little weird, even for me. But after a couple seconds into it, she stops. Because I guess she's figured out that I'm not really into it. Or maybe she thinks I get so little that this gets me off just fine. Or maybe I'm just some bed humper, bumping and grinding myself into the rough cotton fabric. Or maybe I just can't get it up. But whatever she's thinking, her hands just go back up to my traps. Scritch scratch. Scritch scratch. Scritch scratch. All light and scratchy and weenie. And somehow I feel like I hurt her feelings. I'm sorry.

orchid

Fourteen

I started to prefer dating Asians somewhere in my mid-twenties. I can't say whether it was some kind of resolution at the end of the line or just another phase in the ongoing Hapa identity process. Because in many ways I still haven't found my way out of the maze yet. Sometimes I can't even smell the cheese. I keep waiting for Mr. Miyagi or Jerry Garcia or His Holiness the Dalai Lama to step out of the clouds and tell me I've reached some kind of dating enlightenment or ethnicity nirvana. A place where nothing seems to matter and no one judges me by my dinner partner or my bedroom playmate. But looking around me, I don't even see a cloud to step out of. I don't think anyone's coming anytime soon, and I might be waiting here a while. Better put *American Beauty* on again and press the repeat button. Pass the popcorn and pomegranate seeds.

This preference for dating someone of a similar background didn't come overnight. It didn't come without pitfalls, and it wasn't an easy place to get to. I don't really know how I got there, or even how long it took me. All I know is the transition wasn't smooth. At nineteen, I wasn't real good at paying attention to the world around me—so by the time I figured out the significance, I had already rushed in. There wasn't any thought involved and there definitely wasn't any planning. There was a pretty Asian girl living in the dorms with me at UCLA, and one day I asked her to dinner. Simple. It was a spur-of-the-moment thing. I didn't set aside any time to contemplate and reflect. I had already jumped the gun. I had already popped off. Misfired. Skipped the record. Burnt the pancakes.

Asking your first Asian girl out isn't some run-of-the-mill decision. It's not some dress rehearsal or fire drill. There is magnitude involved. I stepped completely over the line in asking Yvette Wong out, and I did so without even thinking. Why didn't anyone warn me how serious this was? I totally botched the segue. I bumped the table so hard my needle skipped over half the album. In the time it took me to say "You wanna get dinner sometime?" I went from white girls and white girls only straight into hostile foreign territory and uncharted waters. I mean, I jumped right into the deep end with all my clothes on. I skipped from "Friend of the Devil" to "Attics of My Life" without a ripple—and the worst part was I didn't even have a clue I had done it. It's like all of a sudden you look around and you're in the wrong part of town. You fell asleep and missed the stop at 110th. Everyone's staring at you.

>-

I open my eyes and it gets worse. You see, more than being my first Asian date, Yvette is my first *Chinese* date. And more than that, in a freak coincidence of coincidence—Yvette happens to be *Laura Louie's roommate* at UCLA. Talk about a recipe for disaster. What are the odds of that? I can't make up better stuff than this. And here I am trying to whistle and walk through the rose garden like everything's okay. I keep waiting for Allen Funt to come tap me on the shoulder and point out some hidden camera stashed away in the cafeteria, somewhere between the ground beef and the rice pilaf. I keep waiting for the laugh track. I keep waiting for some kind of sign. But the man never shows up, I don't come down with a cold, and my car doesn't get stolen. There's no spontaneous act of God. So fine. I can deal with it. I don't care if she's Chinese. There's a first time for everything.

Let's get ready to rrrrrrrrummmmble.

Checklist.

Beautiful.

Glossy, black hair. No bangs.

Nice smile.

Clean nails. No colored nail polish.

Good taste in shoes.

No visible panty line.

All major pluses in my book. No warning lights are showing. All systems are go on this end. (I don't care if she's Chinese.) Houston radios in and confirms. Start countdown.

>-

Okay, I'm a spaz. And she's coming by any minute. It's my first Chinese date and it's just starting to hit me. I'm excited and nervous. I'm brushing my teeth every fifteen minutes. Aim tastes good.

Just like any other date.

Just like any other date.

Just like any other date.

Spit.

Just like any other date.

Just like any other date.

Just like any other date.

Rinse.

Just like any other date.

Just like any other date.

Just like any other date.

Dinner.

I put away my toothbrush and we decide to go to House of Louie for Chinese food. I know. Not a good move.

We're at dinner, and as far as I can tell, things are going pretty good. Yvette has worn this really classy burgundy dress and matching pumps. Good taste in shoes. She's got on baby pearl earrings, a pearl necklace, and an ultra-thin gold bracelet on her left wrist. She looks great.

Good heavens, Miss Sakamoto, you're beautiful!

On my side of the table I'm wearing 501s, pink Sperry Top-Siders with no socks, and a pink Maui & Sons madras shirt. Come on, it's 1984—I could be looking a lot worse. At least I wasn't wearing some bronze Members Only jacket or some shirt with a bunch of nonsensical Japanese characters on it. What were we thinking in that decade anyway? I mean, have you ever actually looked at any of your old Duran Duran albums? Forget the hairdos even. Have you ever checked out what they were *wearing*?

We talk some kind of small, insignificant date talk. The usual gossip about other people in the dorms. Stuff about work. Class schedules. Summer plans. The waiter comes up to take our order and I realize neither of us has even glanced at our menus yet. No, no, that's okay. We'll order. Opening up the menus, Yvette and I start improvising together—and suddenly, we both spontaneously realize the person across the table from us is Chinese. It's hilarious. We both look at each other and we both know the routine. It's like finding out we went to the same piano teacher all those years, or we grew up on the same block. It's like finding out we both know the words to some completely esoteric song. Ordering food in a Chinese restaurant is just another standard family ritual—a sing-song dance between us and the waiter, filled with smiles and shaking heads, pencil scribbles and eventual nods. It's like your duty to bring fruit over to your auntie's house, and her duty to yell at you for doing so. *Aiiyaaa! So much trouble!* It's like trying to refuse a red envelope from your grandmother. It's like fighting over the check. Both of us know them all by heart. And actually, between the two of us here, it's kind of a nice revelation. Menus? Who uses menus? We're improvising.

"You have a sautéed shrimp—a *ching chao ha yun?*"

"And let's get a steamed fish, too. What kind of fish do you have?"

"And can we get a clams with black bean sauce? A *dao see* clams?"

The waiter nods away while he's scribbling everything down, muttering to himself in Chinese. Not bad. I think we actually may have pulled this thing off. I guess all those years of Chinese school finally came in handy for something. We may have gotten a little carried away and ordered too much food for the two of us, but overall I think we did okay. I'm just wondering how much it's gonna cost. Since we didn't use menus I don't have any kind of idea. I'm figuring, what . . . thirty bucks? Forty bucks maybe?

The waiter turns around to go, still scribbling, when Yvette stops him.

"Oh, one more thing," she says, grabbing his arm. "How about some vegetables? A vegetable dish?" She looks over at me for confirmation, raising her eyebrows.

Forty bucks already.

"Uh . . . sure," I say.

Yvette pulls one of the menus from under the waiter's arm and flips to the vegetable section. Her eyes scan the page. Then her eyebrows pop up again.

"How about this one—*Buddha's Feast?*"

The waiter scribbles it down.

"Okay," I say.

Ten minutes of nervous conversation later, the food comes. The shrimp looks good. The fish looks good. The clams look good. But this Buddha's Feast is revolting. It's a bunch of steaming, smelly vegetables. It's some kind of crazy concoction—soggy bamboo shoots, baby corn, Chinese spinach, water chestnuts, black tree fungus. Everything's soggy and gross. I mean, this stuff is swimming in here. This stuff is alive. But it's this *sauce*. The smell—this smelly, thick, brown, sticky sauce. The smell makes me want to gag. I hate bamboo shoots. The stuff smells like my cousin's kitchen with newspaper all over the floor, or my grandmother's bathroom with those weird vials of mystery liquid all over the countertop. It's got that full-on Chinese Tiger Balm smell to it. And you want me to eat this stuff? You want me to eat Tiger Balm? What are you thinking?

Yvette and I are eating quietly. We politely spoon portions of each dish onto each other's plates. We chopstick the food off our own plates and into our mouths. We're trying to look smooth and refined doing it, but it's impossible. No matter what you do or how careful you are, everyone eating Chinese food looks like a pig. You just deal with it. I'm sticking straight to the seafood, and trying to make the best of it, when Yvette looks over at me with her mouth half full. She points at my plate with her chopsticks.

"You're not eating any of the vegetables."

Buddha's Feast.

I try to be polite. I mean, what choice do I have? I take a small bit and put it in my mouth.

. . .

This stuff. *This stuff is vile.* What did we do—piss off the waiter? I can taste every bit of Tiger Balm and black tree fungus on every leaf and root and stem. I'm eating in some Chinese herb store, complete with dried lizards and tiger paws and rhino horns and bear gallbladders. Tastes like a mouthful of my grandmother's underwear. I reach over and grab my ice water, hoping to flush the stuff down me like a storm drain. My eyes are watering. I look across from me through the fog, and Yvette is chowing the stuff down like there's no tomorrow. I mean, she's eating this stuff like the Lawnmower Man. You can't be serious. This is a joke, right?

I do what I can with the rest of the meal, until we can't finish any more of the food. The waiter comes by and starts scooping up the leftovers into little paper boxes. He's using two spoons like chopsticks.

Please don't put the Buddha's Feast in.

"You want to take it all home?" he asks.

"Sure," Yvette says, looking over to me for confirmation with her eyebrows up again. I just smile back. I mean, what choice do I have? I leave the cash on the table. Yvette grabs the warm paper bag. And we head out to a movie.

⌇

We're watching *Red Dawn,* some kind of Communist-paranoia patriotism movie. It's pretty bad. But it's also a first date with a beautiful girl. And on first dates with beautiful girls it doesn't matter how bad the movie is. Because you're not paying attention anyway. You're just trying to figure out how close your legs are to each other, and whether your shoulders are ever going to touch. You're just trying to build up the guts to put your arm around her in your 100+ minutes of darkness. And

116

none of this back-of-the-chair stuff either. That doesn't count. We're talking on-the-shoulder or nothing. Halfway through the initial Commie invasion, I go for it. The Russian paratroopers are swooping in and taking over the school. Just as the first soldier bursts into the classroom, I put my arm around her. For an awful moment I'm stuck in that no-man's land—waiting to see how she's gonna gauge the whole invasion. This is the date, right here. Friend or foe? It all comes down to a running bank shot at Boston Garden and there's two seconds left on the clock. Inbound pass to Magic—*two . . . one . . .*

Yvette moves in closer and leans her head on my shoulder.

It's up . . .

It's good!

It's a winner. The date is officially on, and the movie isn't even half over. Things are going good. Yvette's silky black hair falls against my neck and rests there. This is good. I feel her left hand go to my knee in the dark. This is better. I undulate a little, cuddling her up closer. She nuzzles up to me and

Buddha's Feast.

I smell Buddha's Feast. What is this? I smell the steaming, soggy vegetables. I smell my grandmother's medicine cabinet and undergarments. Is it her breath? Is it on me? I feel like I'm going to gag! What's wrong with me?

I slowly lean away from her towards the aisle, and take the kind of sideways breath you take when you're changing a diaper.

Breathe in deep.

Hold. 2 . . . 3 . . . 4 . . .

My arm nonchalantly moves off her shoulder to the back of her chair. Her hand stays on my knee and her hair remains on my neck. She's got no clue and I want it to stay that way. I can deal with this. The Haz-Mat guys have arrived and they're dressed for a Level 1 incident. They're walking up and down the aisles looking for mercury gas or cyanide or H_2S. I want to tell them it's not that big a deal. It's not. You guys can take off—everything's under control. But I figure it's their job. Who am I to interfere? I let my air out gently, and begin to cautiously sniff the evening again. I don't smell anything. Everything seems to be okay, sir. Just a false alarm. Routine incident. Houston radios in and reports all systems still operative. They're just waiting for my go-ahead. Standing by. I'm watching a cheap propaganda movie in a half-empty theater with a beautiful girl. The smell is all in my head. The smell is all in my head. The smell is all in my head. Everything's cool.

An hour and a half later we're back at her dorm room about to say goodnight. She stops at the door and unlocks it. We stop. She whispers to me that her roommate might be sleeping, and tells me she had a really good time tonight. I look at her in the single light. I see her glossy, black hair and delicate features. She looks beautiful. Quiet. Still. Poised. Somehow the game is in overtime. There was a foul on the last-second shot. It's Laker ball again. They use their last twenty-second time out and bring the ball to half court. Worthy is inbounding and the crowd is going crazy. Everyone's on their feet and I'm tingling head to toe. I move my face closer to Yvette's, and her chin lifts slightly at my approach. Her eyes close. Her lips part slightly. I'm going to kiss her and

Buddha's Feast.

This smell comes up in me again. It's in my mouth. It's in my nose. I can smell it on me. I can taste it. What is going on? It's all in your head, man. It's all in your head. It's all in your head. It's all in your head. Relax.

Yvette's eyes are closed. I move closer. I can do this. We're almost touching and it's getting stronger. I think I can. I think I can. I think I can.

BUDDHA'S FEAST.
BUDDHA'S FEAST.
BUDDHA'S FEAST.

I've got no control of it. It's going through my nose and I can't stop it. No brakes and I'm heading down Mulholland at rush hour. No use steering now. I'm convulsing deep down like I've got some crazy kind of Chinese hiccups. All I can smell, all I can think—all I can see, feel, or taste is Buddha's Feast. I try to make it a quick peck. I mean, I've got to do something. It's the least I can do, right? A token gesture. A modest physical connection for all our suffering in Chinese school and piano lessons together.

I touch her lips and it just overwhelms me. Before I can even feel her, I'm already pulling back—mumbling some kind of goodbye and walking away down the hall. I mean, I'm in and out like bad Mexican food. I don't even know if I actually kissed her. For all I know, I might have just made some kissing sound in the air like a bunch of Europeans greeting each other. I don't care. I'm not turning around and I'm not stopping. I'm trying to look as slow and nonchalant as I can, and move as fast as possible at the same time. I'm like a race walker in the Olympics. Left. Right. Left. Right. Think hips. Getting around the corner, I break out of visual contact and go into full stride. I'm out of radio range and running all the way back to my room and my floor and my own little world, staying quiet and under the radar. I've got soft shoes on and they hide my footsteps. There's no trail here and nothing to follow. Top-Siders are like that.

Inside my room, I close my door and take off my shoes. My roommate isn't home. It's almost 11:00. I pop *Enter the Dragon* into my VCR, sit on the couch, pick up the remote, and press play.

What was that? An exhibition?
We need *emotional content*.
Try again.
. . .
I said *emotional content*—not anger!
Now try again.
With me.
. . .
That's it.
How does it feel to you.
DON'T THINK! *(slap)*
Feel.
It's like a finger, pointing away to the moon. Don't concentrate on the finger, or you will miss all that heavenly glory.
Do you understand?
. . .
(slap)
Never take your eye off your opponent. Even when you bow.

Somewhere in the next few years, the transitions get easier. I'm not quite sure how. Jerry Garcia never drops me a line and I eventually get tired of listening to Bruce's broken English. I think I may have missed a lot of heavenly glory. Over time there is magnitude in other dates, just as there are slow changes in my consciousness, self-awareness, and tastes. But the changes are subtle and constant. Before you know it, it's Christmas season again. They're advertising for Nintendo 64 and racing sets. Your car needs to be smogged and your puppy has grown up. Before you know it, you're searching out Asian girls like sunflowers at farmer's markets. Sometimes you can only see changes after long periods of time and distance. And the farther I get from beautiful Yvette Wong and her baby pearls and nice shoes, the more I kick myself for not kissing her, and for not following up with a second date. The farther I get from Yvette Wong and her burgundy dress, the more I wish I could meet her in my life now. I guess, in a weird way, that's progress.

Fifteen

Six years later, I felt like I had it worked out. I had gone through my whites-only stage. I had gone through my Asians-only stage. For the first time in my life I felt like I had actually and successfully integrated my tastes. No more ethnically biased SAT. No more firefighter quotas. No more segregated schools. For the first time in my life I'm actually dating women and actually dealing with them as women, period. No primary and secondary adjectives. For the first time in my life I'm actually realizing the enormous amount of complexities outside race and ethnicity. I feel like I'm finally ready for all that heavenly glory.

I'm dating a Chinese woman named Mandy Chan who cuts her hair with a shaver. She's nineteen to my twenty-four, with a real sexy bit of independence and confidence. She's a strong Asian American feminist. Done her reading. Done her theory. Done her marching. I'm into it. Strong women are strong women wherever they are. We meet at a conference and argue about Maxine Hong Kingston and Frank Chin. Yes, it's tired, but it's an excuse to politically flirt. How much of yourself do you put into what you say? And how much of her is she letting in? Mandy holds her own. Strong and forceful, but at the same time sexy and flirtatious. She's got muscular Cantonese calves, smooth skin, and bangs across her eyes to balance the crew cut in back. After a few more years, phone calls, and conference run-ins, she ends up at my house for the weekend.

This is a bit unusual even for me. She's come up for the weekend—which essentially makes this our first "date." But we've never even kissed. She gets to the door and rings the doorbell. I open it and we hug each other because we don't know what else to do. Our heads pass each other, and in those two seconds of awkward forever, we both internally wonder where she's gonna sleep tonight. *Never say never.*

"How's it going?"

"Good."

Things are going fine. We go out for Thai food and end up watching TV. Some *Dukes of Hazzard* rerun or something. I'm not really paying attention. The TV's just kind of on. Four hours have gone by and we're still no closer to figuring out where she's gonna sleep than when she came in. We're just more full.

"So what do you want to do?" I ask.

"About what?"

"About where you're gonna sleep tonight."

She laughs a little. "What do you mean?" It's the kind of nervous laugh where you're caught with your hand in the cookie jar.

I'm going for broke. "I figure it's this way," I say. "You're here for a weekend. I invited you here, and you came here so we could be together. We've got about forty hours. I figure we spend them together." Which makes sense to me. We've been toying with the idea of being lovers for enough years now, and the current situation doesn't give us the time to coy around. I figure we go for it.

Which isn't to say I want to fuck her. I haven't decided. I just want to be skin to skin with her. Hold her, kiss her, that sort of thing. She's into it. We share a communal sink and do all the things we can do together—brush our teeth, wash our face, etc. I leave and she does all the things we can't do together yet—adjust underwear, check hygiene, pee. We switch positions and I do the same. I come out of the bathroom and get into my futon with her to my left. I turn out the light.

"So what do you want to do?" I ask.

She laughs, but not as nervously as before.

We begin kissing the way you begin kissing someone you've never kissed before. Your skin tingles against theirs because it's new and uncharted. You tentatively touch and hold each other for the first time horizontally, which is a world apart from the hello/goodbye doorway hugs we're used to. We bring our faces closer together in the black. Even in the darkness you can sense her face approaching. The first kiss is light and dry, barely touching our lips together. You kiss again, both of you thinking about when your tongue's going to get involved and whether or not you should be the one to initiate it. A few more dry kisses get progressively stronger and puckier. I feel the dart of her tongue like a snake. Touch and go. It strikes and disappears. (She initiated. I like it.) Our tongues start darting lightly along each other's lips in synch. Mine. Hers. Mine. Hers. Until we finally meet and taste each other for the first time.

We retract instantly—enjoying the nervousness. One second. Two seconds. I can barely see the light of her teeth grinning in the dark. I'm smiling, too, and wondering if she can see me as well. It's a wonderful place here. A place that only exists for a moment. Like striking a match, it flames quickly, and just as quickly disappears. Sometimes all you remember is that first chemical reaction. Sometimes all you want out of life is that sulfur and friction. You can strike match after match, but in all your life you only taste someone for the first time once. We both know this. And we both want to hold on to it as long as we can, savoring it. Slowly, we come back together, sensing each other in the darkness. Touching our lips together again we gently relax into a groove. Our tongues get used to each other's company. We set a pace, and fall into a rhythm.

Mandy, the Chinese girl, the strong Asian American feminist with muscular calves, tastes pretty neutral. Maybe slightly bitter but not in a bad way. These are important things. Everyone tastes and smells different, and sometimes you just don't match.

ト

I remember a Hapa woman I dated in high school named Dana Apollinaire. I loved both her names, first and last. Dana was Italian, Swedish, and Chinese, though you couldn't tell by looking at her. To me, she just looked great. I don't remember much about her, except she was sort of an edge girl. A darkie. Full attitude. A real tough cookie with a long history. She wore sheer black skirts and a black tank top and cowboy boots. Dyed her hair black. Silver earrings, bracelets, and rings. She sang in a band and did modern dance. I don't remember much else about her besides I really liked her and my parents really didn't like her. Dana was a seventeen-year-old lesbian when I met her, a seventeen-year-old bisexual when we dated, and an eighteen-year-old heterosexual when we broke up. That I remember.

She lived up in Glendora, which is about five miles towards the foothills from Covina. And when I'd pick her up or drive her home, we'd always pass an In-N-Out Burger on Grand Avenue at Arrow Highway. And since this is back when I ate meat, and back when I considered In-N-Out to have the best burgers, we often stopped to eat there together.

This would all be fine if In-N-Out didn't have a distinct taste and aftertaste to all of their food. It's like McDonald's. No matter what you order—Quarter Pounder, fries, McNuggets, shakes—after you finish eating, your mouth always tastes the same. You always have after-McDonald's mouth. You can smell it in someone's car, on their skin, or in their hair. *You just ate McDonald's, didn't you?* In-N-Out is the same way, but their aftertaste is actually a little more disgusting. I guess it's something in the way they fry their burgers or what kind of meat they use or something. But you end up getting this fatty coating slicked along your tongue and the lining of your mouth that you can't wash out. You can't drink it out either. You can't even brush it away. You have to take a napkin and physically wipe the coating off your tongue. And this only helps a little, because usually your tongue gets all bumped up and irritated from rubbing it with a paper napkin, which just adds to all the oral confusion already going on.

Now try eating this stuff together. A Double-Double, fries, and a strawberry shake—coating your own mouths and smelling it in each other's clothes and hair. Then driving back to your parents' house and making out for the first time. Because this is how I got to know Dana's taste. And even though Dana and I ended up having great sex and the beginning of what could have been a pretty serious relationship, my leaving for school, my parents hating her, her smoking, and her ex-girlfriend trying to kill me pretty much finished it off before it ever got a chance.

I wasn't stoked about Mimi coming after me, but I could care less about her being Dana's ex. I didn't care about Dana's sexuality so long as I was involved. Being bisexual or lesbian or whatever just didn't register with me. I couldn't care. All through our dating, Dana was so embarrassed to tell me. She'd keep hinting about it without coming out. Until finally, in a moment between In-N-Out kissing on some throw pillows in the TV room, she gets real quiet. She looks me deep in the eyes, and says,

"I have something to tell you."

"Bisexual?" I ask. This just throws her for a loop.

"*What*—how did you know?"

What's to know? I just figure human beings are just attracted to the human beings they're attracted to. That all these categories of straight or gay or bi don't make any more sense than ethnicity questionnaires. Human beings are naturally open to love, befriend, and fuck whoever they naturally want to love, befriend, and fuck. Whether that's a man or woman isn't really important to me. But once we start attaching stigma and rules and categories, we start limiting ourselves. And that's a bad thing in any respect. You get raised here and you no longer have openness. All you have is choice. And making a choice to be straight, gay, or bi is a bad choice to have to make. But in this world you don't get the choice not to make a choice. That's the way it is. No customer service hotline and no manager on duty.

I'd like to be able to follow my own advice, but I know I'm at the point now where I can't be with a man. I mean, I'd like to be open enough to be able to be with whoever I'm attracted to, man or woman.

But I've been pretty well conditioned over the last twenty years or so. And the thought of some other guy's dick in my mouth pretty much does it for me. No, thanks.

Dana tries talking to me about Mimi one day.

"Mimi's really pissed off that I'm seeing you," she tells me.

Why are you playing the pronoun game?

"Well, no shit," I say. Of course she is. Here you have a two-year relationship with her where you've come out and defined yourself within her own lesbian limitations. Then you go off and fall for some high-school letterman? *I'd* be pissed.

"Why don't you just see her, then?" I ask.

"What?"

"Why don't you just see her?"

Dana hesitates for a second. "You wouldn't mind?"

And I tell her, "No," before I can even think about it. Which doesn't make sense to me. Here I am falling for this beautiful Hapa girl with the beautiful name. A girl who I really like and my parents really hate. She's telling me she might want to start seeing her ex-lover again and I'm saying go ahead like it's no big deal? But the thing is, the more I think about it the more I realize it really doesn't bother me, for some reason. I don't have any jealousy about it whatsoever. If it was a man I would. But somehow because Mimi's a woman, it just doesn't register as a threat. It's too different.

Meanwhile Dana's saying, "Wait a minute—you don't mind *at all?*"

"Not really," I say. "It doesn't bother me."

"You're saying you don't mind if I see Mimi *while I'm dating you?*"

"No," I tell her. "See all the girls you want. Just let me watch." Which really ticks her off. I knew it would, but I couldn't resist.

"Don't fuck with me about this!" she yells.

"You know I'm not into that," I laugh, trying to cover my tracks. "I'm just kidding. Bad joke."

"It's a bullshit joke!"

"Sorry."

"So it *does* bother you?" she asks.

"Well . . . no. It doesn't."

"But it would bother you if it was a guy, right?"

"Yeah, that would kill me."

"That doesn't make any sense!" she says.

"Of course it does," I tell her. "It's a whole different ball game. How can you compete with or even be threatened by it? It's totally different!"

"Because it's a *relationship*! Because it's my *affection*! It's me wanting to be with *someone else*! Whether it's a guy or girl doesn't matter!"

Which all makes total sense to me. She's right. It should matter to me. It just doesn't. And I still can't figure out why it doesn't. Maybe it's all between our legs. I've got a cock and I'm thinking I can do everything Mimi can do and more. There's no threat here beyond the physical. There's no thought about me not having the pussy or breasts that Dana might want. There's no register that maybe what she loves about me is somehow beyond the physical.

Later that day, I go down on Dana for the first time. She tastes like In-N-Out. I finish her. She says to me,

"Pretty good . . . *for a guy.*"

乑

Mandy, the Chinese girl, the Asian American feminist with muscular calves, has settled into a groove with me. We tap a slow rhythm of catch and release. My hands rub her stubble crew cut as we explore each other's mouths and bodies for the first time. I'm enjoying it okay, and it seems like she is, too. No major snafus of Dana In-N-Out tastes or clicking teeth. But at the same time no major fireworks, hooks, or drives.

We roll around horizontally underneath the covers of my futon. It's late October in Santa Barbara. Usually cold, but this year has kept me in mind and stayed warm. Santa Barbara should always be like this. My windows are open and a light blanket over a top sheet is enough to keep you comfortable through the night. The two of us are already partially disrobed. Her in a t-shirt and panties. T-shirt and boxers for me. Our legs intertwining, we rub smooth skin to skin here in a late summer that refuses to let go. It is a good feel. My hands roll across her back and grab her ass as we kiss. Her ass is tighter and meatier than I expected, but still bears the characteristic flatness of Asian jeans and genes. The feel of her panties over it is strong for me, stronger than if she was totally nude. And something about this silk panty barrier covering her most intimate privacy—this last line of clothing defense—elicits a deep-seated drive in me. Whether it be from thoughts of conquest, forbidden zones, or rape, I don't know. But I can feel the pulse in my cock tighten under its wings. She senses it and intuitively responds by clawing stronger into my back. This is how sex should happen.

Our shirts come off and I'm on her breasts. Small and firm with small nipples. For some reason they don't do much for me. I'm not really a breast man to begin with, although I realize its necessity to me. I used to think of myself as only an ass man, and this was the way I'd instantly assess any potential sexual partner. I learned this working at Raging Waters at eighteen. It was the opening year of the first major water park to be built in SoCal. Twenty slides, 10,000 waves, and a million overpriced souvenirs. This man-made beach and wave pool sits in the middle of rolling brush hills, oak, and smog, playing Beach Boys and Jan and Dean over its speakers every day. I do all the things I've learned to do. I watch my water. I present a proper image. I keep my emotions in check. The music helps. Every day I'm reminded that, in this post-Carly life, girls need to be kept away from my feelings. Girls and feelings need to be kept separately, like male bettas. Don't get attached, don't get hurt. It's step one of learning to be an asshole and I'm on fully armored autopilot. Barbed wire, electric fences, Plexiglas, and sentry towers. My fins are raised and my gills are splayed. I'm like Iron Man. I'm like Manzanar.

It's hot enough at the park's 10:00 P.M. closing time to go shirtless, walking off the imported sand and out to the unpaved employee parking lot. On windless summer nights you can leave the top down on your car all the way to your friend's house, any random party, or any twenty-four-hour Taco Bell. A good three-month summer in this ultimate inland California dream means never having to wear a shirt. My best swim-team friends work alongside me, and we take over the slides after hours, doing all the things we enforce the public not to do. Headfirst. Backwards. Airborne. Pairs and trios. During the day we make legitimate life/death rescues in between getting free food from the food-court girls in exchange for a kiss behind the snack stand. It's an eighteen-year-old male's perfect paradise. The fishbowl hierarchy goes from brine shrimp to tetras to gouramis to African ciclids. You have clean-up crew, food court, parking, ticketing, raft rental, and security. Lifeguards own the place.

Because it's the first year of the first park, they haven't really worked out operating procedures yet. Some mammoth investment company underwrites the park's construction. They draw up some plans, advertise the California dream until cash flows in, then go on to the next community or town. Like a SoCal version of Wal-Mart. We are left behind as mindless workers. Honeybee drones with no leaders or collective vision. We turn to embezzling whenever and whatever we can. What else are we supposed to do? Like tan rats with chlorinated blond hair, we scarf up everything in sight—money, food, supplies, or sex. It is all part of growing up in the inland empire of

Covina, Glendora, San Dimas, or La Verne. We grow up in high school with no stimuli or goals past Friday night football games, drugs, and sex. Friends are gained and forgotten a year after graduation, without reprieve. Girls are challenges in back seats and guest bathrooms while you learn that the worse you treat women, the more they desire you. I keep blank scraps of paper for phone numbers in my backpack and wait for sixteen-year-old girls—sometimes fifteen—to walk into the park in their one-piece swimsuits. It's just another method of stealing. Mark (in parking) takes an extra $20 a day by not giving receipts. Steve (in rafts) takes in $30 to $40. Justin and I clock in for each other on our days off, and we all learn that the fastest way to size up a girl is her ass.

I . . . I . . . I love little girls, they make me feel so good . . .

You look at a woman's ass and you know the rest of her body instantly. It is early June here, and the promise of continual heat through November is like a check in the bank. It's an equity-income mutual fund. We sit on our lifeguard towers like vultures with erections, talking on the phone as the 10 A.M. opening crowd filters in the front gate.

Old lady . . .
Family . . .
Kid . . .
Kid . . .
Kid . . .
Family . . .
Family . . .
Girl—too young . . .
Guy . . .
Guy . . .
Family . . .
Kid . . .
Kid . . .
Kid . . .
Kid . . .
Family . . .
Mom . . .
Dad . . .
Daughter. There's one. Check her out, fellas.

"We've Been Having Fun All Summer Long" plays on the park loudspeakers, and I put Coppertone 25 on my already dark arms. I still can't hear that song or smell Coppertone sunscreen without thinking Raging Waters like some swim-team Pavlovian dog. There are a lot of things you learn and remember by repetition, smell, and song. And, dog behavior or not, that smell still brings to mind a good feeling, a good time of life to have lived. A lot of this stuff I'm not proud of, but that's not going to make me diminish the memory. Everywhere in life you learn lessons. Some good. Some not so good.

Sitting in our towers, we talk on the phone about each girl walking down the path to the wavepool, competing over how quickly we can say "yes" or "no" to the desire potential of any nameless, lonely inland girl spending a day at the water park. We average less than a second a woman. Do their parents have any idea what their $20 has gone towards?

Kid . . .

Kid . . .

Kid . . .

Old lady . . .

Mom . . .

Guy . . .

Guy . . .

There's one. No.

For them and for us, this is where the "Are we having fun yet?" bumper sticker originates. These barefoot, walking white girls two steps from trailer-park trash are in their prime here at fourteen to sixteen. Before manipulative and abusive letterman boyfriends. Before abortions, divorces, and dreams of fashion design and modeling give way to dyed hair, body fat, alcohol, and finding cigarettes in their own eleven-year-old daughter's purse, or a used condom stuck to the bottom of her wicker trash basket.

But here, now is now. We celebrate youthful bravado and the ability to make our penises erect. Girls here are always frozen at fifteen. You get older. They stay the same age. And as you continue to return to the job year after year, they get further and further away from you as you struggle to recognize today's music and ignore your wrinkles and receding hairline. Some lifeguards become permanent members of this go-nowhere club. Like college professors or politicians who recycle their wives and girlfriends every few years for the current model. It's a scary thought for me now, but at eighteen it's like some kind of weird joke. I recognize thirty-year-old lifeguards flirting with fifteen-year-old girls. I know why the girls flirt. I know why the men flirt. I know both reasons are a little sad.

When they're around they make me feel like I'm the only guy in town.

Counting girls coming in, towers 7 and 9 have an advantage because they get backside views.

No . . .
No . . .
No . . .
Yes.

We used to think you could tell a woman's body from her legs, but this isn't true. Usually it is, but sometimes you see a girl who looks great from the ground up with really skinny legs, but as you scan up higher she's got this really big butt. Potato with toothpicks. Like the "Time-for-Timer" guy on Saturday morning TV shows singing, "How 'bout a wagon wheel?" A physical trait that we, the young old-boys' network of Raging Waters, dub a problem as a million women joggers wear sweatshirts tied around their waists and Suzanne Sommers rakes in the dough with Thighmaster after Thighmaster. It's no secret that men invent games to keep themselves in power. And this game is in full force. If you want to get good at it, you just don't trust a leg shot.

On the other side, there's no such thing as a woman who's got a really small, tight butt and at the same time really big, fat legs. Doesn't happen. Just physics, I guess. And from this logic we learn to watch hundreds of fifteen-year-old asses in one-piece swimsuits walk into an amusement park, honing our skills for a lifetime.

No . . .
No . . .
No . . .
Yes.

We learn a lot of things early on that stay with us long after we leave transplanted beaches and mini malls. It's a coming-of-age ritual. We're getting taught an eighties version of hunting for food, building a log cabin, fixing a leaky faucet, and never crying. The only catch is, we're teaching ourselves. There is no elder here. No alpha male. Every single lifeguard at Raging Waters is eighteen—even if his birth certificate says he's twenty-five or thirty. We're all the same. It's like *Lord of the Flies* and we don't even have a conch shell. Everyone's a competitor. Piggy's already dead. We're fighting each other for who can move in the fastest, and who can score the most points. Phone numbers are field goals. Dates are touchdowns. Sex is a shutout. We're stuck in some individually separated betta display stack at an aquarium store, twelve cups high and twenty cups deep, displaying our fins and trying to fight each other through Plexiglas cups and airholes. Our whole world is looked at through throwaway, unrecyclable plastic cups. Everything is grossly distorted. Everything seems bigger and more important than it really is. We're Dolly-cloned peacocks that you can't quite get to know, turning our heads in unison when a pretty girl walks by. How much is that puppy in the window? How much is that fish in the cup?

Although male bettas are often kept in community aquaria, this is not the proper place for them. While they will fight viciously with their own kind, in an unfamiliar situation they can become quite passive and fragile. Their trailing finnage is a great temptation to other fish who will often harass the slower-moving fighter and nip or tear his fins. This puts him under stress, which can lead to both bacterial and fungal infections and eventual death. Females, on the other hand, seem to be able to fend for themselves in the average community aquarium of non-aggressive fishes. They are generally more hardy and active, and make ideal additions to any healthy tank.

Inside the water, we are completely certified inland idiots. Purebred and pedigreed. Big fish in a chlorinated natural reservoir who take some YMCA advanced lifesaving course and think they own the world. We learn how to inflate our clothes with air in case we're ever on the Titanic, and how to cross-chest carry a panicked water victim in case we ever want to be drowned on the job. I spend an entire summer working there, then another. By the time some corporate guy with a walkie-talkie comes up to promote me, I've made thirty rescues and graded thousands of asses. I've put in my time. He tells me headquarters has created a new position, Lifeguard Supervisor, and they want me to fill it. He says things have been running a little lax lately, and they want the park spruced up and shipshape. They want the guards more controlled and professional. They want all this horseplay corralled. What do you say?

I think about it for a second. If I take the position I'm suddenly responsible for the other thirty guards who all know how to float their clothes and come too close to a victim but have no idea how to spot a rescue or prevent an accident. I barely know how myself. It means I'm responsible for teaching these guards how to work, how to think, how to respond, and how to behave. It means I'm instantly going from worker bee to alpha male. All of a sudden I've got the conch. I've got Piggy's specs. I can make fire.

What do you say?

The walkie-talkie man is waiting for my answer but I don't know what to give him. I don't know what to say. Things look different somehow. I look at his polo shirt with the company logo. I look at his hairy arms and thick fingers and Casio G-Shock watch. I look at his brown mustache and dirty smile and cop glasses. The sun is still on my back, the chlorine still in my eyes. Everything is a uniform pale yellow behind my Vuarnets, but things are different. I see my nephew coming in the front gate and I suddenly want him swimming in my water—my water and no one else's. Keep in sight. Wave to me now and then so I can see you, okay? I see my teenage daughter walking in and I want her staying away from here altogether. Are you listening to me? I don't want you going there. She gets pissed off and says I never let her do anything. She says she just wants to hang out with some of her friends, and all of their parents are letting *them* go. I catch the scent of Coppertone 25 on my skin, and see her walking in the front gate while thirty Siamese fighting fish turn their eyes in unison towards her.

What are you looking at?

"So, you up for it?" the walkie-talkie man asks, still smiling.

I've always wanted a daughter. I mean, I'm sure I'd be happy with a son, too, but I've always had this idea of raising a girl. I'd want her to have her own mind and her own set of values, and I'd want her to never, ever date me at eighteen. The cycle stops here. Natalie or Tara or P.J. or Rachel will know better. She's secure in her own body. She doesn't need some Raging Waters man/boy to tell her she's got a good ass or not, and she doesn't need to feel beautiful in others' eyes. She calls her own shots, completely comfortable alone or in public. Men come to her for her confidence and fire and she demands appreciation and desire because she deserves it. This is all it takes and this is what she has. I want my daughter riding horses in the desert and swimming in the ocean just for the joy it gives her. She sings when she feels like it, without worrying about where she is, who's around her, or whether she's out of key. *You don't like it? Like I care.* She is all attitude, with armies of followers backing up her every word. She plays water polo and walks into any bar she feels like. *You want to buy me a drink? Gimme a break.* She finds her own homecoming date and insists on meeting his parents and kissing him goodnight because she paid for dinner. She plays a '59 Les Paul with a custom sunburst and she surfs Oxnard, Lunada Bay, and Wind-N-Sea without getting dropped in on. This is what makes her beautiful.

A feminist man is no more feminist than the next man. For all the openness you covet and empathy you acquire, you still carry with you your own tastes and desires and these depend on a person's demand. I love a trophy girl as much as the next guy. Probably more. Tall and beautiful with long hair, thin ankles, and a tight ass. I like to be seen with her and for heads to turn when we walk down the street or enter a restaurant. An individual man can't control his attraction any more than any other man, and I cannot physically desire an unattractive woman. I can try, but nothing happens. An unattractive woman elicits only soft desire in me. Soft desire. Soft penis. Soft heart. This is always constant and recognizable, and it's not something I'm proud of it. It's just the way it is.

Yet women become attractive when they set their own terms. And looking back through past lovers I find short hair, short stature, thick ankles, and an occasional fat butt. All on women I considered completely beautiful at the time. Few of whom I consider beautiful now. What is it that draws you in? What is it that makes you toss all your baggage aside? A woman insecure about her small breasts calls my attention to it as much as a video artist apologizing for technical difficulties beforehand. Telling us you're really sorry the image we're about to see is so green makes us see green. Telling me you wish your breasts were bigger makes me wish they were bigger, too. I love perfect mouth-size breasts. But if you make me want you without them, you make me want you without them. Go ahead. I'm game. Beauty and my attraction are never constants. They're just recognizable.

I tell the walkie-talkie man I'd like to think about it, and his face drops. He puts his dirty smile back in his pocket and turns around, walking away brusquely. Is it something I said? The next day I walk into the main office and tell them I'm not interested in the supervisor position. They tell me it doesn't matter because they've already given the job to someone else. Two weeks later, I move down to San Diego to start school. The next summer I begin lifeguarding at the state beaches there, and Raging Waters records its first drowning.

ト

The other day I was a guest artist in a local college class. An Asian American student asked me to talk about the major turning points in my life. When were they? What happened? What were the epiphanies?

The question stumped me for a second. I hadn't really thought about it before. So to stall for time a bit I asked her the same thing.

"Lemme think for a second. What were *your* major turning points?"

"I don't know. That's hard to answer," she says.

"But you ask me and expect me to answer."

"Yeah."

"But you can't answer it yourself?" I ask. "That doesn't sound fair."

"Well . . . *I'm* only twenty. You know, I haven't really . . ."

"Oh, so now I'm old, too!" I interrupt.

"Well . . . *yeah!*"

The class enjoyed this exchange. They laughed a bit and it lightened the mood. Plus the girl had spunk, which I appreciated. So I started answering her question. I talked about a couple of near-death experiences in my life—getting trapped in a subway during a fire, going over a cliff skiing, etc. I talked about how after each of these experiences, little bits of life meant more to me.

I figured I had answered her pretty well, and I saw a lot of heads nodding up and down while I spoke. So either the class was with me or they'd completely mastered the look-like-you're-listening posture and behavior. Maybe both. But when I glanced back over at the girl who asked the question, she had a quizzical look on her face.

"What's the matter?" I ask. "You don't like my answer?"

She hesitates a second, slightly embarrassed. "No . . . it's not that . . ."

"What is it, then? Come on!" I say, snapping my fingers for effect.

She bites her lip in thought for a moment. Then says "Well, you talk about all this stuff in the ocean and how important it is to you, right? You lifeguard, you surf, you . . . shoot fish, whatever. But all these important things you're talking about that supposedly changed your life—none of them is in the ocean. You know what I mean?"

I nod my head to her. Go on.

"I mean—okay, *I'm* scared to death of the ocean, right? I mean, I can swim and all. I mean, I'm not super good or anything, but I can swim. I was on swim team for a while when I was a kid. But the ocean's just really scary to me. So when I hear you talk about all these, you know, near-death things, I'm just wondering how come you don't talk about that. I mean, was that always like—natural for you, or what?"

Got me again. I had never really thought of it before either. Two good questions in five minutes from the same girl. Not bad.

I think about it for a second, replaying experience after experience in my mind. I guess I've had close calls in the water. I've been held under for two waves on the north shore. I've had my leash caught on a lobster trap in San Diego. I've vomited through my regulator at sixty feet. And I've been tossed around like a rag doll more times than I can remember. But these don't register to me as near-death experiences. They're frightening at the time, but frightening in a different way. Sure, I panic, but it's a different kind of panic. For some reason, deep inside me I know without a doubt that I'm never going to die in the water. And that makes it all very different from any other experience in my life. Sometimes I'll be scolded. Sometimes I'll even be stricken. But I'll always be held.

I look back at the girl. "This may sound kind of silly," I tell her. "But water will never hurt me."

It hurts others, though. Like sacrificial virgins, they get sucked down and penetrated. It enters through their mouths, noses, and ears. It fills their lungs and cavities until their bodies start to sink. They get held down and raped everywhere at once. Sometimes I can intervene and stop the process, and sometimes I work jobs that pay me to do that. Other times I can't intervene, whether I'm being paid to or not. I just have to watch without doing anything. And I always watch. Because no matter where I am, I'm always on duty.

Like any relationship, ours is tenuous at times. I never know if my connection with the ocean is all part of some larger balancing act— how much of what I do is reacted to or simply ignored, how much input I really have. Am I just some Cirque du Soleil act or Sunday afternoon SoCal Venice chainsaw juggler? Does it make you angry when I drag people out of your pull? Do you really caress me when we play, or am I just another one of your million enamored lovers? Do you miss me when I'm away? When the only part I have of you is inside my eyes? Do you realize that no matter what I'm doing or who I'm with, I still see everything in the world through you? That you are with me everywhere I go? Every involuntary blink brings you back and coats my vision again. I feel and see every person who enters you. Some feel right. Some don't. I want to try to stop them, but they're out of shouting distance, and I'm always in slow motion. By the time I get there it's almost always too late.

At Raging Waters, every person walking in the door is worth $70. $20 on entry. $20 on food. $5 on raft rental. $5 on parking. $20 on souvenirs, video games, and forgotten sunscreen. If you get crowded, you can always open up another dirt parking lot or break open more sunblock, but you can never rent enough rafts. The sand-bottom wave pool is churned up and murky on a summer holiday, and no one figures out you've got to limit people in the space. Yellow inflatable rafts come in by the dozens, covering the water with rubber and bodies. When the "waves" start—really more chop and soup than waves—hundreds of people on hundreds of rafts scream and yell. Six eighteen-year-old lifeguards from YMCA pool training make $6 an hour to blow their whistles, pick up phone numbers, tell people what time it is, and say things like "Keep off the ladder" and "No running."

Some trusting father pays for one raft and puts his family on it. Two daughters, one son, and himself. A black family entering the water in the SoCal recreation dream. When the waves and screaming start, his youngest daughter, twelve-year-old Tanisha, slips off quietly. She is immediately buried in a sea of rubber rafts and white people. It's not dramatic. It just happens. Kicked and prodded, she is forced under a giant yellow raincoat like some evil Morton Salt girl, listening to garbled screams and water and the Beach Boys. She involuntary inhales freshly chlorinated piss water and drowns under the yellow tarp without ever seeing sunlight. Body cavities filled, she sinks to the bottom. Her one-piece child's body sits in the imported sand until the ten-minute wave cycle finishes. Above her, the father looks around the calming water without finding his daughter. He gets out to look around the park

Go find your sister.

while the new raft lemmings close up the surface again to wait for the next cycle of waves.

My friend Doug Williams is working tower 7 when a nervous black man approaches and tells him he can't find his daughter. Doug starts to call Lost & Found to give a description when the man says,

"I lost her in the wave pool."

I've talked to Doug about this. He's a good friend. We used to play in a garage band together, playing covers of X and U2 and the Ramones and taping ourselves to laugh at later. We've heard this phrase countless times, and countless times we've ignored it and waited for the kid to turn up in the bathroom or video arcade like they always do. But Doug says this time something was different when the man told him. "It wasn't the words. It was just something in the way he said it." He puts his goggles on and jumps in the water. He searches blindly along the bottom, feeling with his hands, rising with enough time to ferret out sunlight between rented rafts and surface for air.

Second dive.
Scan . . .
Surface . . .
Breathe.
Third dive.
Scan . . .
Surface . . .
Breathe.

On his fourth dive, Doug touches a human arm. He surfaces and screams to tower 3 to clear the water, and he and another guard go down and feel for Tanisha. They find her and bring her to the surface as other guards clear the water and running walkie-talkie supervisors look concerned and think about getting sued. No one screams like in the movies. It's very quiet. Doug wants to try CPR, but he can't get Tanisha's father off her body. All Doug remembers is the man wasn't crying. He appears calm. Eventually a walkie-talkie man with a knit shirt pries the father off, and Doug unsuccessfully tries CPR until the paramedics take over. The paramedics unsuccessfully try CPR until they bring her to the doctors at the hospital. The doctors at the hospital unsuccessfully try CPR until they tell the father that Tanisha died of water asphyxiation and we're very sorry. She swallowed the cat that caught the bird. She swallowed the bird that caught the spider. She swallowed the spider that caught the fly. I don't know why she swallowed a fly. I know an old lady who swallowed a horse . . .

Raging Waters settles out of court for a few hundred thousand dollars and Doug quits his job after working one more day to prove he can. "I just didn't want it to be on my last day, . . ." he says.

Ten thousand guests per day at $70 per guest equals $70,000 per day. Five days at $70,000 per day equals $350,000. I think if I hadn't left the job to guard the beach, I would have been there working tower 7 and living with this guilt now, holding the conch in one hand and a walkie-talkie with low batteries in the other. Thinking to myself, over and over, that five days at Raging Waters equals one twelve-year-old girl. Either that, or Tanisha would still be alive. It's always one or the other. As it is, I just live.

Sixteen

Mandy Chan, with the short-shaven hair and small breasts, is still going at it with me. We're horizontal, lying intertwined on my futon. She's down to her panties, and my hand is on her crotch, rubbing. I can feel her warmth and moisture beginning to soak through the imitation silk. She's not real wet and sloppy. Just calm, warm, and moist. I rub her softly for several minutes, until I can feel her lips parting slightly underneath my fingers like a smile.

Her panties are wet through now, and with all our attention downstairs we take turns switching mouth positions upstairs. Left . . . right . . . turn . . . As if we're both not thinking about where each other's hands are, where they're going, and what it is they might do. Mandy wonders if I'm going to reach under her panties, touch her directly, maybe penetrate her. I'm wondering if this woman is ever going to come anywhere remotely near my cock and why she hasn't even attempted yet. What's wrong with this picture? I have a crotch too, you know. She's thinking about my hand being on her pussy while I'm thinking about both her hands staying completely on my back and going absolutely nowhere near my cock. Yes, I think it's a problem when women don't want to touch men's cocks. Which is different from *a* woman not wanting to touch *a* man's cock. Sex is a give-and-take. An exploration. A communication and openness. And if you think it's about my ravishing your body with my mouth, my hands, and my body while you lie there waiting for some mysteriously pleasurable pressure to enter you and rhythmically bring you to orgasm without even some kind of visual introduction or response on your part, you've either been reading too many supermarket romance novels or too much evil-penis feminist theory. If you don't want to be with me, that's fine. If you don't want to be with men, that's fine. But don't confuse these two, because they're not the same thing.

Our lips break off from each other's to explore. When I venture off, my mouth goes to her eyes, her ears, her neck. On her interval she moves more conservatively, breaking off to kiss tentatively along my neck a few times. Softly, with only her lips. No teeth. No sucking. No commitment. Her hands stay to my back even though I've been rubbing her crotch for several minutes, to her enjoyment. What's the deal? I push my cock through my boxers along her thigh as we start

to grind together. Her hands stay where they are, and again I'm vib-
ing that Mandy is, plain and simple, just not into the penis. She's had
every opportunity to move forward without seeming cock hungry or
desperate or sleazy while I'm practically placing my cock in her hand
and it's no takers. And the thing is, it's not that she isn't into my
penis—that's just the end result. It's that she's not into the total *idea*
of penis.

I give up on the hope of fulfilling sex and set my sights on adequate.
I remove my hand from her panties and start to enjoy the bumping and
grinding of simulated intercourse. This should be okay. Face to face, she
responds with hip pressure and release against me. Pressure. Release.
Pressure. Release. It's nice. I rub up against her and feel her moisture
on me. Maybe this will be fun after all. We roll about, kissing and grop-
ing, and I go to move behind her for some real grinding. I love being
behind a woman, holding her tight and pressing against her ass. I try to
get behind Mandy and she rolls with me. She stays face to face. She's
lying on her back as I gently try to wedge myself beneath her to roll her
over onto her stomach. Basic physics. Fulcrum. Lever. Torque. She
responds by resisting, pressing her shoulders and hips and back firmly
down against the bed. She stays face up and I'm lying on her side. I try
harder to wedge in and roll her over, and she resists even harder.

Its hull is made of pure neutronium, Captain!

I realize she won't budge. She's staying put. It's like we're in the
middle of some Ultimate Fighting Challenge match—Dan "The Beast"
Severn and his Pan-Am wrestling vs. Royce "The Python" Gracie and
his Brazillian jiujitsu. It's like the announcer says. She won't let me
assume the "mounted position." Everyone's yelling and screaming and
the introductions are over. This can't be for real. All I want to do is get
behind you. You know, it's not like I'm armed or anything. Jesus.

Her kisses become more deliberate as she comes more and more
out of the throes of sex, and goes more and more into the don't-you-
even-think-about-it-I'm-not-letting-any-man-get-behind-me mentality.
And I realize this woman has brought the shit to bed with her. She's
brought her books. She's brought her seminars. She's brought her theory. And she's brought the entire history of misogyny, sexism, sexual
harassment, and women's power to bed with me. And she's brought it
at the expense of stilting every other form of natural behavior and normal human desire, like I'm just some nameless cog in the oppress-
women game.

How dare you bring this shit into bed with me? Why do you assume
I'm part of the monster? How can you cast me in some random role
while you pretend you're neutral? (You're not.) Why can't we just

enjoy each other's bodies here together without all this baggage? And we've got to spend a whole weekend together?

Take us out of here, Sulu. Maximum speed.

Some strengths depend on stance and posturing. And I realize that, side by side, I'm lying in bed with a woman who is all stance and all posture. I'm embracing Mandy, and Mandy's embracing her politics.

Q: How many feminists does it take to change a lightbulb?

A: I don't find that funny.

How many times am I gonna have to deal with this? How many activists do you know who can't enjoy anything in life, because all they're looking for and all they see in anything, anybody, anywhere is race, sexual preference, and gender? How often do I have to be with a woman who's afraid to be a woman? How many men are afraid of being what they think a man shouldn't be? Sensitive. Caring. Hurt. Jesus, Mandy. My getting behind you doesn't make you any less a feminist or any less a person. It doesn't make you subservient to me and it doesn't disempower you. Your resisting it does.

Body language out. I try one last effort of communication. Giving up even the hope of adequate sex and setting my sights on survival, I try to talk.

"How you doin'?" I ask.

Mandy responds, "So you want to do it?"

What? What is going on here? Tell Big John McCarthy to call time out. Stand the fighters up again, send them to their corners, and start the match over. I mean, this doesn't make sense. Here we've been going through this whole can't-touch-this and no-dominant-position-for-you routine and then you spring this one on me? What are you thinking? Can someone please explain this one to me? *Cliffs Notes,* somebody. Hello?

"Pardon me?"

"I said do you want to do it? Do you want to make love with me?" she says.

Big John McCarthy's standing over my shoulder.

(Are you ready?)

". . . That's an odd question."

"Why's it odd?" she says, entering discourse mode.

(Are you ready?)

"It's just surprising," I say.

(LET'S GET IT ON!)

"Why's it surprising?" she continues in discourse. Careful here. Any reference to her not seeming like the type to be so forward is sure to land you in oh-so-a-woman-can't-be-forward land. Careful. Slow. Bring it back to you.

"It's just that we don't know each other that well," I continue, trying to get out of telling her why I really don't want to fuck her. I mean, you can't just come out and tell someone you think they're afraid of being a woman without getting them a little bit angry.

"You seem to know me well enough to do *this* much," she says, lawyerly.

So all of a sudden she wants it now? How do I take this? On one side it's kind of a nice surprise. While on the other it's a completely sexist insult. You won't touch me. You won't let me act natural with you. You won't let me enjoy myself. But you want me to make you feel good. I'm not sure which way to look at it.

I think about it. After all this, I really don't feel comfortable making love with her. There's just too much misunderstanding. Too many arguments are left unsaid. On the other hand, she's a beautiful woman who's got me excited again with her forwardness. Something in her spunk is really exciting. So, as every man does, I draw my line.

Most men draw their line somewhere around if it's a woman and you can get it, get it. Others remain celibate or stick it out with serious girlfriends. I draw my line at oral sex. I've been with enough women to die without fretting about my masculinity, and at an average of one partner a year since becoming active, I'm quite proud of the somewhat limited number of women I've had intercourse with. It's not about safety and it's not about some kind of belief. I know oral sex is intimate. I know intercourse is intimate. It's just where I draw my line.

Sexism is as natural to men and women as the desire to be seen with a beautiful lover. But there are always underlying laws. There are always desires beneath the surface. Sex with any man is by nature a violent act. Sometimes it is also an act of violence. And in any new sex situation, particularly nervous ones like this, you need to feel each other out. It's cat and mouse—sensing how far you can push each other, how far you can let yourself go, what their fighting style is. Is she a striker or a grappler? Or is she just going to shoot me? It takes a strong person to let go in a newly sexual situation. And even though a lot of people may look strong on the outside, when it comes down to it, most just wear the clothes.

I take inventory on the situation here. We've bobbed and weaved through the opening rounds. Some slight scoring take-downs and body blows, but neither of us is really hurt. We just know our opponent better. Neither of us can get an arm bar or a submission hold on the other.

Mandy won't let me grind behind her, but she wants to make love with me. I don't want to do it, but I've invited her down for the weekend and it's only Friday night. T-minus 36 hours and counting. Not the opportune time to create a scene. Long weekend to go.

"You know, Mandy?" I tell her. "I know it sounds funny . . . but I really feel I don't know you well enough yet."

She looks at me in the dark with her short hair silhouetted in the window. I'm waiting for her to stick me with the "but you'll do this much" comeback again. But it doesn't come. She just looks at me and remains quiet. I've reached her. I see her in the dark, open again. Baggage behind, she looks like the strong, beautiful woman I wanted to be with originally. She looks great. Her hands are still on me and one of them slides down gently from my back to my butt. She doesn't say anything. I feel the ginger scratching of her nails. What am I *doing?* My cock is still fully rigged at red alert. Part of me starts kicking myself for telling her I didn't know her well enough. At the same time, I realize in my head it's the right thing to do. You're doing the right thing, okay? You're doing the right thing. You're doing the right thing. Look at the whole situation. This whole baggage bit. This whole first date. This whole weekend thing. None of it is quite right, and none of it is comfortable. It's too much too fast.

Mandy's hand starts stroking my butt, and I realize that this too-much-too-fast stuff is all fine and good in theory. But right here and now, with her hand on my butt, I don't want to fuck *theory*. I want to fuck *her*.

I don't bother chasin' mice around . . .

Take the "t," the "o" and the "y" out of "theory" and what do you get? "Her" and "Toy." Enough of this stuff. The trailers have started. The soundtrack is going. Make a move.

I slink down the alley, looking for a fight,
I owe it to the moonlight on a hot summer night . . .

I make an internal compromise and move back to my earlier line in the sand. I look her in the eyes and tell her,

"I'd love to taste you, though."

(Cat class)
(Cat style)

And this girl starts *laughing*. She's cracking up. Like I just told some great joke or made an insanely funny face. All I offered to do was go down on her. I mean, she's the one who wanted to do it in the first place.

"I don't get it," I'm saying. "What? What's so funny? What'd I say?"

Mandy doesn't answer. She just keeps laughing, burying her head in my chest and covering her face. I can feel the bristle of her spiked hair and semi-hardened holding-gel along my neck. How come they can't make hair gel that stays soft?

"What? What? What?" I keep asking as she keeps laughing. "What's so funny?"

I start replaying the tape in my head. Okay. I told her I don't feel comfortable making love. I told her I'd love to taste her, though. *Yeah . . . ?* Maybe she doesn't get the reference or something. Maybe she thinks I want to lick her skin or bite her. Maybe she thinks I'm making some kind of cannibal joke. Maybe she's just a kook.

Mandy brings her head back, still laughing, and I realize the laughing isn't regular laughter. It's nervous laughter. More about taking up space than enjoying life. I stop asking questions and wait for her to stop giggling. It doesn't take long. She stops laughing and gets serious in the dark again. All that stuff about reaching the strong beautiful woman again? Out the door. I can feel it. She's back where she's comfortable again. Sleeping in a bed of books, snuggling up in politics and feminist peer pressure. *Don't let him do that to you. Men only want one thing. Men are all the same.* It's all a cover. It's all a cloak. And it's all over. If I close my eyes I can still make out her face in the dark, looking at me as she says,

"That sounds good. But often, when there are offers like that, there's an implicit idea of reciprocation. And I *really* don't want to do that, okay?"

(Players cannot place two feet in squares 1, 2, 3, or 6)
Do me, don't me, will me, won't me . . .

The night turns into both of us sleeping uncomfortably and sexually unfulfilled. The weekend pretty much stays the same. Mandy and I eat breakfast together, take a walk on the beach, and rent a movie on Saturday night. I wanted to rent *Barb Wire* but I didn't think that was such a good idea. *Don't call me Babe.* When we go to bed, I give her a quick kiss and roll over. It takes me a while to fall asleep, but I don't talk and I don't move. She tosses and turns. I can feel her watching me—her eyes burning into the back of my shoulders and neck. Throughout the night, I never face her. She stays behind me. Neither of us sleeps very well.

Roller skating, skipping, fading . . .

On Sunday morning she drives back up north, no doubt wondering why I can't wait for her to get in the car and go. I do the obligatory goodbye watch-and-wave as her car exits the parking lot and turns the corner. I'm tapping my feet as it passes behind the trees one by one, gritting my teeth. What if she hits her brakes? What if she runs out of gas? What if the bell rings and we go into overtime? The car passes the last tree out of sight, and I run back to my apartment at full stride— still fearing the honk of her car horn or the sound of her Nissan Sentra that needs its tire rotated. Inside, I take off my shoes and lock the doors. I open all the windows, go upstairs, and take a thirty-minute shower.

In a lot of ways, I knew from the first night there was no hope. But the whole thing was my mistake. I invited her here. As the weekend progressed, I just removed myself more and more from the situation. The more I got dragged into the arguments, the more I wondered whether it would ever make a good story. It was my only way to keep going. I'm looking at it now and I'm sure it doesn't. It's not very funny. I don't have any revelations or insights or ironies to share, and if I saw her today I'd probably still feel uncomfortable. For the first time in my life, I was actually dating a woman and dealing with her as a woman— without all the complexities of ethnicity and race thrown in. And it wasn't any easier. In fact, it was harder than ever. How many more Mandys are coming down the line, locked and loaded? I know strong women are strong women wherever they are. I know some are more able to be strong than others. And I know some women keep their sex and their politics very, very close together. I just wish they came with warning labels.

delphinium

Seventeen

Across the world the water feels the same. Seventeen hours in a plane and it's like I never left.

I'm in Japan visiting my friend Brian, an old classmate from Japanese class and a longtime surfing buddy. He's got blond hair, blue eyes, and he's teaching English here. Basically every telltale sign, except the equation doesn't add up. Brian's not a rice chaser. He's one of the few here who's not. Because most Americans teaching English in Japan are male, and most of these guys have Japanese girlfriends from one of their classes. It's a problem. Growing up over the years, Brian and I have talked a lot about these kinds of issues. About the difference between someone who explores a culture to experience it, and someone who explores a culture to make up for some cluster of social inadequacies back home. The answer seems to always come down to respect and intent. What is the right way to investigate your interests? What is the right way to have interests? And how do you work and exist without utilizing a power structure that favors you at every turn? This is a hard thing to do in a country where you simply walk around as an American and beautiful college girls run up to you on the street yelling "Fine, thank you! How are you?" and "Nice to meet you!" and "This is a pen!"

I know I prefer Asian women. That goes without saying. But what if I wasn't Asian myself? How would I deal with that? What if I was some token UB40 white guy who loves playing reggae? Could I do it without trying to wear those embarrassing, white guy, dental floss dreadlocks? Could I do it without Vanilla Icing?

In late September, typhoon #12 comes up the southeast coast of Japan and brings with it gale winds and surf. It is just what I need before school starts again and I have to start mixing who I am with who I pretend to be. Somehow, here in Japan I don't have to do that. Brian and I pack up his 1/2-horsepower mini–Suzuki van with every surfboard we can find and head down the winding, two-lane road that runs along the Miyazaki coastline. Brian is about my height, with pale skin that freckles and burns at the very thought of sun. Worse than my dad's, even. He tells me the one bodily thing he'd trade for in this world is better skin, meaning darker. I tell him the one bodily thing I'd trade for in this world is better eyes, meaning less blind. I wouldn't change skin for the world.

A black/Chinese artist friend of mine has a theory about the whole skin thing. He tells me the white man invented everything in this world that tears apart our ozone, making sun exposure and skin cancer our next black plague. The white man made it all. The industrial revolution. The internal combustion engine. The beef industry and its rainforest depletion. He tells me the white man caused it, so the white man burns first.

I've lifeguarded for sixteen years without burning, and for sixteen years I've lied about my eyes. It's the question on the form right next to driver's license number and ethnicity boxes and the questions about previous felony convictions.

"Do you now wear, or have you ever worn, contact lenses?"

"No."

There's more to lifeguarding than 20/20 uncorrected vision. I've learned that by watching a lifetime full of bad lifeguards and a handful of good ones. When you think about lifeguards, you think about confidence and know-how and capability and grace under pressure. And, as much as I hate to admit it, you think: *Baywatch*.

Baywatch is the scourge of every beach lifeguard who takes his or her job seriously. I mean, where do you want me to start? It's all the episodes of giant squids and mystery currents and tsunamis. It's the silicon-breasted models who can't swim, making ocean rescues without wearing fins, or with their hair down. It's the beaches filled with gloriously beautiful people, when in reality the beach brings together the absolute *ugliest* people on the face of the planet. It's every single female lifeguard in America having to hear the same idiotic comment every single day she works.

"If I start drowning, will you rescue me?"

I start lifeguarding at the beach as a way to get closer to my water. I start it as something to come home to. Fresh out of Raging Waters at nineteen, I move to San Diego and realize I can get paid to watch the ocean eight hours a day. Is this a joke? Where do I sign?

A cold April morning finds 200 of us trying out in 54-degree water without wetsuits. My lungs freeze when I enter, but I know I'll be okay if I can just get through this. I know I'm not going to die in the water. We swim 1,000 meters in six-foot surf, returning to shore with hypothermia. Everyone is shaking frantically. No one can sit still. No one can talk. Half an hour later they take the top fifty of us and make us do a run-swim-run. Another half-hour later they take the top thirty of us to interviews. Then they take the top ten to the academy. Eventually seven of us start working the rookie towers at the South

Carlsbad campgrounds. It sounds pretty hard now when I write about it. But it wasn't so bad, really. At nineteen, you just don't know any better.

I had these wonderful dreams of beach lifeguarding. Growing up in Covina, my ocean experience was limited to Wednesday afternoon swim-team carpools in the summer, or whenever I could convince my brother to let me tag along with him as a kid. A beach lifeguard was a whole other class of existence. These guys were watermen—equally skilled at swimming, surfing, paddling, diving, and fishing. They *lived* by the water. They knew the ocean inside out. They answered any question you could throw at them. They solved problems. Going into training, I felt like an impostor waiting to be discovered. A pool swimmer who just bought his first used surfboard and was too embarrassed to ask for assistance from the blond, sunburned kids in the shop. A two-year veteran of a man-made water park and man-made waves. A lover of the ocean for the way it holds me, sitting in a room full of beach kids. Who's gonna tell me I don't belong here first?

My parents keep asking how school was. It's like asking, "How was that drive-by shooting?" You don't care how it was. You're lucky just to get out alive.

My dreams shatter fast. The academy is a week of hazing and intimidation, with some first aid and CPR mixed in. The real job is no better. The 150-person San Diego Coast squad is like some kind of mini army battalion—complete with hierarchies, social cliques, and bullies. Everyone is white. Almost everyone is blond. And everyone outside your seven-person rookie class is watching you. Everything is regimented like a fraternity, and rookies have to pay their dues. Older guards play tricks on us, calling in fake CPRs or sending some kids out in your water to "drown." It's all part of training, they tell me. It's all part of "making you a better guard." I thought I would relish watching the water each day, but the job took the joy out of it. I'm so worried about screwing up that I dread every sound, every visit, and every telephone ring. I begin hoping that no one enters my water. Because if no one is in it, I can't make a mistake. If I don't make a mistake, I can't get in trouble. I find myself praying for foggy days and rain.

Sitting in my tower, I slowly learn what a bunch of predominantly go-nowhere people do when they're stuck in boxes by themselves for eight hours a day. Some of them do pushups. Some of them write graffiti. Some of them watch women and masturbate. Believe me. I quickly learn all the tricks to take care of bodily functions, and all the attitudes of the old-boys' network. If you have to pee, piss in one of your swim fins and pour it out on the sand next to your tower. If you have to shit, shit in a bucket and hope there's enough clean gauze left in your first aid kit after wiping to bandage any accidents during the rest of your shift. *Baywatch* it's not. You learn to treat Mexicans as second-class citizens and you learn blacks can't swim. You learn to smile at your women co-workers and to talk about what they'd fuck like when it's just you and the boys. You can go into the main lifeguard headquarters and still find the hard-core porno mags that used to be sitting around the bathroom a few years back. They have to hide them now, but they're still there. Look in the file under "Reading Materials." As a rookie, you can't really do anything but smile. You can't really do much later, either.

※

Four years later, I'm a veteran guard. I've put in my dues and earned my reputation. I've worked every tower, made every rescue, and answered every question. But sitting here in some eight-hour advanced first aid class, I'm completely dumbfounded. It's worse than traffic school. I'm listening to an instructor tell me to watch out for Mexican doctors and Vietnamese stingrays. I'm listening to thirty-year-old veteran guards watch a childbirth video, yelling "Eat me!" and "Gash!" in front of fifteen-year-old female trainees who look around the room and smile uncomfortably. What are they supposed to do? I'm watching everyone else laugh the boys-will-be-boys laugh and continue on with their lives. How many more hours?

At the end of the class, we have a general discussion on how to improve future classes. I listen to everyone talk about more hands-on work, more scenarios, or more focus on primary and secondary surveys. I listen to people talk about which drills worked the best, and which were a waste of time. When they're finished, I take a shot and say my piece. I talk to an audience of about thirty white men, five white women, and a Chicano rookie named Victor Sanchez about basic things like respect and professionalism and racism and sexism. I tell them I don't care what you do on your own time, but there's no place at work for this kind of shit. Afterwards, I hear the basic after-speech responses.

"Those were really good points."

"Thanks for saying that, Kip."

"You've given us a lot to think about."

Most of the guys just look at me. I know what I'm getting into and I'm ready to leave anyway. I want to find a better way to be around the water.

After the meeting, the various people get into their various Toyota trucks and drive away to their various destinations. I'm pulling out when I see Victor Sanchez running over to my car. He comes up and taps on the window. I roll it down.

"Thanks, man," he says.

"For what?"

He just smiles and nods his chin at me.

Victor and I shake hands and he takes off. It's the type of handshake a lot of white guys give colored people to be "down." Sort of like getting a tribal band tattoo around your arm and going shirtless at the next Coors Amphitheater concert. Fine. I've never understood the idea of white people in this country desperately searching for *culture*— Guatemalan clothes, Black English, Indian sweat lodges, tribal piercing, whatever. King Arthur shields and Irish clovers I can understand. But Polynesian arm bands and kanji characters? Maybe I'm missing something between all the seven-string guitars and backwards baseball caps. I start my truck, turn on the radio, and head off to buy a burrito.

The old-boys' club at the California State Lifeguard Association shuts me out. It's what I expected, and I'm ready to leave anyway. My schedules get slightly worse. My conversations get a lot more professional. Not all of the guards participate. In fact, some were and still are good friends. But that doesn't matter. You have to realize that, overall, this is an old-school organization. A fraternity. An academy. A lodge. The kind that makes high-school rookies walk into a circle of 150 veterans and introduce themselves on opening day, while the veteran guards yell insults at them. Not everyone yells, but that's not significant. It doesn't matter if everyone doesn't participate. Because when you're in the circle, you don't hear who's not yelling. You only hear who is.

ト

In Japan, Brian and I drive down the Miyazaki coastline for nearly an hour following typhoon #12. Most of the coast is unsurfable, with typhoon gales coming in. The surf report is calling the waves five meters, but in some spots they seem bigger.

We pull into the dirt parking lot next to a *takoyaki* restaurant that marks a reefbreak called Uchiumi. As usual on a Sunday morning, there are carloads of Japanese guys wearing Rusty and Quiksilver clothes, standing around looking at the ocean and smoking. Most of them have these brownish red streaks in their hair from trying to lighten it. Brian and I mesh into the crowd and check the surf. The right is working, with fifteen guys on it. The left looks unsurfable. Too big and too gnarly.

"You should see this left go off, Kip," he tells me. "It really fires on the right conditions."

"It looks almost surfable now."

"Almost," he says. "Let's watch it a while."

Brian is like me. He'd rather surf a medium break with no one on it than a good wave that's crowded. Even here in Japan, where, for the most part, the vibe in the water is polite and friendly by American standards, it's just a matter of time until everyone learns to be jerks in the water. Too many people. Too much testosterone. Too much insecurity.

We're looking at the Uchiumi left and at something that keeps resurfacing in the impact zone.

"What is that? A log?" Brian asks.

"I don't know."

Another wave comes through the log zone and exposes the object's white underside. It's a surfboard or part of one. We watch, waiting for it to wash in, scanning outside for a swimmer on half a board. But we don't see anybody. The logboard stays out.

"Where's the other half?" he asks.

"I don't see it."

"Why isn't it moving?"

The typhoon surf is full of white water and foam, especially in the impact zone, and we lose sight of the board piece again. It's part curiosity and part concern about a surfer who might be driving back to Fukuoka with half a board, pissed off and cursing. The impact zone is about 300 yards from us. A hundred down the hill to the reef, and 200 over the reef into the water. Maybe it's swimmable if you're careful and slow, but it's not something I'd want to have to do.

A whitewater wave catches the board again and pulls it towards shore. We're relieved for a second as it gets behind the board and begins to tractor it in, until the board dips under the wave and resurfaces, sticking straight up in the air like some kid waving in front of a jetty. It's a universal sign that anyone who surfs recognizes. Tombstone. Someone's underwater, pulling down against the leash.

"*Shit!* Somebody's caught under there!" Brian yells, running back to the car like any decent human being would think to. What's he going to do? Paddle out? Get help? From whom? I'm probably the best swimmer in this city and I'm standing on a hill looking at a broken board in the ocean and thinking.

We're gonna need a bigger boat.

"Come on! We gotta go!" Brian yells from the car, changing frantically into his surf trunks. *"We gotta go!"*

I have five friends who have lost someone in their water. Some their fault, some not. One victim was on PCP. One was in the glare. Two just had their hearts explode in the water, and one just drowned. I always wondered what I would do if I lost someone in my water, because sometimes you just miss things. You can feel them when they're happening. Sometimes you can even see them. And there's still nothing you can do. Happens to the best of us.

I'm still standing and thinking—exactly what you're taught never to do as a lifeguard. No matter what you do, react. Make a decision. Show initiative. Brian is in his trunks, running up to me with his surfboard under his arm.

"What are you doing?" he asks.

"What are *you* doing?" I say.

"We've got to get that guy!"

"We don't even know if it's a guy or not."

"You saw the board stick up!"

"The leash could be caught on something."

"And it could be a guy under there!"

"I'm not convinced it is," I tell him.

And Brian asks me, "Are you willing to take that chance? Are you willing to risk that? . . . *You're* the lifeguard."

Check. Obviously, I'm willing to risk that, because I haven't moved. In the states I'd be out in a second, but here something is keeping me. Maybe it's indecision. Maybe it's unfamiliar surroundings. Maybe it's fear. Why haven't I moved? Brian is looking for me, waiting for me to make a decision, and I'm not making one. A bigger crowd has gathered around. Fifteen or twenty people now, pointing and watching the board in the water. No one is doing anything but wondering what to do. Somebody gets out a pair of binoculars. Someone else, a camera.

Without thinking, I jog back to Brian's 1/2-horsepower mini–Suzuki van and start putting on my surf trunks and looking for fins. Brian follows me. I still haven't made a decision.

"You're going to swim out?"

"I don't know," I tell him. I mean, if I go out with a board, how am I going to get this guy in through the impact zone? *If* I can get out. *If* there's a guy. I find a pair of fins a size too big. I've got no rescue buoy and no backup on this beach or in this city. Maybe in this country. For all I know, they've never even heard of lifeguarding.

I mean, we could radio back and get a bigger boat . . .

We get back to the cliff, walking now, and look out at the logboard again. It's still in the same place, swirling around. Brian is still holding his surfboard and looking at me. Then the board. Then me. Then the board. Then me again. The crowd is bigger now, about fifty, and in the distance we can hear a siren approaching. I'm standing, as a four-year collegiate All-American swimmer and fourteen-year veteran lifeguard. And I'm not going out. I'm just standing.

"So you want to go or what?" Brian asks. He's calmed down off the initial hero rush now and has settled more on the quiet observation of the Japanese on the cliff.

"The guy's dead, you know," I tell him. Mostly to convince myself, but partially because it's true. It's not a matter of life and death. It never was. It's a matter of conscience and guilt. How many times can you say to yourself, "I'm sorry"?

Brian's looking at me, wanting to believe. He wants to believe the guy is dead. The sooner we convince ourselves of this fact, the sooner we get on with our guilt-free lives and go surfing somewhere else. If this were film theory, we'd be talking about escape and suspension of disbelief. If this were psychotherapy, we'd be talking about avoidance and denial.

"The human brain's got four minutes without oxygen," I tell him. "The guy's been down at least fifteen. He's dead. Even if we try and get him, it's going to take us another ten minutes to get out there, and he's more dead—if we can get out there to begin with."

"So we're not going?" Brian asks.

"We're not going."

I swallow it and try to get on with living. I have never *not* gone on a rescue in my life. No matter how futile. No matter how dangerous. This is my virgin time, and like most virgin times, it's not something you like. You pretend to like it for your partner's sake and ego, but there's nervousness and self-doubt and pain and guilt. Everything we get taught since birth. We stand around on the cliff a while longer as more and more Japanese show up. Over 100 now. They're doing the same thing we're doing. A couple of fire trucks pull up, and a bunch of guys in bunkers storm out and join us on the cliff. One has a camera. We stand watching the logboard that might or might not be tug-of-warring a dead man and we listen to the flood of ambulances pulling into the dirt parking lot. The *takoyaki* restaurant here is making a major business rush.

Two surfers from the right-hand break paddle over across the channel during a lull. When they get about five yards from the board, they start slowing down. When they get about two yards away, they stop and sit on their surfboards. Neither wants to be the one to pull up on the leash and check. Would you? The crowd of rescue workers, *takoyaki* eaters, surfers, and guilty lifeguards watch from the cliff like *Survivor* fanatics, without making a sound.

One of the surfers swallows deep and pulls up on the leash. The crowd watches with binoculars and telephoto lenses as he turns around and starts waving frantically. Three other surfers paddle over and start to pull the board and its attached man over the reef and in to shore. None of them makes it. Three of them get washed around the impact zone and into the reef, and no one even tries to paddle back out. They walk in with their boards under their arms and their heads filled with something. I don't know what because I didn't go. I just stood on the cliff.

Eventually a boat comes out of the harbor and anchors about 200 meters outside the surfline. The two surfers who didn't get washed in paddle the broken board and its man-anchor out to sea to the waiting ship, out of the range of binoculars and telephoto lenses. The Asian male reporter starts interviewing bystanders, and Brian and I run down the road towards the harbor. There are four fire trucks and an ambulance waiting for the boat to sail in. They transport the man-cargo into the ambulance, which takes off with its lights flashing. Some police take down vital information from the two surfers, whose hair is still wet. I notice that one of them has a board shaped by the same guy in San Diego who shaped mine. Small world. The twenty or so rescue workers mill about, as rescue workers do when there's nothing left to be done and they don't want to return to the station and go back into waiting mode. As they say, all dressed up and nowhere to go.

This whole thing takes maybe an hour. And during that hour, I shot maybe fifteen frames on my Minolta. Brian and I get back into his 1/2-horsepower mini–Suzuki van and cruise farther down the coastline looking for surf, but our hearts aren't into it. We both know it in ourselves and we both know it in each other, but we still go through these sets of outside motions because that's what men do sometimes. Neither of us tries to console the other's guilt because we know the facts. The guy was dead. There was nothing you could do. You could have been killed trying. It's not your responsibility.

Etc.

Etc.

Etc.

Sometimes it still doesn't stop you from looking at fifteen still frames and wondering if you could have done anything. Or if you were supposed to.

The newspaper comes out the next day and says the guy was from Fukuoka. Twenty-five years old. Drove down for a crowded Saturday surf and he might as well have been the only guy out. We didn't go on him, the firefighters didn't go on him, and Gamera the flying turtle didn't go on him. I guess for firefighters it's hard to swim in bunkers. And I guess Gamera only rescues children in the movies. Adults are supposed to take care of themselves anyway. Sometimes they're supposed to take care of each other, too.

Tsuyoi zo Gamera!
Tsuyoi zo Gamera!
Tsuyoi zo GA-ME-RAAAAA!

Eighteen

As an adult, there's a part of me that wants to be taken care of. And in graduate school I thought I'd found the girl to do it. Katherine was one of those rare rice chasers who was a straight white woman. I guess I should have picked up on it when she wanted me to teach her all the Chinese I know—about twenty-words' worth—or when she wanted to name our dog "something Chinese." I guess I should have noticed when she started making videos about how Asian men really are sexy, or how when we broke up she immediately started dating another tall Hapa filmmaker. *Hmmm.* But I'm pretty slow at these things. Sometimes all I want to do is believe someone is telling me the truth.

Katherine pledged a sorority. (Warning.) But I didn't really pay attention, since the only kind of "rush" I knew was Neil Peart, Alex Lifeson, and Geddy Lee. She was one of those I-wish-I-wasn't-white kind of people who desperately search for something ethnic in their lives. Foods. Customs. Clothing. Lovers. Some of these people end up in positions of power later—teachers, best-selling authors, Academy Award–winning filmmakers—and they want to stay friends to the community because they understand our hardship. They donate their money and their name to up-and-coming colored artists who sleep with them. And they say things like, "Even though I'm white, I understand." Katherine had already gone through her European and Latin and black stages. I was next.

"So," I ask on our first date, "what do you want to eat?"

"Sushi!"

We go to a hole-in-the-wall sushi bar in San Diego. Katherine butchers Japanese words while ordering and puts *shoyu* on her rice, trying to look suave. I don't say anything. I mean, what's the point, right? We go through *toro* and *hamachi* and *amaebi* while she tells me of all the great sushi bars she's eaten at around the world. Like I care.

Sixty-seven dollars later, we go back to my place in Cardiff and end up watching a *Batman* video. Not a Val Kilmer one, either. We're talking the original one with Mister Mom. The wannabe-Asian white girl starts kissing my neck, and the next thing you know, we're in bed. I mean, what are you gonna do? My roommates aren't home, and you can't really expect me to watch *Batman*. We get in bed naked in the dark and start kissing. I don't want this thing to go too far because something's wrong. I'm not sure what. Peter Parker, the Amazing Spider-Man, calls it "spider sense." Daredevil Matt Murdock, the man without fear, can tell if you're lying just by listening to your heartbeat. I'm not in a Marvel comic book, so I'm just going with the flow and ignoring the warnings.

"How about we just talk for a while?" I say, trying to stall for a minute. I mean, Jesus, I'm scared. This is our first date, okay? I've never had sex on a first date before. In fact, I haven't had sex for two years. What if I can't remember how to do it? Listen. It's just like riding a bike. It's just like riding a bike. It's just like riding a bike. But what if I have bad breath? Does that affect riding a bike? What if I come too fast? What if I can't get it up? What if the old kickstand doesn't work? 90 percent mental. 90 percent mental. 90 percent mental. Relax.

"I like talking," she says.

Five minutes later, we're fully naked, kissing on the bed, with Katherine on top of me. She's bigger than other girls I've dated. She'd call it voluptuous. I'd call it fat. Not *real* fat, but definitely big and carrying extra packages. She's on top of me and I can feel her wet pubic hair on my stomach. It's cold. Her big breasts are squashed down and flattened out all over my chest like giant jellyfish.

"Say something in Chinese," she breathes into my ear, with her hair spilled out over my face.

"What?"

"In *Chinese*—tell me you want me in Chinese or something," she says, as she reaches down and grabs my cock, aligning her massive hips on top of me like I

(I want you in Chinese?)

have any choice now in fucking you and what did you say you want? I don't know any Chinese. I just know the essentials. How to order *dim sum*. How to say "thank you" and "sorry." No one teaches you how to say "I want you." Suddenly I'm regretting dropping out of Saturday morning Chinese school. I missed the *one day* where they teach you how to say "I want you." I should have gone. I should have gone. I should have gone. You were right, Ma. You were right, Ma. You were right. If I had gone, I'd know what to say.

Her hand places me to her opening and I can feel the head of my cock touching up against her pussy. Jesus, I'm just lying here. I thought we were gonna talk. But her pussy isn't like the five or six other pussies my cock has touched. It's cavernous and alive. Like some hungry, slimy sea cucumber or sea anemone that's got all its tentacles splayed out, looking for little Chinese cockfish swimming by to grab and throw into the oven. *Arrrrghh!* It's some black hole, some horse eating oats, coming after me as Katherine lowers her big behind down on me and I smother. I feel ever so slightly the sides of her colossal walls undulating and eating and digesting me like a snake swallowing an egg. Did you know they can swallow eggs twice their body size?

"Mmmm," she moans as she starts to fuck me and I just lie there. "Tell me in Chinese."

"Mmmm," I moan back, hoping she'll forget the request and move on to the kind of nonverbal groan conversations you make when you fuck. My hands go to her hips and I start to move with her groove. She's so big it's like I'm fucking some warm tarp or something.

"In Chinese," she moans. "Tell me you want me in Chinese."

"Mmmm," I say.

"Tell me you want me in *Chinese.*"

"Uhhm . . . ummmm . . ."

"Tell me."

"Uhhm . . . ummmm . . ."

"Tell me!"

"Uhhm . . . ummmm . . ."

"Tell me!"

"Uhhm . . . ummmm . . ."

"Tell me! Tell me! Tell me! TELL ME TELL ME TELL ME TELL ME TELL ME TELL ME!"

"NAY HO MA!" I sputter out. (Like what? I don't know what to say. "How are you" is as good as anything.)

"TELL ME!" she screams.

"NAY HO MA!"

"YES!"

"NAY HO MA!"

"YES!"

"NAY HO MA!"

"YES! TELL ME! FUCKING TELL ME!"

"NAY HO HO HOOOO MAAAAAAAAA!"

⸎

I'm worked. I've never had sex on the first date before and I definitely never shouted *nay ho ma* during sex before. Katherine and I are lying in my bed together in Cardiff and a full moon is shining in on us through the sliding glass doors. Outside is a Jacuzzi we never use that's full of algae. Inside I'm wondering what the hell I'm doing. I'm just staring at the ceiling when she tells me,

"You're a very sweet lover."

(Smile)

". . . Sweet?" I say. (Really?)
"Yes. You're a sweet lover."

I put my head into her chest and let her cuddle me up to her, still smiling. My emotions are running haywire now. This is the first time I've made love in two years. It can't be a one-night stand. We've got to keep going out. She says I'm a sweet lover. No, she said a *very* sweet lover. What a beautiful thing to say (smile). She's pretty terrific. Katherine Katherine Katherine Katherine

"I have something to tell you," she says.
"Tell me?"
"Yes. Something kind of important," she says, stroking my hair with her nails.
"Tell me."
"I'm not the healthiest person around."
"What do you mean?"
"I'm dying of cancer."

Whoa whoa whoa whoa hold on a second. Here you've just seduced me, placed me to you. Here you've just mounted me while you've made me yell out some ridiculous Chinese greeting like it's the sexiest thing in the world, and now you're telling me you're dying?
(Relax)
"Do you have an, uh, E.T.A. on yourself?" I say, trying to affect a mixture of nonchalant caring and callousness.
(Smile)
Oh my God. Relax.
"The doctors told me I had six months."
(Keep talking. Keep talking.)
"How long ago did they tell you six months?" I ask—casual casual casual casual
"Over a year ago," she tells me.
"Mmmm," I say to her chest and no one else.

(Smile)

(Relax)
(Smile)
(Relax)
"Now can you take me home?" she asks.

～
ᚱ

I drive her home at 3:01 in the morning to her poorly built, overpriced
condo in La Jolla. I kiss her goodnight and drive the fifteen minutes
north to Cardiff. It's a long fifteen minutes.

That night I keep waking up, thinking she's dead. *(Inhale)* Oh my
God. Relax. You just met her and she's a rice chaser. No, she's not. How
can you say that? The poor girl's dying! Sleep again. *(Inhale)* Oh my
God. Relax.

At 7:15, I call my brother Dave. He's an oncologist, like *I'm* supposed to be, according to Ma.

"What are you doing calling so early?"

Panicked and tired, I tell him I've got a close friend dying of ovarian cancer.

"What kind of treatment is she getting?" he asks.

"I don't know."

"Who's treating her?"

"I don't know."

"Well, how old is she?"

"Twenty-two," I say.

"Why is she having this kind of problem at such a young age?"

"How am I supposed to know? *You're* the doctor. I barely know her!"

"I thought you said she was a close friend."

"Well she is . . . kind of," I tell him.

"You're crazy!"

"You're the doctor! Come on, help me out!"

"Well, has she had chemotherapy?" he asks.

"I don't know. I don't think so."

"What do you mean you don't think so?"

"I mean, she's got all her hair and stuff . . ."

And he tells me, "I think you should find out."

At 9:31 the first florist in La Jolla opens and I'm at the door.

"A blue iris, please. No wrap," I say.

"Would you like any fern and baby's breath with that?"

"Um . . . no, but give me one of those plastic water-tube things."
"Okay, how about a card?"
"No, thanks."
"Just a flower?"
"Just a flower."

At 9:39, I'm at Katherine's overpriced condo, $2.11 poorer, ringing her doorbell.
(Inhale)
"Well, good morning to *you!*" she says smiling.
(Exhale)

She looks healthy to me. And she's alive. Thank God.
"I brought you a flower," I say, without much disguise of nervousness. That random mixture of caring, nonchalance, and callousness? Hit the showers. I just want to put my arms around her. I just want to hold her and make her better. I just want to do more than I can.
"How sweet!" she says. "Come on in."
I go into her overpriced condo and hold her like she's gonna die tomorrow. No girl deserves this kind of disease. It's not fair.
"So, you miss me?" she asks.
"Yes."
"Say it," she says.
"I missed you."

ተ

We talk about her ovarian cancer. Her calm, me trying to act calm. Diagnosed two years ago. One cycle of radiation. Terminal illness. It's not fair. I tell her my brother's an oncologist and she doesn't react much. Tells me she doesn't want to see him. She'd feel uncomfortable, she says. Her dad's gotten her the best doctors available anyway. Flown in from Sweden. So why would she need to talk to anyone else?
"How about we just call him and talk?" I ask.
"No, I don't think so. I'd be uncomfortable."
"But he's my brother. He's one of the premier oncologists in the western United States," I tell her.
"Really?"
"Of course, really," I say. "He's one of my ma's kids. We don't have any choice. We *have* to be the best at things."

Katherine and I start dating. If you can call what we did on our first night a "date." We eat together, sleep together, and fuck together. Sometimes we rent movies. She likes to get foreign films or old American movies while I usually head to the New Releases section, which means we end up watching a lot of foreign films or old American movies. Zhang Yimou films with Gong Li. Hong Kong gangster films. Sometimes Godard or Sirk or Fellini or Hitchcock. Once in a while I can pull off a new release, but that's once in a while. It's good for me, I figure. My dad loves her because she's busty and speaks French. My ma seems to love her because Katherine seems to take care of me. But mothers always have that spider sense operating on some level. Me, I'm just clueless.

Girls, watch out for those weirdos.

We are the weirdos, Mister.

On one of several trips to the family place in L.A., I notice my brother Dave outside on the porch talking with Katherine. No one else in the family knows about her cancer. Too much hassle. Too much fear. They walk back into the room together, and Katherine is politely smiling and laughing. As they separate, she turns and cuts me an icy glare. Complete evil eye. What? What? What did I do? From across the room, she walks up to me in slow motion like a cat going after a sick bird. My wings don't work. Something's snapped inside and I can't move. I've fallen and I can't get up. Whatever it is I did, I didn't mean to. I'm sorry, okay? Okay? I don't know if I should smile at her or run. But before I can even think, it's already too late. Katherine is in striking range.

"I told you I didn't want to talk to him about it!" she hisses.

"But I didn't ask him to . . ."

"Yes, you did!" she spits.

"No . . . I just . . ."

"Yes, you did!"

꒜

Dave calls me the next night.

"You know, Katherine doesn't have the slightest clue what she's talking about," he says.

"What do you mean?"

"I mean, she doesn't know anything about her condition. Nothing at all."

"Are you sure?" I ask.

"What do you mean, am I sure? Of course I'm sure."

"So what then?"

"So what then is whatever treatment she's getting, the doctors aren't explaining anything to her. She's confused. And no matter what's going on or what treatments she's getting, the bottom line is she should know what's going on."

I tell Katherine about it at dinner. Tonight we're at a Thai restaurant. Before dinner we buy matching kimonos at a Japanese gift store in Kearny Mesa. I know. I'm an idiot. We all got to learn somewhere.

"You're going to bring this up again?" she warns.

"Look, he just says that maybe your doctors aren't giving you all the right information."

"I don't want to talk about it."

"I mean, couldn't you maybe just ask them to clarify things on your next visit? I can go with you if you want."

"That won't be necessary," she says coldly.

"Or you could just tell your dad to check it out," I say (which shouldn't be a problem—he already hired a P.I. to investigate me). She puts her fork down, pissed off.

"I'll think about it," she says, and goes back to eating.

Two weeks, eleven fucks, and a million nightmares of losing Katherine later, she comes bouncing into my bed one evening.

"It's over!" she's yelling. "It's over! I'm okay!"

"What?"

"I'm okay!"

Turns out these "doctors" were frauds. Embezzling funds from her rich father while fabricating terminal cancer on her. I'm at once completely stunned, euphoric, and disgusted. What could be sicker than taking advantage of a person's compassion and care? What kind of person can lie like that? These people should be sentenced to *Jerry Springer*. It's bread and circuses. *The Decline of Western Civilization. In the Company of Men*.

Euphoria takes over. I call Dave at home and tell him the good news. He's completely stoked.

"I knew it!" he yells. "I knew it!" Even over the phone I can feel him pumping his fist.

He's happy with himself as a doctor and as a brother. He's good at both of them. I'm happy with myself as a brother and a lover. I think I'm good at both of them. And I think Katherine is happy with herself, too. There are no side effects. She's completely healthy. She can bear children and we can lead a normal life together. More blue irises are bought, and we celebrate by going out for Chinese food. What a relief. What a story.

Seven months and thirty-seven fights later we're flying over the Atlantic to stay with her friend Ben in England. Later Ben and I become great friends and we remain so to this day. We do things like surf and plant trees and test-drive Jeep Grand Cherokees together. At this point, we're just meeting.

"You'll love my friend Ben," Katherine tells me. "He's totally great! He's a professional motorcycle racer and he models on the side and he's really well known in England and he taught me how to ride a motorcycle and blah blah blah blah blah blah blah . . ."

I stop listening because Katherine is always dropping names and feats, trying to embellish herself and her mediocre white suburban American existence. Like I care if she knows a *Sports Illustrated* swimsuit model. As if knowing one makes *her* better looking.

"And one time we just cruised on his motorcycle up the California coast for two weeks together. It was the funniest . . ."

"Whoa whoa whoa whoa hold on a second" I say, immediately suspicious. I mean, just whose place are we staying at anyway? "I thought you said you guys were just friends."

Katherine starts laughing. "Oh my God!" she giggles. "Oh babe, don't be jealous—it's just *Ben!* He's just a *friend*," she says as she turns up her charm output. Big smiles and rolled eyes under waves of hair project the complete ridiculousness of her and Ben ever being lovers, until I join in and start laughing with her. And the crazy thing is, I know this charm is just another part of her arsenal. I've seen her do it to cops to get out of tickets, and I've seen her do it to professors to get into classes. I fall for it anyway. Men are stupid. I'm a man. Do the math.

"All right, all right," I tell her, looking at big smiles and batting eyelids without even having met the guy. "All right, all right, I'm being silly."

"Yes, you are," she says, still laughing. But for different reasons, maybe.

We get to England and stay at Ben's place in Reigate, outside of London. He's a good guy. Funny, personable, attractive. He's busy setting up a motorcycle racing school for a week as Katherine takes me all over England, doing every manner of things that I hate. A guided tour of Westminster Abbey, the Royal Family replicated in wax, the Tower of London to see the crown jewels. I mean, what kind of tour is this where they don't even let you hold the swords or try on the crown? And like a swimsuit-model friend who makes you feel prettier yourself, or a motorcyclist friend who makes you feel more a rebel, all this crap is just another transparent attempt to make you feel more cultured, more worldly, more special, more ethnic. Anything but white American suburbia because look at me, I'm more than that. I'm more than that. I'm more than that.

See, I don't really care about any of this because I'm not more than that. I grew up in *Covina*. There is no more desolate congregation of liquor stores and mini malls. I grew up in inland suburbia and I'm proud of it, like battle scars. Who else got through and still functions? Things mean more to me now. The ocean means more to me because I had to work to get to it. No cigarettes and alcohol mean more to me because I had to fight to keep them out of my body. Love means more to me because I've hardly ever had it and sex together at the same time. Sex by itself doesn't mean much. That's one of the downsides of growing up in Covina, where there's not much else to do but fuck.

ꝋ

Katherine is two weeks late for her period. She tells me so as we're standing in line to see *Miss Saigon*, which is your typical white-G.I.-fucks-Asian-woman-and-leaves-her-with-kid-and-she-kills-herself musical. Except this one's marketed as "the classic love story of our time."

"Are you sure?" I ask.

"Of course I'm sure!" she snaps back.

"Well, what do you want to do?"

"I don't know yet," she says, looking away.

She's been on the pill since I've known her, which is since the first night. To regulate her menstrual cycle, she tells me, because what single woman wants to say she's on the pill because she wants to be able to fuck whenever and wherever she pleases?

"Well, you know, you could just be late," I suggest hopefully.

"I'm never *two weeks* late," she says.

I'm working on a real liberal-male dilemma here. I want this child aborted. I've got no moral problem with that whatsoever. Bringing an unwanted child into this overpopulated world?—*that* I've got a problem with. But I know deep down that I don't really have much of a say here. It's totally her decision and I've got no right to pressure her. It's her body, right? I figure men shouldn't even be allowed to vote on this issue in the first place, let alone legislate it. Then again, from my point of view, there's absolutely no way I'm ready to be a father. I mean, I can't even get myself to school on time. And even if I was, Katherine is certainly not who I'd want to be a father with. I guess after seven months and thirty-seven fights my spider sense of self-protection is finally starting to kick in. Come on, you've got to abort you've got to abort you've got to abort . . .

"So I guess if you are, we'll just get an abortion?" I beg, nonchalantly. Take the bait take the bait take the bait

"No."

"I mean, I'll pay for it and everything. And I'll be

(What?)

there with you the whole time through the whole thing." (Did she just say no? What happened to this full feminist independent woman thing? Now all of a sudden she wants to be Mom?) "And I've got a lot of friends who have had it done and they tell me it's really no big deal."

"No, I can't do that," she says.

"Pardon me?"

"I don't think I can do that."

Whoa whoa whoa whoa hold on a second. Regroup. Let's get the teams straight. This is the girl with the Pro-Child/Pro-Woman/Pro-Choice bumper sticker, right? This is the girl that's gonna take care of *me*. And I'm the guy with the men-shouldn't-even-be-allowed-to-vote-on-let-alone-legislate-it position. What is going on here? I thought we had rules. I thought we had referees. When it all comes down for real, it's just rhetoric?

"What do you mean you can't do that? I thought you were pro-choice," I say, entering debate mode. Slowly but surely I'm moving towards war here.

"It's different! You don't understand, and it's none of your business anyway!" she spits.

"Well, I'd like to think it's some of my business," I tell her. "It's my kid, too!"

"You don't even know if I'm pregnant!" she yells, while a bunch of English people in line turn around and look at us. They're all wearing tweed, and flannel scarves.

"Shhhhh," I say.

"DON'T SHHHHH ME!"

"Come on, Katherine let's just . . ."

"I HATE IT WHEN YOU DO THAT!"

". . . not make a scene, okay?"

"IF I WANT TO MAKE A SCENE, I'LL MAKE A SCENE! IF I WANT TO YELL, I'LL FUCKING YELL, OKAY?!"

"Okay okay okay . . ."

"DON'T JUST 'OKAY OKAY OKAY' ME! LISTEN TO WHAT I'M SAYING!"

"I'm listening."

"YOU'RE NOT LISTENING! YOU NEVER LISTEN TO ME!"

"Yes, I am. I'm listening."

"YOU'RE NOT LISTENING TO ME!"

"What do you want me to do? How do you want me to show you I'm listening?"

"I DON'T WANT YOU TO SHOW ME YOU'RE LISTENING! I WANT YOU TO LISTEN!"

Do you ever get into these conversation traps where you don't know which way is up anymore? Where you don't know if it's you or the other person who's really operating on three cylinders? Maybe it's me. Maybe I'm really not listening. Maybe she's just a lunatic. I mean, the signs are there underneath the smiles and the eyes and the cleavage.

I'm not going to be ignored, Dan.

We stay silent and the line starts to enter the theater. Katherine puts on her charm for the ticket taker, the usher, and the gentleman who drops his program next to her, while I'm getting the silent treatment and wondering how it is I'm supposed to listen to somebody who's not talking to me. The lights darken and for two hours Katherine cries at every melodramatic scene in the horrid musical while I just try to control my anger at the whole production. Are they serious? I see the Asian male roles as soldiers, barkeepers, and pimps. I see the Asian female roles as dancers, whores, and trophies for American G.I.'s. I remember the whole fluff over Actors' Equity boycotting the production because they felt an Asian should be playing the Eurasian role. As if an Asian would be any more appropriate than a white when it comes to playing it. If you want accuracy, cast a Hapa. And I witness a basic truth in this country—it's easier and more acceptable to make a white man look colored than to make a colored man look white.

During the second act, Katherine runs out to the bathroom for more Kleenex. She comes back and sits down next to me and reaches out for my hand. What, so now we're okay again? Do I have the ball now?

"I got my period," she smiles.

Finally, after a week of tourist torture with Katherine the I-wish-I-wasn't-white girl, she leaves for France to embellish herself with more Euro stuff. I stay back in Reigate with Ben for a few days and have a blast. We do all the things you do normally as you live your life in a land. Which is precisely the kind of thing I want to do when traveling. Anyone can see the crown jewels and buy a postcard. Ben and I rent movies and eat falafel at 2:00 A.M. Sometimes we work on his Audi or go run errands in town. It is the beginning of a friendship that continues well past the next year, when Katherine and I break up in San Diego. It's the kind of nasty break-up you'd expect, full of her tantrums and demands and ultimatums.

We're barely a week apart when she appears at my door one night, just before midnight, crying.

"I have leukemia."

(What?)

"Whoa whoa whoa whoa hold on a second—what?"

"I have leukemia."

As if I don't have enough guilt going on over this break-up already. For the first time in two years I'm not on daily eggshells, and now she gives me this? I'm finally able to talk with someone without feeling pressured to prove I'm listening. I'm finally able to spend time with the friends I've ignored and the sports I've missed. I feel like, after being leashed for two years, I'm outside.

We talk about her situation. She's calm, I'm trying to be calm. The worst thing you can do for her right now is come back to her out of sympathy. Remember that.

Katherine just got the preliminary tests confirmed. Things look bad. She's got to go through chemo again, get braces for weakened bones, etc. This isn't fair. She's crying while I hug her at the door. Hugging back, she whispers, "I never want to let go," and I almost keep her there for the night. I'm not sure if it's out of guilt or love, but I figure it's more guilt. Sounds like me. How do you explain loving someone who's about to leave?

I call Dave at dawn for the second time and tell him about the situation.

"That poor girl," he says. "What kind of luck is that?"

"What kind of prognosis does she have?" I ask, ignoring the question. "How old is she?"

"Twenty-three."

"Not good."

Katherine shaves off all her beautiful hair because it's coming out in clumps from the chemo. She has braces fitted for her weakened teeth and her face swells from the treatments. Sometimes I go visit her and smell the pot that she smokes to control the nausea. My roommates stay with her through the night several times a week as she cries about dying and cries about me. I still keep my distance. Mostly because I'm a jerk and don't want to go back to being leashed, getting yelled at, and walking on eggshells again. Plus I've started to realize how much of a rice chaser Katherine really is, and I want no part of it. Sick or not, I'm still looking out for *número uno*. The few nights when my roommates and I are actually all in our place together, we talk about Katherine's situation. They try not to make me feel guilty. They try not to call me a jerk for not being there for her now. But I see how they really feel. I'm condemned and everyone knows it. I try not to talk about what I can do to help, besides going back to being her boyfriend again.

As I've mentioned before, Katherine and I had bought a dog together, a pug we named Gao-Jye because she wanted it to have a Chinese name. Another warning ignored. So with the current situation I've got to see her several times a week to exchange dog duty, like some post-divorce child-custody battle. Sometimes she looks pretty good. Sometimes not so good. Sometimes she's out getting chemo treatments and I say hi to her roommates. They say hi politely and wonder how it is I can be so cold. But what no one seems to understand is, it's not that I can't deal with having a sick lover. It's that I can't deal with Katherine—sick or healthy. Yeah, I wish she wasn't sick. But that wouldn't make me any less wary of her. How do you explain that to roommates and friends who just look at you and see someone abandoning ship? Is anyone here not on the jury?

Ben has heard the news. He flies out from England to see Katherine and ends up staying at my place for several weeks. It is one of the many late nights after watching *Cheers* where we just stay up and talk.

"You know, you can't be guilty about this," he tells me. "Kathy is a tough one to be with, believe me."

"I know. I keep telling myself 'You can't be with her out of sympathy—you can't be with her out of sympathy.' I mean, I know that's just not the right reason . . ."

"It's true!" he interrupts. "You've got to live your life doing the things that you need to do. I mean, take me and my mum. I haven't seen her in years but I still try . . ." and Ben goes off on a long tangent about his relationship with *his* family. I'm not listening. I'm just thinking about how sick Katherine looked the last time I saw her, with her pasty skin and no hair.

"And you really have to make certain decisions about what is positive or not," he continues. "No one makes them for you."

"I know, but this leukemia just isn't fucking fair with her," I tell him, "especially after all that crap with the cancer."

"Cancer?" Ben says. "You mean heart condition."

"No . . . cancer," I tell him. "You know, that thing with the Swedish doctors who conned that whole thing about that ovarian cyst and . . ."

"No, it was a heart condition!" Ben interrupts. "I'm sure of it."

"No no no. I'm talking about the cancer she thought she had, that those doctors faked."

"No, I know. I'm *sure* it was a heart condition."

"Look, I was there!" I'm saying. "My brother is the one who dis—"

"In fact," Ben interrupts again, "when we used to date, she had this one time where she almost . . ."

"Wait a minute. You used to *date* her?"

"Of course. You didn't know that? We drove all up and down California together on my bike, and she got so bloody sick one time . . ."

"And she had a *heart condition?*"

"Yeah, in fact when she was having this one attack or something I thought she was really gonna die! I mean, she was on the back of my bike barely holding on! Something about having to get back to get this specific prescription or something. I mean, I just wanted to get her to a hospital, right? But she insisted she had to get this specific medicine at her place in San Diego. I mean, I was flying! We're doing like 110 trying to get her there, and I'm trying to keep her conscious and keep her on the bike . . ."

"Jesus . . . ," I'm saying.

"And the craziest thing of all was this whole time with the heart attack or problem or whatever you want to call it—this whole time I'm flying down I-5 full throttle, we're thinking she's bloody pregnant!"

"*Oh my . . .*"

"I mean, it turned out it was nothing. But Christ! For a couple of days there, it was pretty frightening! I mean, she was . . ."

"Two weeks late," I interrupt.

"Yeah . . . how did you know?"

Ben and I share experiences and stories almost in the way men share sexual conquests. Except this time we're sharing sexual embarrassments and trying to outdo each other in terms of how badly each of us was taken. Until the subject comes back to the poor girl and her terminal "leukemia." And Ben looks at me and says,

"You know, neither of us really wants to say this now, do we?"

𝔶

Four years and lovers later, I run into a guy at a film festival in New York. He's the other tall Hapa filmmaker Katherine dated. This guy Tom. So Tom and I start talking as best you can when all you have in common is you went to the same school and you fucked the same woman. We're two minutes into the conversation before he tells me she lied to him about the leukemia, too. Ditto another boyfriend, Larry, who stayed with her through a terminal brain tumor, or my friend Ben and her heart condition with the mysterious mystery drug. The difference here is she admits everything to Tom. And because she confessed everything to him, he forgives her.

"I mean, how can you not forgive her, right?" he says.

I'll tell you how. I'm a confessor. All my artwork is confessional and narrative to some degree and I know every hook and angle you can run. I've got the playbook. I know how to cut and praise, how to fictionalize and disguise, how to seduce and distance. I know how to prevent criticism through aggression and through sympathy, and I know sympathy works better most of the time. People come up and tell me how courageous I am for being able to open up and share my pain, when it doesn't take any courage to confess anything to strangers. Family or friends maybe, but strangers? Sure, what the hell? I did it.

Which is why I don't buy the confession. I know how easy confessing is. I know how little it really means. Katherine's confession of all the lies and all the manipulation of all the lovers doesn't count for anything more than just another notch in the make-believe-I'm-sick-for-attention file. Except now, instead of cancer, heart disease, or leukemia, it's moved on to "Oh my God, look how *mentally* sick I am." Until we run in with padded concern and attention and blue irises. Until we call our doctor brothers and beg for medical information. Until we pretend a Hapa fetish is really all in our heads and it's just about love. Pretend pretend pretend pretend pretend. No, really. Doesn't love have anything to do with it?

All the king's horses and all the king's men can show and tell you otherwise, but you still don't believe what you're seeing and what's happening to you. No person could take advantage of another's compassion and care. No person could steal from the elderly or rape a mentally retarded girl. No person could hit their child. No person could litter the beach. No person could eat veal. No person could buy gas at Exxon.

I get an HIV test after washing Katherine off my skin because who knows what else she lied about? Sometimes at night I still scrub myself in the shower, trying to get her stupid white-trash taste off my body. I crank the temperature as hot as I can tolerate, while the soft water sprays my back and chest. It bounces off me like rainbirds at a public fountain, or an endless supply of non-penetrating bullets. It flows down my ribs and hips and thighs, taking microscopic bits of skin and loose hair along with it. Everything pours out together, forever connected. They spiral counterclockwise down a steel drain. Counterrotate camera. Slow dissolve to Marion Crane's eye. Slow zoom out . . .

Mother. Oh God, Mother! Blood, blood!

Cut.

᠇

Three days of solid, winter rain have maxed out the token flood controls of our southern California desert. No one expects floods here. No one expects real rain. The storm drains have all opened up like arteries, washing the fertilizer, animal carcasses, used motor oil, and chocolate sauce down the streets and into the ocean. Outside my window, toxic rivers are flowing along the curbside. Twenty minutes down the pipe and everything ends up mixed, shaken, and stirred. At the end of the line the water is bubbling and churning and brown. Its blood is infected with pesticides and broken egg shells and there's not a thing I can do about it. I want to run to it. I want to jump in. Every part of me wants to flow out to the storm drains and back to the ocean. But there's no safe place for me to enter. The virus has already taken root.

1
3
21
903
1,631,721

You take the blue pill, you wake up in your own bed, and believe what you want to believe . . .

I take a shower every morning and every night, but nothing on me is getting clean. I can't get this memory out of my head and I can't get this black-and-white film off my skin. Nothing makes sense. It's all steam and mirrors. A 2,000-gallon goldfish bowl.

You take the red pill, you stay in wonderland, and I'll show you how deep the rabbit hole goes . . .

My shower head scatters $C_{17}H_{19}ClN_2S$ intramuscular injections around the bathroom, while my hands are covered in $C_{11}H_{17}N_2NaO_2S$ anti-bacterial soap with vitamin E and aloe. I'm washing my hair with pancurium Br, conditioning with KCl, and using a saline wash between each. Nothing's working. I might as well be washing with Comet and Simple Green or scrubbing blood out of the carpet. I might as well be standing in the rain and hoping.

Somewhere there's a queen's crown with your name on it. You can wear it with your kimono and your cleavage and your eyelids and your smiles. You can wear it when you eat Chinese food you can't pronounce, and you can wear it when you fabricate diseases to capture colored boyfriends. As long as you wear the crown, you can always be queen of the wax museum. You know, if you hold really still and just let your hair bounce, maybe no one will notice. The lovers will stay faithful and the tourists will snap pictures on throwaway cameras. Maybe if you keep smiling, no one will ever talk about it after they find out. Poor girl, can you feel them staring at you? Poor girl, can you hear them saying you don't look real?

I fall asleep without major complications. There's no difficulty in finding a vein. No violent physical reaction. No overly tightened leather straps preventing chemical flow. No safewords and no clogged tubes. My respiratory system stops and the KCl reverses my heart polarity. Everything shuts down quietly. Twelve witnesses watch me through one-way glass and look for movement, but there's nothing much to see. I just stop what I'm doing. There's no show, no spasms, no twitches. One by one, the witnesses leave their metal chairs and slowly walk to the exit. At the door, the last one looks back at me for a second, like in the last episode of *The Mary Tyler Moore Show*. No change. Filmed before a live studio audience. Thanks for coming. Number 12 turns and hits the lights. The door closes and I feel the room go black around me. Left alone now, everything just slowly burns. After a while, there's nothing left but dirty needles and some wilted iris petals that'll get cleaned up in the morning.

The next day the rains stops. The rivers slow to trickles. The gutters go empty. The storm drains pool and drip like bathroom fixtures with bad washers. Twenty-four hours later, health commission workers who don't swim tell me it's okay to go in the water again. Seventy-two hours later, birds rise.

Things always look different on the outside, and afterwards. Things always look different when you wake up. I open my eyes and look at the new world around me. Everything is okay now, they tell me. Everything is clean again. Everything is safe.

A week later, my HIV test results come back negative. It's just another "get out of jail free" card in a lifetime of chances and close calls. It's like we all slept with the same whore, but I'm the only one that lived to tell about it. Everyone got infected but me. I look at my new body and promise myself "never again," but all the other men have either died or forgiven her, and all the witnesses have left the room. There's no one around to hear me make hollow promises. I collect my $200 and go home.

morning glory

Nineteen

I started to understand life in a tunnel with my friend Keith Alexander. Keith had a studio across from mine at UCSD when we were both in art school trying to make art. The guy is about 5′8″, stocky, and black. Built like a linebacker with a little paunch of stomach goo and thighs the size of my waist. I was having some trouble moving a wall in my studio, so I go over and ask if I can borrow some of his strength to help me out with the move. Keith gives me a "Sure, man," and thirty seconds later we're trying to move this thing.

The wall runs about 8′x 10′ and weighs close to 200 pounds. We get on either end of it and try to shove it down the hall. But while Keith is holding up his end of the bargain, I don't seem to be covering mine as well. My side doesn't even budge. It stays on the ground and the wall stays pretty much in the same place.

"You know what?" he says, assessing the situation. "Why don't you just steer the thing while I push it?"

And he says this in a straightforward manner. No criticism whatsoever. Just an acknowledgment of the fact that he's a stronger wall-pusher. And his candor here puts me at ease because it doesn't make me lose face. There's no suggestion that my wall-pushing incapabilities might reflect any other kind of male deficiency. The kinds of implications you get when for whatever reason you're unable to hit a baseball or feed your family or participate in a gang rape. There's none of the you're-not-a-man-if-you-don't kind of garbage that makes men do things in life they shouldn't.

"Sounds good to me," I say.

I move into steering position while he puts his shoulders down and sets his shoes into the ground like some monster bull. Without even grunting he shoves this thing across my studio like it's nothing.

"Thanks."

"No sweat."

"How'd you get so strong?"

And Keith looks up at me straight faced and says, "Been poor all my life." We leave it at that and our friendship begins.

Keith's artwork involves taking journeys with him as a guide. He basically takes people on tours of particular spaces that either he or the participant decides are interesting, for whatever reasons. And what comes about through this artwork is based on their interaction with each other and with the space and with other chance elements. He might take you, for instance, under a bridge along the catwalks to explore the space you never see, or he might take you inside a slaughterhouse to see the efficiency or inefficiency of the machines we make to kill animals, and how far removed it is from the sterile shrink-wrapped pork loin and beef shank you've been buying at Safeway or Foodland or Albertson's.

And the beauty of Keith's work is that it really dances the border between art and life. Which makes it on the one hand fascinating for its real-life experience, and on the other extremely difficult to categorize as an art form. And while I would tend to classify it under that pervasive umbrella of "performance," I don't think Keith would be very happy with that. So I'll classify it in his words.

"I take people on walks."

And it happened we were sitting in our studios shooting the shit one night, when the topic of the tunnels under campus came up. Both of us had heard the rumors that an elaborate labyrinth of tunnels existed underneath UCSD. Both of us had friends who had friends who had friends who had actually been down in some of these tunnels and come back full of stories. Both of us had heard the rumors that the tunnels were built for the CIA or the FBI or for National Guard riot control during the student uprisings of the '60s. And both of us had also heard that any student caught in the tunnels would be expelled without question. And it seemed that out of all the rumors we heard, this was the most believable. Because if anything seemed plausible about this, it was that you could get expelled for it.

So between a combination of our being fairly bored and our trusting each other as partners fairly well, we decide to embark on a tunnel tour.

Now neither of us really knows how to properly prepare for a tunneling expedition, but we figure to take the basics—warm dark clothes, flashlights, crowbar, Swiss Army knife, running shoes. The dark clothes so you don't get spotted and the running shoes in case you do. Keith, for some reason, also brings along a pair of pliers.

"You can never have too many pairs of pliers with you," he tells me.

We enter through a manhole cover by the Biomed Library at about 10:00 P.M. And the tunnels are real. They're noisy and claustrophobic and layered with pipes and bare light bulbs in wire cages. For the next few hours, Keith and I traverse underground across the university, surfacing now and then at various indoor and outdoor locations. A few doors are locked, and these frustrate us a bit. Because, to be honest, after the first half-hour the excitement kind of wears off. Every tunnel starts to look pretty much the same after a while. So to liven up the stakes, we convince ourselves that all the rumored CIA riot gear and civil defense supplies are stored behind some of these locked doors, which we take turns trying to pick open without success. It's something to do, anyway.

There's a lot of graffiti down here from previous tunnelers, and it falls into two categories. Because, if you think about it, you can probably guess which two groups of people might be exploring tunnels at the risk of being expelled. The first group is the fraternities, which give you all the SAE PLEDGE CLASS WAS HERE stuff. The other is the guys who are a little too involved with some esoteric fantasy game. Which gives you all the HALT ELF and WIZARDS DO IT WITH MAGIC WANDS Dungeons and Dragons–type graffiti. I don't know which guys seem sadder, really. The frats because they operate on the whole group mentality of you're-not-a-man-if-you-don't, or the fantasy-animation guys because they just don't care.

So we're wandering around, getting quite bored and cold by now, and we come across this spray-painted warning:

TURN BACK

So of course we keep going. I mean, do we look like sissies? And walking farther along the tunnel, we see some more doomsday graffiti:

NO ONE HERE GETS OUT ALIVE

Which we attribute to just some no-life Jim Morrison groupie, and keep walking until we come to:

LAST CHANCE——TURN BACK!

Which actually gets us a bit interested. Maybe we'll find something forbidden in these tubes after all. So we trudge another fifty yards until we just come to the end of the tunnel. It dead-ends at a locked door, and that's it. No pot of gold. No toy surprise inside. No dinosaur coin. Nothing.

There comes a point in learning any skill or hobby where you get past the initial hesitancy and clumsiness of it all and begin to understand the physical concepts. Your body starts to pick up the movements at a comfortable level and you break past the novice phase. When you ride a motorcycle, there's a distinct turning point where you finally get past the conscious clutch/throttle/shift mentality and actually start to lean into your turns, downshift, and accelerate out of curves without thinking. In karate, it's somewhere around brown belt. In surfing, it's your first time without a leash. And anyone in any field will tell you that this critical shift—this departure from novice to intermediate—is the most dangerous time. You have the beginnings of physical understanding, but without refinement. In other words, you have all the beginnings of power and absolutely no way to control it. This is the gambler after a big payoff. This is the skier on his third day. This is a snowboarder any time. And as with any false sense of mastery, you quickly lose respect for simple things like roads, girlfriends, or power tools. And you should never lose respect for things greater than yourself. Believe me.

This is where Keith and I are in terms of tunneling. We've come along just far enough, after three hours of exploration without incident, to proudly declare ourselves tunnel veterans. We're the seventeen-year-old Ninja rider without a helmet, and all our lights have turned green.

"Let's do it, man," I say.

Taking out our credit cards and matching Swiss Army knives, we go to work on our door lock. There's no guard, so it's just a matter of time and friction until we pop it open. The success feeds straight into our newfound tunnel stardom. We might as well ask each other for autographs. We're so excited we boldly go where no man has gone before, ignoring pussy Dungeons and Dragons weenie warnings. We cross the threshold into the forbidden tunnel, which should hold some now-unleashed horror, but we find it's just the same old thing. No guns. No riot gear. No minotaur and no Pandora's box. Just another dimly lit tunnel disappearing into the darkness. Disappointed after our 007 lock-picking success and fallen expectations of adventure, we two tunnel stars let the door close behind us and lock ourselves in. *Tin . . . roof!* Rusted.

"Is it a girl?"
Is what a girl?
"Whatever it is you're upset about."
Oh . . . no. I'm just sort of disturbed about things.
"In general."
That's right.

It's interesting to watch how fast realization awakens and how slowly it sets in. We realize fast that we're screwed. Right away we both notice there's a metal guard along the inside door edge so we can't pick our way back out. We look at each other for a moment before Keith says to me, "Well . . . only one way to go now."

But, like getting stung by a scorpion or losing a finger in some machine accident, your realization is much faster at awakening than it is at registering. In other words, you may realize right away that you've lost your index finger, but you don't really consider the implications of this fact. You recognize the initial incident. You got stung by a scorpion, or you trapped yourself in a tunnel. Nothing else. No magnitude. No panic.

Me and Keith walk about 300 yards along the tunnel before we come to another door, which is chained and padlocked. And we realize there's no other way out. We're trapped forty feet underground. All of a sudden I've got no problem with that magnitude stuff. I remember now that I'm claustrophobic. I remember now that I'm cold. I remember now that I'm thirsty. I remember a lot of things.

Keith and I walk back along this 300-yard tunnel slowly looking for airshafts or passageways or anything, and we realize we're rats in a cage. On one end of the tunnel there's a 1' x 2' airshaft covered with chain-link fence, heading into the dark. On the other end of the tunnel there's a huge, humming, screaming metal fan. That's it. We can't get through the fence on one end, and this six-foot-wide fan thing is spinning and whirling and humming and hungry and drooling like it can't wait to take a bite out of two careless brown-skinned Boy Scouts. But it's got patience. It's got nothing but time. It'll just keep sucking in freezing cold air down the chain-link airshaft, pulling it the length of the tunnel, and spitting it straight to hell at 5,000 rpm. *Feeling lucky, kid? Come a little closer . . .*

Apparently my claustrophobia is showing because Keith looks me straight in the eye and tells me,

"I'm gonna get you outta here."

I go into survival mode, quick. I had noted four spigots and some overhead piping that might hold water, which could mean living another couple weeks or so. Longer if I killed Keith and ate him. I also noted an alarm system that I'm using as a psychological backbone. Because, expelled or not, if it comes down to dying of thirst in some tunnel, I can think of plenty other schools to go to.

Keith figures our only chance is to try to break through the chain-link fence and hope the airshaft leads somewhere. Neither of us wants to think about trying to get past the Satan fan on the other side. Keith goes to work on this thing with his pliers (because you can never have too many pairs of pliers with you), and I pace around thinking about how thirsty I am. I think about all the things I haven't had a chance to do in this lifetime. I think about how I suddenly have to go to the bathroom. I figure we better use the end by the Satan fan for our latrine since the air is getting sucked that way anyway. I mean, how mad can Satan get? Hell probably smells pretty bad already.

After about forty-five minutes Keith isn't making much progress on the chain-link fence and I'm starting to panic. Finally I've had enough. I'm not gonna die down here. And with Keith busy on his project at the other end of the tunnel, I trip the alarm. Or I should say I *try* to trip the alarm. Because it doesn't go off. It's just a taunt. A placebo. I press the button again, but it's just another rescue ship on the horizon for Gilligan and the Skipper to yell at. I guess they don't have much need for alarms down here behind locked doors and manhole covers. So why put one in? Just to tease us? I'm barely controlling my breathing now, frantically trying to think about other things for another twenty minutes or so. There's nothing else to do but hyperventilate or shit my pants, and I'm not gonna walk back down there and tell Keith our 911 phone is a decoy. Next to me the Satan fan keeps humming, while my brain makes it sound more and more like laughter.

Mrs. Robinson, if you don't mind my saying so, this conversation is getting a little strange. Now, I'm sure that Mr. Robinson will be here any minute now . . .

Keith eventually breaks enough of the chain links to squeeze through the teeth with just some minor cuts and bruises. He disappears, squiggling down the airshaft for a while into the darkness until I hear him say,

"Well, come on!"

Come on? I don't think you understand. I don't like tunnels. I almost lost it seeing Ray Charles at the Hollywood Bowl, because when you leave they funnel you under Highland Avenue in these pedestrian tunnels that immediately get people-jammed. And people keep pouring in from the entrance, but there's no room to move at the exit. It's like a compression slaughterhouse. We've got limited oxygen here. And all I can think of is earthquake earthquake earthquake earthquake. I know I live in California and earthquakes are part of our everyday lives. But I'm in a tunnel here, okay? I don't like tunnels. And Keith wants me to crawl into an *airshaft?*

"What can you see?" I say, trying to avoid the subject. But there's no response.

"Keith?" I'm calling out. "Keith? . . . *Keith?*"

Tell us where you are, Josh!

. . . *I just want to apologize to Josh's mom . . . and Keith's mom . . . and my mom. I am so sorry. Because no matter what he says now, it was my fault. I was the one who led us into the tunnel. I was the one who insisted we weren't lost. I was the one who insisted we keep going . . .*

I squirm through this thing like Rambo, because it's either squirm to Keith or die alone in a tunnel. I come out the other end and I'm in some kind of silo with Keith. He's smiling.

"I knew if I answered you, you'd never come," he says. Good one.

This silo goes up about forty feet to street level by our flashlight beams. Keith climbs up the side to the top and I feel my first twinges of comfort, because I can hear an occasional car above. But Keith can't get out. The only opening is on the opposite side of the wall ladder he's holding on to. So to get out he's got to swing across this forty-foot chasm and try and kick at this thing with his foot. And while he's doing that, I'm supposed to stay below and catch him if he's falling like in the Kinks song. That's the plan, anyway. I don't like it.

In any emergency you need leaders. You need leaders not only to run the circus but, more important, to keep the freaks from freaking and freaking out all the other freaks. It's like walking down a row of caged chickens, which is sad enough on its own. No matter how slow and nonthreatening you walk, it's just a matter of time until they go berserk. Hundreds of birds, four to a cage, sit completely still and watch you until one individual loses it. One bird starts clucking and panicking. Which gets the other birds in its cage clucking and panicking. Until you've got this pandemonium of clucking and panicking and squawks and feathers and blood. The birds tear their claws off on the cages. They scratch and bang themselves against the wires. Everything is chaos until the fox walks away, the grain belt starts running, and the antibiotics kick in again.

We've reached a point, Keith and I, where he's almost lost the reins. I can see it in his dim silhouette up in the silo. His shoulders are hunched. He no longer commands leadership through invincible promises of bravado and salvation. He no longer motivates the troops. He's tired, frustrated. For ten minutes he's kicked at this grating. Enough to have gotten a small opening. He can get both feet and one arm out the hole to freedom, but he can't muster the courage to let go of his safety arm and risk the forty-foot drop to my token safety net. He climbs down, sets his jaws, and sighs.

"Why don't you go crawl back and set off that alarm?" he says, defeated.

(Oops.)

"Alarm?"

"Yeah," he tells me. "Go back and set off the alarm. I give up."

"What alarm?"

"The one back in the tunnel."

"I don't remember any alarm," I say.

"Quit being a funny guy."

"What?"

"I said quit being a funny guy and go set off the stupid alarm!"

You mean . . . lemme understand this 'cause I—you know, maybe it's me. I'm a little fucked up, maybe.

But I'm funny how?

You mean funny like I'm a clown?

I amuse you?

I make you laugh?

I'm here to fuckin' amuse you?

What do you mean funny? Funny how? How am I funny?

Keith is looking at me like I'm crazy. "What the hell are you talking about?" he asks.

Now, I could tell him I already tried the alarm in a moment of panic and it doesn't work. It's just a taunt. A placebo. And I could tell him if you don't get us out of here by climbing up out of that silo (that's *you*—not me, because I'm afraid of heights) we're gonna stay down here until the police pick us up. I could tell him a lot of things. I know at least we're not gonna die anymore, since now we can scream for help and just deal with being expelled. Keith has already resigned himself to this expulsion by asking me to set off the alarm. He's given up on the great escape and is ready for the cavalry to arrive. And that makes me a little sad. It's like watching Captain Kirk or Bruce Lee or Michael Jordan give up. It's not supposed to happen. Keith *is* the cavalry.

So we switch positions. I do breaths and he does compressions. I become the coach or the father or the mother, telling him to get back up the silo and goddammit get us out of here. Because he can do it and I know he can do it. *So go!* And Keith climbs back up this wall and starts swinging out his feet and his free hand like before.

"DO IT!" I scream. "DO IT!"

And Keith makes some kind of weird barbarian yell and lets go of his safety hand. He dangles and wiggles for a second.

"GO!"

And wiggles and dangles

"YOU GOT IT!"

until he finally shimmies out feet first and he's free.

"YEAH!" I'm yelling from down in the silo. "YEAH! YEAH! YEAH!"

"Okay, come on up," he yells through the opening forty feet above me.

(Come on up?)
What you talkin' 'bout, Willis?

"No man . . . Go back around and open up the door in the tunnel!" I reply.

"I told you I'd get you outta here. Now, come the fuck up!"

I climb up the wall not looking down, like they tell you, and I reach the top. I swing my feet out and Keith grabs hold of my ankles.

"Okay, I got you. Now let go of your hand."

"No."

"Come on! It's getting light out here! Let go!"

"NO!"

"*LET GOOOOOOOO!*" he screams and pulls on my feet. What if my shoes come off? What if he pulls me just enough for me to fall down the silo?

"LET GO!"

And I make some kind of weird barbarian yell and let go of my safety hand. I'm wiggling and dangling while Keith's pulling on my ankles.

"GO!"

I get my knees out. Then my butt. Then my torso.

"YOU GOT IT! GO! GO!"

And all of a sudden I'm squeezed out like a newborn. I'm out.

Me and Keith look at each other. Two mud-covered, brown-skinned burrow rats straight out of pet-shop jail. And then we just start yelling and screaming and hugging each other. We're outside this busted air vent dancing around with our pliers and flashlights in the sunrise. We run back through the eucalyptus to our studios and wait for the cops to arrive. We watch them look around for a while, then shake their heads and leave. Everything is wonderful. Everything is giddy. We head out to a twenty-four-hour taco shop and I order the best burrito I've ever tasted in my life. I go back to my girlfriend Hanako's place and take the most wonderful shower I've ever taken. I love the smell of the shampoo. I love the feel of the soap. I love the way the faucet turns. I wake her and we make love in the morning.

Air tastes better. Her skin feels warmer. A blanket touches softer. I like to think of that as a successful piece of art. Thanks, Keith.

Twenty

Like everybody else in this world, I'd say most of my experiences with cops have been bad. What's different, though, is that most of my experiences have been with campus cops—who most people think of as a half-step between mall security and toll-booth operators. In reality, though, they're actual police officers with guns and badges, and they're more than eager to prove it. They just don't have many opportunities. Keith and I were lucky enough to have avoided campus cops for the most part, and I've tried to keep it that way ever since. I had only dealt with them a few times before in my life. And none of those times has been pleasant.

I figure most of them must be fairly unhappy individuals. They spend their days ticketing and arresting and hassling anyone younger and happier and more successful than they are. Then they change out of uniform, get inside their American cars, and go home to more alcohol, guns, and pornography. I originally thought all UC police were like this, but apparently it's only the older San Diego cops. The cops at UCSB where I work now are fairly nice, so I guess it has to do more with demographics or pay scales or entrance exams. Or maybe it's just something in the water over time. Either way, I got introduced to them over a parking meter and a penny.

I'm usually not one to give away choice scams. It kills them off. But this one deserves additional life on principle alone. And since this scam has already lived its heyday in SoCal, it won't hurt to share. Things tend to disappear around here. You wake up one morning and everything's over. Gone the way of frozen yogurt and DiMarzio pickups and Herbalife. Up the 15 past Barstow and beyond. Endangered species.

Should I call you Logan, Weapon X?

Take a penny—a fairly recent aluminum one rather than copper, and find yourself a concrete curb. Not asphalt. Rub the penny on its edge, flattening one side of it until its diameter equals the diameter of a dime. This takes about thirty strokes or so. Put the penny on its face and drag it along the curb with your foot a few times until Lincoln's face rubs off. This should only take a few drags, and you need to be careful not to flatten it too thin or it won't work correctly. Place it in the dime slot of any random parking meter, flattened side up, and use a dime to push it in all the way. Crank away and rejoice. If you do it right, the penny will fill up the entire meter without damaging it. (I've heard.) Campus meters cost you a quarter for fifteen minutes. A penny and a couple strokes on the sidewalk buy you four hours. Which sounds like a better deal to you?

I'm not much of a thief by nature. I just think of parking as a natural use of space that belongs to everybody. If everybody respected it and respected one another, there wouldn't be a problem. Of course there are idiots who will park their cars for weeks in prime zones, but there are always idiots around here and there. That I can deal with. I'm much more against some monster institution gouging students for a buck an hour, just so they can park closer to the bookstore and spend more money at the same institution that's charging them in the first place. Since when do we have to pay to spend money? I'm even more against the parking "officers." Glorified meter maids who take joy in ruining people's days to make up for unfulfilled areas in their own lives. Can you imagine going to work every morning knowing you're going to ruin people's days? Can you imagine getting paid for that? I consider parking as much a God-given right as pissing outside. So I shave pennies. I'm just doing my part—like buying a black-market cable box or calling the phone company over a 10¢ overcharge. It's like Robin Hood. Robin Hood would definitely have shaved pennies. He certainly peed outside.

We're shaving pennies in college. Myself, my friend Pablo, and a few other buddies before water polo practice. I felt vindicated in this practice since UCSD was a Division III school and didn't offer any scholarships. We're practicing six hours a day for some coach who thinks he's Napoleon. We're representing the school and paying full tuition. We're bringing notoriety and prestige to the university. And they expect us to pay to park by the pool? Do they have any idea how much that would cost?

So me and Pablo are shaving away on the main street through campus one morning, when we notice three of our penny-shaving friends getting arrested down the road from us. Spread-eagled against the paddy wagon. Handcuffed. The works. It takes a moment to register, before me and Pablo figure out it might be a good idea to cease our Robin Hood activities for the time being. We toss our modified Lincolns under a nearby car and nonchalantly start to meander towards the pool. As nonchalantly as you can meander when you realize you're about to be arrested.

And this is where I propose the UCSD parking patrol and UCSD police force have way too much time on their hands. Because not only do they have this parking lot covered with three officers, two parking cops, and a paddy wagon on a weekday summer morning, they also have some video guy recording us through one-way windows in an unmarked van. Pretty elaborate stakeout, I have to admit. Either they were expecting us or they're *really* bored. Which doesn't matter much to me either way, so long as they're not bothering me or using my money. They're doing both.

Pablo and I are about to cross the street when this parking guy pops out of nowhere. He's like some troll jumping out from under a bridge to stop the Billy Goats Gruff.

"FREEZE!" he yells.

Someone yelled "freeze" at Yoshi Hattori when he was dressed up as John Travolta and rang the wrong doorbell on Halloween. He didn't stop and he got killed. I figure I'd better stop. Pablo and I put our hands in the air and stand there, watching this little man in a parking uniform walk up to us with a grin on his bearded face. He's got the full rent-a-cop uniform. Sears polyester pants and a two-inch-wide plastic belt holding his gut in. He walks around us in a circle, going through radio codes and static on his walkie-talkie like some little kid playing fort. Until he finally reaches under a car, picks up one of our shaved pennies, and shouts,

"AH HA!"

Fuck the police, comin' straight from the underground . . .

Getting arrested is like getting shot. You've seen it thousands of times on TV, but you have no idea what it's really like. It's not even close to what you think. Nothing works like it's supposed to. The officer who drives up is a Vietnamese fellow about my age named Bau Tu. He gets out of the police car and he stands about 5′6″ at a stretch. Short cop. Warning sign. He's got a close-cropped flattop, and he's wearing those Ray-Ban reflective cop glasses and knee-high black leather boots. If he's got a boner I'm gonna freak out. Without saying anything, he pushes us against his UCSD Vanagon and starts frisking us. And for some reason I start to find this whole situation kind of funny. I mean, it's ludicrous. I'm only wearing running shorts and a T-shirt. What do you expect to find on me? Grenades? So when Officer Bau Tu says,

"You got any guns or knives on you?"

I realize the only thing I can declare that isn't visible is my Speedo. Which makes me chuckle a bit to myself.

"No . . . no knives today," I tell him.

This makes Officer Bau Tu quite angry. If there's one thing that makes a short cop angry, it's somebody laughing at him.

"You think this is some kind of joke?" he yells. *"I'm not McGarrett! This isn't Hawaii Five-O!"* Which I think is even more funny. Funny enough that the gravity of the whole situation doesn't even hit me as he cuffs my hands and slides me in the van with the rest of my criminal element. We drive the quarter-mile to the campus police station and they separate us. We're each in an empty room, by ourselves. What's this about? All of a sudden it's getting a little more real. The plastic baggy handcuffs are making my fingers numb, and they've got the air conditioning in here cranked to maximum. It's like brainwashing time. I'm waiting for L. Ron Hubbard or the Reverend Moon to come in, sit down, and ask me if I'm really happy with my life. And how come I'm in my own room?

Zed? Maynard. Yeah, spider just caught a couple flies.

By the time Officer Bau Tu opens the door, twenty minutes later, I don't know what to expect. How much trouble can I be in for a penny? This is about a penny, right? I don't know if he's here to shoot me or let me go. He walks into the room with his Ray-Ban cop glasses still on, and the door closes behind him. It's just the two of us. No windows and a locked door. I'm half expecting this guy to get medieval on my ass. But he just sits down with his clipboard.

"Name?" Officer Bau Tu asks.

Mmmm . . . Back when I was picking beans in Guatemala, we made fresh coffee. Right off the trees, I mean. That was good. This is shit. But, hey, I'm in a police station . . .

"Name!"

"These cuffs are making my fingers fall asleep."

"NAME!"

"Lawrence Fulbeck," I tell him.

"Height."

"You know, it's not like I'm gonna jump you, can't you just loosen . . ."

"I'M NOT GONNA ASK YOU AGAIN!" he screams with his full 5′6″ volume. "Now, you can do it here, or we can take it downtown!"

And for the first time, I realize that Officer Bau Tu has a heavy Vietnamese accent. He sounds more like, "Oah weah can tekit doun toun!" And suddenly I realize that Officer Bau Tu is the first Vietnamese police officer I have ever met. Everything comes into focus. I see how much shit he must have gone through to get this job because of his size and his accent and his build and his background. For the first time, I realize I might actually carry some kind of respect for Officer Bau Tu.

"Height," he says.

"Six-one."

"Weight."

"170."

"Now . . . just what you think you were doing there in the parking lot, *hmmm?*"

That brief thought of respect? Out the door. Bau Tu is reminding me more and more of some Vietcong P.O.W. torture-hound in a Chuck Norris *Missing in Action* film. I don't think anymore about his accomplishments or his hardships or what he's gone through as a Southeast Asian immigrant. Because accomplishments don't count for shit if you'll still sell your family to save your sorry ass. And, no, I don't think it's entertaining anymore.

I'm struck with a mixture of funny and sad. Funny and sad for me as well as for him. But also for how we feel for each other. We're stuck together in this room with no windows and a locked door. For these next few minutes, the world is only me and him. Just the two of us. Building castles in the sky. If you take away the gun and the handcuffs, we could be playing cards together or having dinner. Kind of funny. Kind of sad.

I think of sitting on Asian Pacific Student Coalition boards in college, with reps from each of the various individually flavored clubs—Korean, Chinese, Pilipino. Christian, Social, Engineering. I remember sitting there watching us fight and bicker over some stupid charter wording. While Joe and Jane fraternity don't know or care—now or ever—about who we are or what we do. Chartered amendments are yesterday's egg rolls. Do you think anyone outside this room really cares whether we're called the Asian Pacific or the Asian *and Pacific Islander* Student Coalition? Do you think anyone outside this room really cares whether I rubbed a penny on the sidewalk or not? Nothing makes a power structure happier than watching its smaller dominions fight one another. You think white L.A. cared when blacks and Koreans shot one another in South Central? You think anybody besides Asian men wonder why every TV station in the country has an Asian female newscaster?

Fu Manchu Officer Tu snickers and glares at me occasionally, while his flattop quivers with each black ink pen stroke. He still hasn't taken off his cop glasses.

"You know," he says, looking up for a moment, "I don't want to say we're making an example of you here. *But . . .*"

He looks down and starts scribbling again. Was he smiling?

(An example of me?)

"Date of birth," he mumbles.

"April 30, 1965."

"Age."

(Think about it. I just told you what year I was born, Einstein.)

"Twenty-two," I say.

"Race."

(Here we go.)

He looks up again, and raises his mirrored cop glasses. He squints at me for a second. And I figure I'll just tell him before I get the comment or question. It'll save us some time.

"I'm half-Chinese and half-Caucasian."

Fu Manchu Officer Tu stalls for a moment, looking over his questionnaire. He pauses, not knowing what to do. Then he abruptly checks two boxes. He puts his pen down and looks up at me.

"I got a cousin like you. You guys sort of look the same."

ィ

I've gotten attitude from Asian guys all my life, and I'm finally starting to figure out why. There are two reasons, and both of them have to do with my being Hapa. The first is that some of these guys just can't handle your existence because you represent what, to them, is the end result of "their" women getting fucked by white barbarians. Plain and simple. In their eyes, you're the product of an Asian woman fucking a white man. So all their hatred of banana women, rice chasers, and white colonialist standards of beauty and desire get put onto you, however misdirected. I know that when you look at all the Hapas in the world, there aren't nearly as many with Asian fathers. But it does happen, you know. Lighten up.

The other reason some full-yellow brothers hate Hapas is this whole exotica crap. The whole best-of-both-worlds hybrid-vigor myth of physical beauty and prowess and intelligence and mystery. Kind of like how everyone talks about mutts being better and smarter and healthier dogs than purebreds. If you want to dispel that myth once and for all, I can bring out some butt-ass ugly Hapas right now, okay? They're out there, believe me. But some men still get bent out of shape because they see women swoon over Bruce or Brandon or Keanu or Russell or Tiger. They feel they get left out in the cold while Asian women jump on the Hapa bandwagon.

Some of this is true. Some women do swoon and some men do play it up. I can't speak for Hapas with black or Latino or native blood, but as far as Hapa haole men go, it's a reality. Some Asian women do chase them because they're white enough to be attractive and Asian enough to pass with their parents. Most Hapa haole men choose to identify white and date white, while a smaller minority choose to identify Asian and date Asian. An even smaller group choose to identify as Hapa. We all just try to date who we want, but it's always political on some level. Whether you want it to be or not. That's a pain, but it's true.

Twenty-one

Hanako was the closest thing I found to a politically correct date. Half-Japanese and half-Caucasian, she filled in all the blanks around me. My hardcore friends couldn't get after me for choosing white and dating white, and they couldn't accuse me of trying to "work something out" by only going after Asian girls. For once, I was untouchable. Even her name was great. I liked the way it sounded, introducing her to my friends or referencing her in public. It answered the question without it's even being asked. How many white girls do you know named Hanako? Basically, she was everything I wanted in a girlfriend at twenty-five. Beautiful, intelligent, and always fun to be around. She could be as happy taking a walk or studying biology as going to a five-star restaurant. Probably more so. Plus she could even deal with me waking her up to make love in the morning after escaping from a tunnel. That's definitely a nice quality in a girlfriend.

No sex, no drugs, no wine, no women, no fun, no sin, no you, no wonder it's dark . . .

We dated for about a year. And it worked out pretty well for the most part. She was never into the politics like I was, though. Maybe she smiled too much to let it get to her, but she was as content reading Amy Tan as James Baldwin or Malcolm X. And I think there was always a question on her part about why I was so into the whole Hapa thing—and how much that had to do with why I was dating her. I mean, she knew I was into her. I just don't think she ever fully understood how much it had to do with *who* she was rather than *what* she was. And how do you convince someone of that? How do you even start separating the two?

And to be honest, I have to admit there was something about her being Hapa that really *was* attractive to me. I know I dated Dana Apollinaire in high school, another Hapa with another cool name. But that situation was so caught up in the whole bisexual love triangle that I didn't even get around to dealing with the basic ingredients of race, ethnicity, and self-identity. We had enough going on and I hadn't even begun coming to terms with that stuff inside myself. How was I supposed to bring another variable into the mix? With Hanako it was different, though. I was in a different frame of mind. A different place. It was like after all the crap and all the arguments and all the observations, I was coming home. I know that sounds naive, but I was twenty-five years old. At least then I had an excuse.

The honeymoon ended when I met her parents. Hanako's white dad hated me from the beginning. For one, because she and I met when I was her T.A. And no matter how hard you try to explain it, no matter how careful you've been, no matter how long you waited, you still preyed on his daughter. Two, because when he asked me how my parents met, I had to tell him the truth—that my dad was my mom's T.A. as well. Funny coincidence. Try explaining that little genealogical trait to your girlfriend's dad. Add to that my long hair vs. his short hair, my L.A. upbringing vs. his High Sierras living, and my opposition to hunting vs. his mounted zebra skin on the living room wall and you've got a fun first weekend with the parents lined up. All he needs to know now is what my hands feel like on his daughter's jeans. Where does this guy keep his guns, anyway?

"I'm gonna help Mom in the kitchen," Hanako tells me. "Why don't you go talk to my dad?"

(Talk to your *dad?* About what?)

". . . Okay."

I look over and he's standing by himself in the living room. I look back and Hanako has already disappeared into the kitchen. I have to move now. I approach him slowly, moving closer and closer until I'm finally next to him. He hasn't moved or made eye contact. But he knows I'm here. He knows.

The demon is a liar. He will lie to confuse us. But he will also mix lies with the truth to attack us. The attack is psychological, Damien. And powerful. So don't listen. Remember that. Do not listen.

"So," I ask him, "how can you kill such beautiful animals?"

(Mental note. Mistake.)

"I've eaten everything I've killed," he says, looking forward.

"What about the *zebra?*"

"That was a gift."

We stand around with our hands in our pockets a while longer, looking at various inanimate objects on the fireplace mantel. What else are we supposed to do? I glance over at the kitchen. Hanako and her mother aren't even close to finishing dinner yet.

"Didn't you say you took a shot at a tiger?" I ask.

"When I was stationed in Thailand. That was a long time ago."

"But you said you eat everything you kill."

"I didn't hit him."

"But let's say you did. You were going to eat a *tiger?*"

(Mental note. Mistake.)

"Listen," he says, turning to look me in the eye. "That was the *one time* I was going for a trophy. And I missed him anyway."

"Yeah, but you said . . ."

Dinner's served and we sit down. We're sitting around in silence when Hanako's brother breaks the ice.

"So, Kip, what's with the hair?"

"Pardon?"

"What's with the hair?" he says, smiling. Dad's eyes are still in his plate but his ears are cocked. I can see them bending towards me as he chews.

"I'm trying to grow it out . . ."

Dad steps in, looking up.

"For what?" he asks.

"For a performance."

"For a *what?*"

After dinner, we go out to a movie. Just the five of us. Mom. Dad. Brother Henry. Hanako. Me. We pack into their red Chevy Suburban and drive through the snow into town. We're seeing Kurosawa's *Ran*, which translates as "Chaos." If I hadn't picked the movie, I'd swear they were trying to tell me something. The movie's long, with an intermission. During the break, we three men excuse ourselves to go to the men's room—myself, Hanako's brother, and Dad. Testosterone's running high. We walk along silently with our radar cranked to maximum. I can feel the popcorn crunching under my shoes and her dad's eyes boring into my back. *Yes, I fucked your daughter and when we park and throw the seat back she can honk the horn with her feet, okay? Why don't you just get it over with and ask?*

It's an old theater in some little Northern California mountain town where everyone's got four-wheel drive. The old theater's got only one bathroom, and it's upstairs. A line of old guys wearing parka vests with plaid flannel sleeves sticking out are waiting in line out the door. Hanako's brother gets in line first. Then me. Then Dad. The line moves slow. We get to the door and there's one sink, one urinal, and one stall. The lights flicker. The movie's going to start soon. Everyone around me is either urinating or about to. We inch forward. The man ahead of Henry goes in the stall while Henry hits the urinal. Both start together, finish together, and flush together. Henry zips up just as the guy comes out of the stall. My turn.

I go into the stall and the seat's already up. I stand there, unzip, and

194

hold. Hanako's dad steps to the urinal next to me. I can hear his big snowboots set down and grind in. We're separated by some thin privacy panel that blocks vision but not sound.

I can't pee.

I'm standing over a toilet and everyone, particularly Hanako's dad, can hear I'm not peeing. Think think think think.

10. 9. 8. 7. 6. 5 . . .

Her dad unzips and immediately opens up like some kind of fire hydrant. Strong, confident, and loud. But not quite loud enough to block out my silence. I can't pee and he knows I'm not peeing. He could be peeing loud enough to shake the building and his big, cocked ears would still know I'm stuck. Think think think think. Yes, I'm having a little problem, okay? Didn't you think that maybe you're making me a little nervous? *Exactly what kind of boy are you bringing home Hanako?*

4. 3. 2. 1 . . . . 10. 9. 8. 7. 6. 5 . . .

His steady stream is in full flow now. Loud, like some raging river or Hoover Dam. I'm standing over my still-as-a-lake toilet thinking pee pee pee pee while Moses is parting the Red Sea next to me. I drop my gum into the water *plink*

The lights flicker again. Dammit, I don't have much time.

4. 3. 2. 1 . . . . 10. 9. 8. 7 . . .

His steady stream is starting to slow down and I'm not even close. I don't have to pee for a week. You hear me? A *week!* People are waiting and I'm sitting in my soundproof chamber stall of silence, realizing there is absolutely no way the human body can mimic the sound of its own urination. Hanako's dad is almost finished. Think think think think. I'm thinking of just zipping up and acting casual. Oh, me? I always pee silently. Oh, I didn't really have to go. Oh, I just came along to keep you company. And in the middle of all this, in a completely spur of the moment panic—I decide to drop my pants. Turn around. And sit down. There's a sure way to impress dad.

I spin around after standing for thirty seconds and sit down on the toilet like a girl. Hanako's dad's stream stutters for a second and finishes. I hear him zip up. I see his thick boots turn around and face my little dunce-hat-sit-down-if-you-can't-pee-chair, just for a second, then walk out of the bathroom. Clunk. Clunk. Clunk. Clunk.

I wait a minute. Flush the empty toilet and my piece of gum. Wash my hands. I walk back down into the theater and sit next to Hanako. The movie's already started.

"*You* were gone awhile . . ."

Everything is a ritual. And everything is a test. Whether I have to prove my politics, verify I am who I am, or pee for volume in front of a girl-friend's father. Sometimes it all kind of feels the same. I know I can hide from it in my personal relationships, but only if I hide from it myself. And as much as with any white woman, I know part of my relationship and part of my attraction to Hanako stemmed from where I was in my life and how I saw myself. She sensed it and I sensed it. We just didn't want to talk about it. Where are you supposed to start? It's so much eas-ier just to make love in the morning.

There was a time when I could live a life of racial ignorance. But that time's getting harder to remember. There was a place I could meet other Asian men and women without immediately assessing where it was they were in their progression of awareness. And for all the years I've spent learning and teaching and raising consciousness, I'm no longer sure if that was such a bad place to be for me. I'm not certain if living a life of racial ignorance is such a terrible thing anymore. I used to press for people to open their eyes, seething inside with each refer-ence and reminder of how many steps back I had to begin, or how much of a head start I could be awarded. I spent my every entrance into every Chinese restaurant preparing myself for either attitude or exoti-cism. I attended my every introduction armed.

Maybe part of me thought having Hanako attached to my arm might bring out more of who I was for others to see. Maybe this is the feeling I had of coming home. I thought being with her might stop some of the questions. I thought it might stop some of the aggression and the forks brought to my table without request. But she was her own woman like any other. With her own particular smell and taste, and her own individual progression of awareness. Politically, she will never be where I am. She probably won't even get to where I was when we dated seven or eight years ago. It just wasn't her interest. Wasn't her spark. But it took me this long to see the value here. It took me this long to under-stand that she could have taught me as much about *not* opening my eyes—about letting things go—as I ever tried to teach her about Asian American politics and focusing in. And in the long run, I don't know who would actually make a bigger impact on the world. I used to be absolutely sure.

In some ways, I think her dad might have sensed it, too. That's part of your job as a dad, and I don't blame him for treating me the way he did. He had his own things going on. I just hope I'll be able to pull it off when the time comes that my own daughter brings back some younger version of me into our living room. Sure, I'd forbid her to date me at eighteen. But me at twenty-five? I probably wouldn't forbid it then. I just wouldn't be real happy about it. Maybe I can get through an introduction. I can even shake his hand. But what do you expect me to do with him after that. *Talk?*

Twenty-two

I was talking with my friend Sophana, who is a Cambodian woman full of fire. She's gone through the whole gamut on her way to becoming who she is. Immigrant refugee. Party girl. Boy toy. Asian American activist. International-relations specialist. She's been through it. Articulate and educated enough that I totally respect her opinion, but also completely accepting of me as a friend, enough so that I can be absolutely honest with her. A rare combination. And I was talking to her one night about possibly spending my life with a white woman. I had been thinking it over and I'd come to terms with it. It's not as simple as "It's just about love" and it's not as rigid as "You can't date someone who doesn't understand the oppression of your people." It's somewhere in between.

She sits there for a second.

"Now, what's that look supposed to mean?" I ask.

"Nothing . . . just thinking."

"And . . . ?"

"Well," Sophana starts, "you know your work's always gonna bring this stuff up. It's not like you're gonna get away from it. Everywhere you go you're gonna get asked what your dating deal is."

"Yeah, but I'm okay with that," I say, going into my well-thought-out reasoning. "Because, look, if it was the same for an Asian guy as an Asian girl to date white, then I'd be a hypocrite. But it's *not* the same thing. I mean, all the simplistic crap like 'Well, look at so-and-so—he married white,' 'You Asian men don't give Asian women any agency,' whatever. I mean, that's all it is. They're totally simplistic arguments. They're sound bites."

"How do you figure?" she asks.

"'Cause they turn these issues into these neat and clean simplistic arguments that you can't even respond to. You can't go into dating and gender politics in thirty seconds or something, and whoever's feeding you this stuff knows it. They give you these quick lines, then they try and base the whole dialogue on some neat and clean argument where there's no way for you to respond. It's like talking about abortion and saying, 'Look. It's simple. Is killing right or wrong?' You know what I'm saying? It ignores all the other issues around it."

"Like what issues?"

"All right, like this agency thing. Of course a lot of Asian women don't fall for this *Joy Luck Club* stereotype stuff. That's obvious. But if you try and pretend you're completely *not* affected—then that's crap, too! I mean, the stuff is everywhere you look! And it gets in there somewhere to *some* level. It's not like you live in a vacuum, you know?"

"I don't know if I really buy that," she says.

"Okay, look. Take this well-I-know-so-and-so-and-he-has-a-white-girlfriend thing. It's real easy to say it's the same thing and everything's cool. But it's not the same thing! An Asian guy dating white isn't even close to an Asian girl dating white! I mean, one operates on all these social policies that totally *encourage* the pairing, and one goes completely *against* the same system. I mean, if I could pick up an *L.A. Times* and find a bunch of white-women-seeking-Asian-men ads it would be one thing. You know what I'm saying? Or even *Asian*-women-seeking-Asian-men ads. But the stuff isn't there. It's just business as usual. Any major newspaper in the country? Same thing. You just can't argue that. You can't."

I sit back for a second to let it sink in.

Did I ever tell you that this here snakeskin jacket is a symbol of my individuality and my belief in personal freedom?

"So you think that your dating white is going against the system?" Sophana asks.

"Hmm?"

"Are you listening to me?"

"Yeah."

"You think you're bucking the system?"

"To some extent," I tell her, "any Asian guy dating white is."

"All right," she says. "Then you've only got one problem."

"Yeah?"

And Sophana tells me, "You're not Asian. You're Hapa."

"So?"

"So it's not the same thing," she says. "You're not some random Asian guy breaking down the stereotypes of being wimpy and asexual and all that bullshit. *You've* got the complete stereotype of being beautiful and desirable and exotic! You can't totally identify yourself as an Asian man because you're not an Asian man! In fact, as a Hapa you've got the *same* stereotypes that Asian women have in this country. Exotic . . . sexual . . . beautiful . . ."

I think about it for a couple seconds.

Tic. Tic. Tic. Tic.

"But when I'm with a white girl I get problems, right?" I come back at her. "You know, like when I was with Katherine . . ."

"No. Don't even try it," Sophana interrupts. "Look. You're not an Asian man, and you don't face the same things they do. *Sometimes* you might. But probably not more than any guy with a beautiful girl does. And most of the time, I bet . . ."

"That's crap! One time we totally got vibed by these white guys at this one restaurant . . ."

"Kip," she interrupts again, "it's not the same thing. It's not. You're gonna have to rethink this."

"Don't gimme that! Were you there? Were you? *Were you there?"*

She's giving me that look again, but I'm on a roll.

"Were you there or not?"

"No," she says sarcastically.

"Okay, then. Look. I'm an artist. I'm making my work and I'm living my life and if people have got some issues or problems or whatever it is they're working out and something I'm doing pushes one of their buttons, then that's *their* problem."

"That's not what we're talking about," she says.

"It's totally what we're talking about."

"You being an artist—that's only tangentially attached to this. You need to come to terms with your whole Asian male thing."

"Oh, great," I say. *"This,* I do not need to talk about."

"Oh, that's good," she responds, nodding at me. "Just write it off. That'll work."

"That's not writing it off. I just don't wanna go into the whole emasculated bullshit Long Duck Dong crap I've dealt with forever! Why don't we talk internment camp next? I'm over it, okay?"

"That's exactly what I'm talking about! You can't say that! You can't just adopt being an Asian man and all the problems that go along with it whenever you feel like it! You don't have that right! Look at you, Kip. How long have I known you? How many girlfriends have you had?"

I take a deep breath.

All I wanted was a Pepsi. Just one Pepsi. And she wouldn't give it to me.

"Sophana," I enunciate slowly, "you don't even know *half* of some of the stuff I've gone through. Okay? Sometimes I just don't wanna deal with this crap."

"So live in a vacuum? Same criticism you guys always throw at Asian women."

Tic. Tic. Tic. Tic.

Deep breath again. "Don't pull this," I say. "You *know* I've thought about this stuff a lot. And you know I've dated a lot of Asian girls . . ."

"Is that something you had to work out or something you had to prove?"

"*Sophana,*" I sigh, "I hate when you pull this crap . . ."

"Just answer the question."

"Neither. Okay? It was just a choice I was making."

"Choice?"

"Yes. *Choice.* Just like when I was younger and I'd be only into dating white girls. It just got to a point where I go 'What am I doing?' and threw that shit out."

"And you started dating Asians?" she asks.

"Yeah, I started dating Asians. And, yes, to answer your next question, it did feel more natural, like . . ."

"Sounds to me like you had something to work out," she interrupts.

We sit in silence for a while. I'm getting pretty pissed off because this feels too much like psychotherapy. Like every public confessor, when you really go deep down, everything is stored, private, and protected. Big secret. Sophana gets up to make some tea.

"You want some?"

"No."

She sits back down next to me with her tea bag and cup and a cup for me anyway. It's one of those Celestial Seasonings berry or flower or spice things that never tastes like it's supposed to. It just tastes like funny water.

"Look," Sophana says, "you know I'm not trying to piss you off. You've just got to think about these things. Better to get this from me than someone else."

"What things?" I ask.

"You've got to think about being with her," she tells me. "It's not the same as an Asian guy being with a white girl because *you're half white.*"

"So?"

"So people are going to see you as choosing your white side . . ."

Just a Pepsi.

". . . and they're going to see you as choosing it *because you can.* Just like any of these other guys that can go either way and go white. They'll just see you as doing the same. No matter what your work is about. No matter how much activism you do. No matter what—some people are just going to say you're choosing to be white. It's just something you're going to have to deal with."

I stay silent for a second, taking it in.

Doesn't matter. I'll probably just get hit by a car anyway.

"I'm just telling you this because I care about you," she says. "You know that."

We sit for a couple seconds sipping our funny-water tea.

"You know I hate this shit," I tell her. "I just want to make my work, send it out, let people deal with it. Period. Just do my thing without all the crap attached."

"I've heard *that* one before," she tells me.

iris

Twenty-three

Sometimes life gets in our face, and we forget for a moment how to make up our own fictions. We spend most of our lives insulating ourselves—changing timing belts before 60,000 miles and double-checking our door locks. But there come certain points where we have to step outside our accustomed shelters and securities or risk sinking into the random landscape of routine and settlement. I love *Seinfeld* re-runs as much as the next person, but I never want to live a life where I look forward to them. I don't want to be satisfied with after-Christmas sales, *Men's Health* magazine, action movies, and an obligatory goodnight kiss. There come certain points where we need to put down our magazine questionnaires and seek out the things in life that scare us, because how else can we learn whether we're really the person we say we are?

For me this happens only in a few select areas. It happens occasionally when I'm making art, or teaching. It certainly happens in love. And it happens when I freedive alone. I've been spearfishing for only a few years, but each time I've entered the water to hunt, part of me inside apologizes. Part of me questions the person I say I am. And part of me is scared. I figure we all spend our lives around death in some way or another. I just tend to look at it a little more directly than most.

Maybe this has something to do with my own version of a reality check. A way to reaffirm my priorities. Maybe it's a way of letting myself know where it is I am and what it is I'm doing. I watch my brother work as an oncologist, and I hear him tell me that every day when he leaves work to go home to his family, he feels like the luckiest man alive. I guess spending your days around dying people will do that to you. As will saving a life, or, I suppose, failing to do so. I look for this perspective when I go visit him at work, but all I see is a waiting room like any other doctor's waiting room. Fluorescent lights, magazines, and aquariums full of marble angels, red swordtails, and blue gouramis. Besides the fact that everyone else in the waiting room has cancer, nothing's out of the ordinary. I can feel for them. I can empathize. But somehow I'm not part of the process. I'm always an outsider. Always a visitor. I need to find my own ways of being scared, and my own ways of being lucky.

ᗱ

An hour before high tide, I walk across the oil fields to the reef at Naples and look at the water. The ocean is 64 degrees and nearly flat. I'm guessing visibility somewhere around ten feet. I put on a 1-ml shirt, a 3-ml O'Neill surf wetsuit, and I go over my checklist. Mask and snorkel. Fins. Gloves. Gamebag. Weightbelt with thirteen pounds of lead. I walk down a dirt hill, delicately stepping over the railroad tracks like a spider web. I look both ways for silent Amtraks, but I don't see any coming. Everything feels okay so far. Everything feels safe. Reaching the sand, I put my key in the key pocket and tuck the safety cap of my spear into the leg of my wetsuit. I've lost enough keys to make sure I zip all the way up, because nothing's worse than looking for a single Toyota key in a universe of silver sand. Except maybe looking for a single gold prince or princess in a universe of golden frogs. That's what they tell me anyway. Sooner or later you get tired of kissing. I spit in my mask and smudge the spit around with my finger before rinsing it in the water. I tie my hair back in a ponytail. I check my mask for a proper seal and place my snorkel in my mouth.

I'm entering the food chain near the top, but not at the top. And, in terms of how you feel, that makes a big difference. People can sense when you're nervous or scared. They cancel second dates, fire awkward talk-show hosts, and draw their weapons faster. Fish can sense it even more. It's like you've got no secrets when you enter the water. There's no place to hide and all the lights are turned on. You never know where the boss is and you never know who's watching. You just know they're around.

Whether you actually shoot or not, diving with a spear and diving without a spear are two very different things. You slip underwater and everyone seems to know your name and what you're here for. They definitely know if you're scared. No matter how tough you act, the smell is on your skin. You're see-through. You might as well be some high school kid trying to sass Mr. Vernon during Saturday morning detention. Shermer High School. Shermer, Illinois 60062. For all your bravado, your bluffs don't have a chance.

Eat my shorts.
What was that?
Eat. My. Shorts.
You just bought yourself another Saturday, Mister!
(Sigh) . . . I'm crushed.
You just bought one more right there!
Well, I'm free the Saturday after that. Beyond that, I'm gonna have to check my calendar.

Good! Because it's gonna be filled! We'll keep going. You want
another one? Say the word—just say the word! Instead of going to
prison you'll come here! Are you through?

No.

I'm doing society a favor.

So?

That's another one right now! I've got you for the rest of your nat-
ural-born life if you don't watch your step! You want another one?

Yes.

You got it! You got another one right there! That's another one, pal!
You through?

Not. Even. Close. Bud.

Good! You got one more right there!

You really think I give a shit?

Another!

. . .

You through?

How many is that?

Kicking out past the surf, my heart is racing. I'm consciously controlling my panic just to move into the deep water by myself. Clouds of
sand in the water explode in front of me like silent smoke bombs and
sea monkeys. They spray my mask with little glitters of gold and silver
and black and brown, reducing visibility to less than a foot in some
places, like an underwater fireworks show. In the clearer patches I swim
over eelgrass, rock, reef, and loose kelp that's waiting to wash up on
shore. The waves push it in and the sun dries it black. Soon the flies
come like a desert sandstorm. First one, then more. Until one morning the man with the yellow shirt drives up in a tractor and drags the
dead kelp away down the beach. No one knows where he goes with it.
Maybe to the next beach. Maybe to make sushi or toothpaste or ice
cream. Maybe he just keeps going.

Thinking of these things keeps my mind busy. It makes me feel better until I come over the edge of the reef and into deeper water. I lose
the bottom. Instantly, I pop up and look around me. I see the world
from above again, 100 yards offshore with no one around anywhere and
a living world encircling me. I see the surface motion of the water, and
the sun reflecting in each cadence. I feel my fins kicking to keep me surfaced and my weightbelt pulling me back down again. For a reassuring

second, I think I see the head of a surfer down the coast, behind the spray of a wave breaking towards shore. I gauge my location, take a deep breath, and pretend to see more surfers sitting all around me as I go back under. They're waving casually and telling me it's okay. *Everything's cool, man. Don't worry about it. A waterman like you? Come on.*

I'm diving in twenty feet of water. Cruising down to about fifteen feet, I scan the bottom for the outline of halibut. I search for any sign of the mouth, tail, or eyes marked in the sand. I look along the edge of finger reefs, where the little fish that halibut feed on might stray too far from the safety of the eelgrass and into range of the buried aggressor. The anchovy hunts the copepod. The halibut hunts the anchovy. I hunt the halibut. And so on. Most of us are hunters in one way or another. All of us are prey. An outline in the sand could designate a halibut as much as a sandshark, a stingray, or a rock. You have to look at it close because some taste better and some are more dangerous. You have to look it in the face.

Human beings are scared little creatures, really. We have the front-facing eyes and binocular vision of predators, but we run away from anything in the wild, unless we're armed. Sometimes even then. Dogs bark. Snakes rattle. People hide. Grown adults run from quarter-ounce mice and bugs. We fortify our apartments with no-pest strips, roach motels, and electric bug zappers. We're afraid of spiders, sharks, and the dark, when the most dangerous thing around us is how we treat one another. I should be more scared driving the freeway. I should be more scared coming home at night, or asking a woman to have dinner with me. But it's all a world away from me, like television. All that's in front of me is life, death, and the world's biggest aquarium. I hold my spear in close, with two hands, somehow taking a small bit of comfort by extending its tip into the darkness of the water.

I feel so visible. I keep trying to slow down my heart rate, thinking I can disappear into the environment if only I can relax. So much about being here depends on how you're feeling. When you're confident and really focused on hunting, your body exudes it. No matter how hard you try to act nonchalant, you swim like a predator. A coyote separated from the pack. You breathe water through your lungs and you sense the fear in the other fish. Everything smaller gives you a wide berth, while everything larger than you stays just outside your vision. All you catch is the occasional glimpse. I see schools of perch part around me like a blanket, and skates scatter under my shadow. Instantly and unconsciously, I feel my body drop into feeding mode. It happens like a sudden shift in your vertebrae, like an involuntary nighttime twitch. And it feels good. It feels natural. My heartbeat drops to nothing and I forget about breathing. My eyesight tightens. The wind goes still and my hands relax. All the dogs have circled now. They're crouching in the tall grass and waiting.

The eelgrass beneath me parts under the surge and reveals a legal halibut lying on the rock reef, camouflaged in color but not in outline. I swim over the fish and hold my spear above it. Easily legal. At least 26" and fat.

Now the decisions of a lifetime come up.

What is the law?

You're a vegetarian. Sort of. You don't do cows, pigs, chickens, or ducks, but anything from the ocean is game. Everyone draws their line somewhere. You wear leather jackets, shoes, and belts but seethe with hatred for people at county fairs who pet the pigs and grab a bacon cheeseburger for dinner. *Oh, look how cute he is, honey!* You'll grab a ladder and glass to take a cricket outside, but you have a snakeskin wallet in the back right pocket of your 501s. I look down at an adult fish digesting its catch on a reef in fifteen feet of water. This is his domain and I'm just a visiting assassin. I should have wiped my feet before coming in. I should have dressed nicer. I should have brought a gift like my ma taught me.

I think about it. If I were living in the mountains and needed to eat, would I be able to kill an animal? Could I shoot a deer or a fawn? What about Bambi's mom? What about the Donner party?

Not to eat flesh. That is the law.

One summer, I yell at a junior lifeguard for swatting a junebug and I watch him start crying. The Junior Lifeguard Program is basically a water-safety camp that I've been teaching for the last ten years or so. My real job, as they say. Ostensibly, the program is about trying to make the kids water-safe—rescue skills, swimming, surfing, first aid, CPR. That sort of thing. Their parents drop them off at 7:30 from sport utility vehicles and minivans and Mercedes, and pick them up four hours later. The kids spend five weeks being happy, getting in shape a bit, and sunburning a lot. While I spend five weeks making sure they're safe, trying to affect their lives—and believing in education again. Sometimes I wonder if I should be paying them instead of the other way around.

Teaching at the university level, I usually start getting antsy around March. I notice my eyes darting around more and my already short attention span diminishing even further. Because every year around this time, my main joys in teaching start losing the battle to all the other garbage that goes along with the job of being a professor. Here, sit on an advisory committee that just argues with itself. Here, write a proposal in triplicate to try to get $200 allocated to pay someone to walk across campus and clean your video heads or reboot your server. Here, counsel an undergrad who's pissed off at this educational system and its funding cuts and all the broken equipment that no one has the skill, money, or time to fix. Try telling him you're pissed off about it, too. It doesn't help. Here comes another one. Another's waiting after her.

There comes a point where the perpetual-motion machine takes over. Sooner or later, you stop teaching and start merely functioning. Most of us don't mean to do this. It's just a matter of survival. It's a matter or realizing that you alone can't change the system. And it's a matter of getting broken, of wearing down. You feel your idealism slipping away like a slow leak in a bicycle tire. It gets replaced with lunch meetings, departmental politics, and bio-bibliographic updates while the virus incubates inside you. Pretty soon you find yourself symptomatic and highly contagious. It goes airborne like Hantavirus or Ebola. You find yourself walking up the back stairs to your office, and you feel yourself looking at an approaching student in terms of what they want from you instead of seeing what they have to offer. And that's a bad place to be. It goes against every reason you became a teacher and it puts you one step closer to growing old. We're all scared of getting tired and giving up our dreams. But I'm more scared of reaching the point where I don't care anymore. Sometimes there's nothing I can do but rest, drink plenty of fluids, and wait for summer.

I remember a teacher in college who changed my direction in life. His name was Phel Steinmetz, and he taught photography in the Visual Arts Department at UCSD. He wasn't a big-name professor, just a guy who really cared about his students, and his teaching. Basically, he would walk into class with a photo or two and a scrap of paper with a couple of notes jotted down on it. And we'd talk. We'd talk for two or three hours about making art and looking at art. We'd talk about the camera and the power behind it. We'd talk about how to use our own focus and intuition and instinct in making photographs, and how to make works about what we thought was important. But mostly we just talked about life. I'd talk about swimming or surfing or my family. Other students would talk about their own individual passions. And Phel would talk about the university and being a professor.

And this was where I first heard that my university wasn't about what I always thought it was about. Phel would just say it in passing.

"The university isn't about, teaching."

"What's it about, then?" we'd ask. But he'd already have gone on to something else by that point. He was that kind of teacher—always a step ahead of you and always forcing you to *learn* on your own. We were left to either ponder the question of what our university was about, or just give up and ignore it altogether. I always chose to ponder. I still do.

I guess the university could be about money. That would make sense. As a faculty member now, I'm always getting pushed to bring in more funds from outside sources. This is the kind of stuff that brings you prestige in the real world. Not helping students. Not teaching. There are two basic ways of getting outside funding in the arts. Some of it you get by getting good at writing grants. Most of it you get by getting good at schmoozing with the right people. I'm not very good at either. I don't want to be.

I guess the university could be about power. That would make sense. There's ego and class difference everywhere you look on a campus. You'd think that by the time someone is good enough at what they do to be a college professor, they'd be successful and secure enough to not let their egos take over. Think again. Because in reality, a lot of people who reach the top of some random, esoteric subject don't have much going on in their lives outside of it. And they somehow carry the attitude that the rest of the world owes them something, just because they spent ten years researching 19th-century Chinese painting or post-colonialist literature or string theory. Like they've earned some kind of real-world social importance. Like a Ph.D. actually means anything outside academia. These are the faculty who treat staff like slaves, students like children, workers like monkeys, and rival colleagues like enemies. These are the nerdy doctors who never got dates in high school, yelling at nurses now and making them cry. These are the short white men walking two steps ahead of their scurrying Asian female students. Sometimes it's just some kind of weird, twisted revenge.

Not to walk on all fours. That is the law.

I guess the university could be about sex. That would make sense. In a world that revolves around fucking, you suddenly find yourself given absolute power. For the first time in your life you can completely manipulate your social situation. Why wouldn't you? Your class is your kingdom. It's your fantasy world. Your lectures showcase whatever it is you want to showcase—your wit, your style, your intelligence. It's your stage, and you've got a ten-week-long captive audience. With each class you can play God to any beautiful sacrificial virgin in front of you. Sooner or later she realizes you're human and moves on. But after she leaves, you can always find another. There are always fresh bodies and searching minds coming in, like an assembly line. You get older. They stay the same age. Your tricks get recycled. Scorsese captured this dead-on in *Life Lessons* with Nick Nolte and Rosanna Arquette. It's in *New York Stories* with a terrible Coppola and a mediocre Allen. Be careful which virgin you watch it with.

Not to spill blood. That is the law.

But if the university isn't about money, power, or sex, what could it be about? Phel never told us. He'd just say, "Some of us are trying to change things," and leave it at that. Class would end. We'd put on our backpacks and walk out into the sunlight.

ᄀ
ᄀ

Eight years later, I got offered a teaching position at UCSB, and I wanted one of Phel's photographs to take up with me. I didn't have the $1,500 to buy it, and I wasn't bold enough to think he might want to trade for a piece of my own work. But I asked him anyway.

"Come by the studio," he says.

We don't talk about money or trades. We don't even talk about photography. We just talk about the usual life stuff. Except this time we're both talking about the same things. We're both talking about the university and being a professor. We spend an hour in his studio looking at prints, even though I've known exactly which one I want the entire time. It's a three-piece panel of the side of a house. The house is white with a red tile roof. A crack runs along the length of its wall and into the ground. Doesn't sound like much. Most people seeing it tell me it doesn't look like much either. It's one of those photographer's photographs—even when I haven't shot a camera for years, it reminds me I'm an artist. I need that sometimes.

I pick it out. Phel wraps it up in butcher paper and walks me to the door.

"Well, good luck," he says, extending his hand.

"Phel, you gotta let me give you something for this."

"You already have," he says.

The whole scene seems pretty corny, but I don't even break a smile. I just walk off with my print and my responsibility. I've got an endless supply of art students ahead of me, each of them waiting for me to tell them they're on to something. As if I somehow have a better idea than they do. I can crit picture after picture of bongs, beer bottles, the beach, and the person they're currently fucking without even coming up for air. It's pretty easy, actually. Maybe they should be telling me. But every year I've still burned out, running back each summer to teach ten-year-old junior lifeguards in Solana Beach. I guess I just like talking to people who don't laugh at recycling. I like being around people who don't feel they *have* to go out on a Friday night. I like watching people who really believe they can change the world. And most of these kids are too young to have given up yet.

Simple math. Tell a cashier you don't need a bag for the bagel or batteries or soap you're buying. The next day, thirty ten-year-olds each tell a Vons cashier.

Thirty bags a day × seven days =.

Fifty-two weeks × ten years =.

Even in a closed-end lease, it's still pretty amazing. Somehow, education works here again. I can talk to these kids about respecting the water and the beach and one another, and I can see them tuning in. Maybe they're only listening to me because I can surf big waves or they really like *Baywatch*. But they're listening. I can tell them about respecting life in all its forms—sandcrabs, bees, and junebugs that they normally toss around or swat indiscriminately, and I can see results the next day. No three-month Rogaine wait here. In between Capture the Flag and rescue training, we talk about little things in life and what they mean to each of us. We talk about what we've got in our brown-bag lunches. We talk about what it means to kill a bug. We talk about what it means to kill a fish.

There is a time between each night and day when each of us takes our turn at being God. We decide whether to squash an ant that's walking along the kitchen countertop. We decide whether to shoot metal spikes through a fish or to swim on by. I know that God is a giant white shark swimming close to shore, a Nissan Pathfinder pulling out in front of me on a rainy mountain road, a pile of loosely crumpled Butterfinger and Abba-Zabba wrappers tossed in the corner, and the beating heart of a sleeping woman. Sometimes I live my life waiting for God to decide what to do with me. Other times a halibut on the ocean bottom waits for me to decide. The anchovy waits for the halibut. The copepod waits for the anchovy. And so on.

I cock my spear without thinking, breathe two deep breaths, and dive down on the fish. Slowly and without bubbles. I'm in complete attack mode now. This fish is dinner. Five feet away the fish senses my presence. Four feet away I point the sling and slowly move its aim over the body of the fish, from the tail up along the lateral line to the head. Three feet away the fish shifts its eyes. It sees me and twitches to run.

pffft

I shoot. Time goes fast here. The shot goes off mark because the fish is bolting. It hits in the gut instead of the head. I jam down and pin the spear. I can hear the prongs scraping through the fish against the reef. I'm kicking as fast as I can to sink the spear further, because nothing is worse than shooting a fish and losing it. Then you're no better than any random drive-by gangbanger or trophy hunter. You're just killing for the sake of killing.

The halibut is struggling, it's flat body undulating frantically. It sends waves of energy up the spear, through my arm, and into my chest cavity. I see its pink liver and stomach come out through the hole I blasted through it. I know it's gonna die. I can't lose it. I'm at the bottom and the fish is spinning clockwise and taking my spear with it, kicking up sand and clouding the water with glimmers of golden dirt and blood. I can't see and my lungs are aching for air as I reach down blindly below the fish and frantically feel for the other side of the spear tip. I touch the prongs, grab them with my left hand, and I reach the defining moment—like when the jackals bring a zebra off its feet or the ball leaves Magic Johnson's junior skyhook hand against the Celtics in game four. Everyone instinctually knows the real fight is over. The hyenas and the zebra and Chick Hearn and Larry Bird just go through the formalities of biting the jugular or calling a time out. The fish still snaps its jaws and struggles, but the chase is over. With one hand on either side, I swim the fish up to the surface and breathe.

The fish is bigger than I thought. Closer to 30″. And the paralyzer prongs, together with the fish's spinning and my bad shot, have opened a hole the size of a golf ball in its gut. The fish is bleeding and dying fast. I start swimming the eighty or so yards into shore and begin talking to the fish. I keep it in the water so it can spend its last moments in its own home. I'm sorry, but I have to eat it, I tell it. Everything has to eat. Everything has to hunt in its own way. The dying halibut watches me and doesn't say anything. It just closes its jaws and bleeds. They are special fish. Brown on one side, white on the other. Everyone sees them as having two sides instead of being just one fish. They keep the white side down where you can't see it, but it's the brown side that gets shot. If I look deep enough, there must be something to learn here.

Are we not men?

ᄀ
ᄼ

Back on shore, I pull the dead fish off my spear and place it in my game-bag. I head towards the car with my fresh kill and a thousand eyes following me. Soon the entire beach will start booing. For all I've done in my life, part of me still feels like just another man stealing from his mother. I pick up cans and bottles in the sand. I buy phosphate-free laundry detergent. I recycle my plastic and boycott jetskis. But I still feel the virus becoming systemic. I still feel like I'm shooting blanks.

Somewhere off the coast, a fisherman replaces the oil in his boat and dumps the tarnished semi-liquid in the ocean. It floats to the top in a dark slick, but the boat has already pulled away to cleaner waters. Two miles south, a white American family on a half-day trip takes several minutes photographing young Jennifer with her catch—a 3″ rockfish. Undersized by usefulness if not by law.

One picture.

Two pictures.

Three pictures.

Hold it up higher, honey. Look at the little fisherman!

Four pictures later, they pull the hook and toss the fish back in the water. It sinks to the bottom, joining a million other suffocated rockfish and finless sharks wiggling in the sand. The hook goes back on a line. Five pictures later a seventeen-year-old Joan Jett clone tosses a cigarette out of her Mustang window while listening to Van Halen—the Sammy Hagar version—and sets our backyard afire in Covina. My tree house burns to ash. My mother's roses melt. My father's birds combust. How does it feel to burn alive in a flight cage on fire? Do birds burn in the air or do they fall to the ground like meteors?

Six pictures later a rich La Jolla woman with too many years of too much sun smokes on the beach, while my junior lifeguards practice rescue breathing in front of her. Do you not see at all? Or do you see and just not care? Put your cigarette butt out in the sand. Drop it on the sidewalk and rub it out with your shoe. Toss your fishing line over the rail and wait for it to snag a gull. We all die a little with your every decision anyway. Do you understand? Every single time you toss your cigarette butt on the ground, I die a little. I know you don't mean it personally. Does it matter?

Someday the birds will descend out of the day sky and peck the eyes out of every smoker who drops butts on the ground. Someday the fish and eels will strike out of our showers and bathtubs and toilets, biting the testicles off every man leaving his empty beer cans at the beach. On campus, students, faculty, and staff run frantically from the clouds and clouds of birds, while some of us walk calmly and watch the apocalypse. The birds only swarm around the chosen ones. If you had no sight then, what does it matter now? They stagger around screaming with their arms and hands extended forward, and dark sockets where their eyes once were. I hear the screams, but I don't show any reaction. I see men bolting out of public restrooms with their pants around their ankles and their knees together, desperately holding their wet crotches with both hands. No more breeding for you. No more heirs to your Budweiser throne.

It's a little sad, all the blindness and castration and all, but no sadder than now, really. A woman means nothing with a comment, and a cigarette is tossed without thought, but a child's innocence and my tree house will never be rebuilt. I notice a child's mimicry and I notice my walking silence. I notice a disregard for common space and common life. I notice an upended tortoise trying to right itself and several crows standing on the desert sand waiting for the turtle to die. I notice mostly things I can do nothing about.

Twenty-four

Two weeks later, a man is killed by a shark. It happens simply. And it happens not far from where I hunted. The man was urchin diving off San Miguel Island, which is one of the Channel Islands off the coast of Santa Barbara. And on a day like any other day, he surfaced next to his boat and began removing his gear. But on this day he gets hit. Before the deckhands can react, the fish has taken off one of the man's legs. It mauls the other in the process, rolling its eyes back and shaking its head vigorously from side to side underwater. The whole process happens immediately—a fraction of the time Chrissie screams and struggles in *Jaws,* and without the benefit of Chief Brody, Hooper, or Quint to enact any kind of retribution. There is no cello prologue, no stunt double. None of us will ever see this on a Universal Studios tour. The deckhands, running over, see only some foam, a half-man floating, and the wet slap of a fin. In this lifetime, Jeff Richards is dead by the time they drag him to the boat.

Four of us are driving to surf that same morning. Myself, two graduate art students named Steve and Bill, and Bill's wife, Cindy. We drive up the coast in Bill's *Brady Bunch*–type station wagon, nicknamed "Carzilla." We're hoping to surf a break called Tarantulas, which is an offshoot of Jalama Campground—the first public access north of Point Conception. Having gotten a late start, we're rushing to beat the wind. Bill drives. Cindy rides shotgun and looks for cops. Steve and I sit in the back and talk about guitars. Bill tunes his radio to 92.9 and we listen to assorted nineties pop-punk through crackly speakers. Green Day and Offspring and Weezer. Ten more years and they'll all be on *Time/Life* "Best of the Nineties" compilations.

Passing Gaviota, I look out to my left and see the trees whizzing by. Beyond that, I see the barbed wire and nondescript signs denoting any of the thousands of military, oil, or cattle acres forbidden to the general public. Beyond that, I see the Santa Barbara Channel and the outline of Santa Cruz Island. And seeing this, a random thought comes to me. No explanation. No cause and effect. Just a simple thought about white sharks off the Channel Islands. It moves to my tongue effortlessly. Without thinking, I ask Steve about it.

"Hey, do they ever get attacks off the islands?"

"Shark attacks?"

"Yeah."

Bill sighs and shakes his head. Cindy laughs. They know the statistics. Better chance of getting gored by a bull. Better chance of dying from a bee sting or getting struck by lighting. Exponentially better chance of crashing and burning right here on the freeway. But Steve, who grew up in Santa Barbara, just looks back at me and answers. No head-shaking and no laughing. He tells me the sharks are always there, and people surf there all the time. So either you don't surf there, or you surf there anyway and you deal with it.

It doesn't really answer my question, but the thought has already passed through me. And from previous experience, I don't think we're gonna reach a better understanding together. Steve and I are friends, but we don't always communicate very well. We surf together, occasionally play guitar together, and for the most part enjoy each other's company. But we don't really understand each other when it comes to talking. He's more toward a heavy metal edge and I'm more towards the bluesy side. We can usually find common ground around Hendrix or Page, but there's always that issue of how loud to turn up our amps. If I were describing it as a girlfriend relationship, it would be one of those three-month deals in my early twenties. Movies. Dinners. Holding hands. Sex. I forget about it. Bill changes the radio station and I don't think anymore about it. No more Weezer.

To this point, I had seen only one piece of Steve's artwork. He had made these three 1-foot-diameter ceramic balls and hung them from the ceiling on cables in the art office. It was a nice sculpture, and I had made a mental note to mention it to him when I got the chance. This is kind of a rule in the art world. If you like their work, you tell them you like it. And if you don't like their work, you either tell them you like it anyway or you just don't say anything. Honesty isn't a way of life in the arts. No Abe Lincolns here. We have our own codes and behaviors, and nobody walks ten miles to return a library book. It's pretty clear. When no one comes up to you after your show or screening, nobody liked your work. You get the message and it doesn't hurt as much. But it also doesn't help. Which is why things like honesty and negative feedback are so valuable in a world of hiding and cheek kisses. Like condoms or broccoli. They may be unpleasant, but they're good for you.

Steve and I jammed one afternoon until our ears rang, then decided to jump in the water.

I got blisters on my fingers . . .

An hour later we're surfing Hammond's, a reefbreak south of Santa Barbara in Montecito. The break is crowded and recent rains have polluted the water. The sets are infrequent and the vibe is mildly aggressive. Everyone is a little frustrated about a lot of different things. Steve and I are sitting in the water as the sun goes down, desperately trying to wait out the crowd and catch that one magic, last wave of the day. But it seems like everyone else has the same idea. There's still twenty guys around us with their arms on their knees, looking out at the horizon and subtly jockeying with one another for position. It's not surfing at its worst, but it's not far away. We just sit there. My mind is drifting from what I'm gonna make for dinner to switching my strings to the chord changes of "Communication Breakdown" when the wind glasses off. The surface texture stills and it slowly gets quiet. I think it's in E.

It's very special, because if you can see, the numbers all go to 11. Look, right across the board.

"Ahh . . . I see."

Eleven . . . 11 . . . 11 . . .

"And most amps go up to ten?"

Exactly.

"Does that mean it's louder? Is it any louder?"

Well, it's one louder. Isn't it?

I'm about ready to give up and paddle in when I remember I liked Steve's hanging ceramic ball piece in the art office. So I tell him so.

"Hey, Steve, I liked your hanging-ball thing."

"What?"

"I like your three-hanging-balls thing," I repeat a little louder.

"Sorry . . . I still didn't hear you. Three *what?*" he says.

"Balls. Your three hanging balls," I say, getting a bit perturbed. "I like them."

You're all the way up. You're on 10 on your guitar. Where can you go from there? Where?

"I don't know."

Nowhere. Exactly.

"I don't know what you're talking about . . . ," Steve says.

"I like the thing you've got with the hanging balls!" I enunciate. This is

218

starting to get me mad. Because it's hard enough to hear in the water to begin with. But since I had my ear operated on, I've had to wear these silicon plugs in my ears and a rubber hood on my head every time I go in. Which makes it even harder to hear. And like a teenage girl with a Walkman on, you tend to talk a little louder than normal when you can't hear very well. Which I guess must make me pretty damn loud since the other surfers are all turned around and looking at me crank the volume on complimenting Steve's hanging balls. I'm screaming this stupid weenie art-office compliment to Steve and he's just sitting there giving me these totally dumbfounded and confused looks, saying,

"You like my WHAT?"

Which is pissing me off because nothing pisses me off more than not being able

"YOUR BALLS! YOUR BIG HANGING BALLS IN THE OFFICE!"

to communicate. Especially when it's just some casual, simple thing you should be able to handle in a second. But no, we can't make it easy. We've got to make this difficult. We've got to make it a burden. We've got to make it really, really hard to give a guy a little compliment. And all this time Steve's just shaking his head, looking at me like I'm some totally incomprehensible idiot.

"WHAT THE HELL ARE YOU TALKING ABOUT?" he yells.

And how do you figure *I'm* the idiot? *You're* the one who made the stupid ceramic ball thing. I'm just trying to give you

"LISTEN—I JUST LIKE YOUR BIG HANGING BALLS, OK? NO. BIG. DEAL."

some positive feedback. *And what the hell are all of you looking at? Haven't you ever seen a*

"WHAT AM I SUPPOSED TO SAY TO THAT?"

hooded half-Chinese surfer complimenting a blond, confused Caucasian's hanging-ball artwork before?

"JUST SAY THANK YOU—I DON'T CARE!" I yell.

And Steve just looks at me. And after all this crap, he doesn't say anything at all. No thank you, no acknowledgment. Not a thing. Jesus.

What we do is, if we need that extra push over the cliff . . . you know what we do?

"Put it up to 11."

Eleven. Exactly. One louder.

So we just sit there in the twilight, silently waiting for the final set with the rest of the lineup. And the rest of the lineup eventually loses interest in us, turning back around and looking at the horizon again.

They slowly lose interest in communicating, meaning, and art. No one seems to care about Steve's hanging balls anymore. Steve and I each catch our last, magic wave and ride in to shore. We go back to our cars, change out of our wetsuits, and drive home in the dark without saying goodbye. And it isn't until the next day that Steve figures out what I'm talking about. He comes up to me and says, "Thanks." I guess some people just take compliments better than others.

E - DAD - E. That's it.

ャ

I ran into the same kind of embarrassing water conversation in Hawai'i. Except this time I was the victim. It was one of those seven-day packages they run after Labor Day. Airfare and accommodations in Waikiki for $499. A bunch of families off my former swim team in Covina had decided to go. I was still pretty close with a lot of them, and school didn't start for another month, so I decided to tag along. I was nineteen. I didn't know any better.

Waikiki is a human sewer. It's everything we've done wrong to the islands rolled into fifteen blocks of plastic leis, prostitutes, and ABC stores. You spend your days walking crowded sidewalks, scamming on other people from California, and dodging island-cruise-flyer handerouters. In the evening, you head back to your forty-story hotel, change clothes, and eat at all the restaurants you'd never think about eating at on the mainland. Denny's. McDonald's. Pizza Hut. Your room gets cable TV, and the hotel bars sponsor nightly bikini contests. A week later you fly home sunburned, wearing a Town & Country baseball cap and a Reyn Spooner aloha shirt. The whole idea makes me feel like a white guy with a mustache.

Our group varied in age—anywhere from eleven to sixteen, plus parents. Arriving at LAX for departure, I immediately see there's no one near my age. Which is fine. I brought a 6'10" pintail with me. I figure I can get there, grab a bus, get out of Waikiki, and explore the rest of the south shore by myself. I like traveling alone and I like not having a plan. Nothing's worse than trying to make group decisions on what to do, where to go, and how to get there. How many times have you stood around for half an hour while everyone talks about where we all should go eat? It's that *Lord of the Flies* thing again and we still haven't found the conch. I can do without it.

Everything is under control until we're about to board the plane, and this kid comes running up the jetway with his suitcase and duffel bag. Turns out he's the last of our group—a fifteen-year-old Jewish boy named Mark Housner. He cuts in line to catch up to us, bumping his bags into other people waiting along the way. There is no awareness. Not even an "excuse me" or "sorry." He finally gets up to us, out of breath and a bit uncertain. Dropping his bags at his feet, he sighs and pushes a nervous smile. He says hi to some of the kids he knows. Some of them nod back. Then he introduces himself by punching me in the shoulder and saying, "Hey! How's it going, big guy?"

Not a good way to start with me. But I figure why get into something when you don't need to? It's a five-hour plane ride and they haven't even opened the doors yet. Seven days to go. What's the hurry? Sometime in our life we all need to learn about male posturing. Mock callousness, indifference, silence. Half-court traps. Free safety blitzes. Imported beer. We've all been at that awkward stage where you don't quite know what to do with yourself. Maybe we didn't half-heartedly punch someone in the arm, but we can all claim our share of dorky maneuvers growing up. They're packed away in our attics next to half-empty Drakkar Noir bottles and black Reeboks. This kid's just gonna need a bigger attic. He's a bit over the top.

It's all so obvious. Before he could wear contact lenses, Mark Housner was the kid who always lost his glasses. He was the kid whose locker you broke into in middle school, tossing his underwear in the urinal for uniform day. By the time you reached high school, you and your friends just ditched him. *Yeah, we'll meet you there. You did? We must have missed each other.* He'll spend his college weeknights on an Internet browser and his college weekends playing "Magic: The Gathering" with a bunch of other guys who got their underwear flushed. If he ever marries, he and his wife will produce little fat kids who play indoors all summer long. They'll eat Twinkies, drink root beer, and watch too much TV. Maybe when they're fifteen, they'll go to Hawai'i. It's not like I'm happy or sad about it. It's just the way it is.

Now, I owe it to myself to tell you, Mr. Griswold, that if you are thinking of taking the tribe cross-country, this is the automobile you should be using. The Wagon Queen Family Truckster.

Inside the plane, the kid stuffs his suitcase (full of wool sweaters) into the overhead compartment. He puts his duffel bag between his ankles and starts looking through the safety pamphlets and complimentary copies of *Highways* magazine located in the seat pocket in front of him. He's completely wound up with all the excitement of leaving home for the first time. Even with the seatbelt fastened firmly around his waist, he's having trouble sitting still. I don't get it. Didn't they have

Cub Scouts where he grew up? How about the YMCA? How about the Weather Channel?

You think you hate it now, but wait till you drive it.

An hour into the flight, the flight attendants serve us our choice of chicken cacciatore or ravioli. Then they come down the aisles with the beverage cart, pouring our soft drinks and apple juices and letting us keep the can. Everyone starts to eat while I pick through the iceberg lettuce and poke at my lemon square. Looking about the plane, I assess the ages and personalities of our group. And it doesn't take me long to realize there's not going to be anyone for this Housner kid to hang out with once we get there. The fifteen-year-old girls are gonna be busy trying to meet seventeen-year-old California boys. The thirteen-year-old boys all think Mark's a fifteen-year-old geek. If they were bigger, they'd flush his underwear down the toilet. I guess that's a little sad.

We get to the hotel and the case gets finalized. The girls immediately take off to find boys. The boys immediately take off to look for girls, surf shops, and video games. The adults go downstairs to the bar to start their first of seven nights getting drunk, and Mark decides to tag along with them. I guess everyone's where they're supposed to be. I'm in the hotel lobby looking for a bus schedule and the number for a surf report, but all I can find are luau flyers and hula lesson brochures. No one seems to have any answers, but they all know when the dinner buffet opens. A minute later, I see Mark come shuffling out of the bar with his hands in the pockets of his Gotcha shorts. ID check. The adults probably requested it. I see him trying to display some confidence and swagger, but his gait gives him away. His shoulders slump. His eyes glance around at strangers with other places to go and better things to do. He's an out-of-shape, middle-aged single man walking into an aerobics class for the first time. Wrong shoes. Wrong shorts.

And looking over at this kid in the lobby, between all the palm fronds and anthuriums, I experience a momentary lapse of reason. I don't know how else to explain it, and I don't know why it happens. I just act without thinking. I sign on the dotted line without even reading the contract. With the scribble of a pen, I join the Marines, lease the car, and let the new roommate move in. And in this soft moment of decision, which I could attribute to my own compassion or my own stupidity or my own loneliness, I call Mark the sweater-packer over to me. And I ask him if he wants to come surfing.

This explodes him. I mean, the kid lights up. Immediately, he starts asking me about waves and spots and moves and equipment, bouncing around like an underfed puppy that's been in the pet store a couple of weeks too long. Which is actually kind of mildly amusing, until he starts striking these mock surfing poses in the hotel lobby and singing the first bars of *Hawaii Five-0*. We're talking in front of real people here. This is not part of my reality. All of a sudden I become even more aware of myself publicly. The spotlight is on. The cameras are rolling and the mics are live. Suddenly, I'm filled with the desire to broadcast the immense distance and hierarchy between the two of us. Nature takes over. Like any alpha male, my eyes look in front of me. My walking quickens without consideration and I move with independence. My emotions disappear. Beta males tag along, watching my eyes for clues like obedience school. I mean, you can tell we're not really friends, can't you? You can see this is just charity, right?

Human nature is always honest. I watch conventionally beautiful high school girls run in packs through indoor shopping malls. With big hair, excited looks, and loud voices. These big-hair packs turn into sororities later, and eventually metamorphose into loosely knit, nomadic cliques of singles-bar-hopping, tanning-boothed, divorced women in their late thirties. I don't know what they turn into after that. I don't want to. As human beings we flock around those who reflect and accentuate our own professed attributes. More insecurity, more flocking.

Walk into any random bookstore and pick up any random *Men Are from Mars, Women Are from Venus*–type book. For $19.95, the answers are plain and simple. We just don't know what to do with them. As men, we're aware of our actions and we're aware of our lies. We continually assert our independence and intimidation. We constantly seek to master our emotions and the world around us. And we always know how stupid we're being. It's just that no one ever taught us how to do anything else. It's like a never-ending Super Bowl Sunday, complete with halftime spectacles and Pepsi commercials. Someone needs to write a book that goes beyond identifying gendered behavior. Someone needs to come up with an answer besides therapy, men's groups, and lack of role models. I've been through enough therapy. I don't want to beat on animal-skin drums. I don't want to run around barefoot in the forest. And I don't want to spend my life standing in the rain, arguing with a priest and a woodcutter about women, men, and bandits. In the end we're all telling the same story.

Men are only men. That's why they lie.

Getting to the beach, Mark the geek is asking me about surfing etiquette. I figure I should clue him in, since this type of thing can really get you into trouble. Especially if you're some sweater-wearing haole kid in Hawai'i. And, unfortunately, him getting into trouble most likely means me getting into trouble. It's another part of that contract I didn't read.

We're standing together on Ala Moana beach and I'm wondering how I got myself into this. I look over at Mark the geek. He's holding his orange boogie board, wearing his Gotcha shorts, and smiling in his Carl's Jr. sunglasses.

"Where's your fins?" I ask.

"What?"

"Your fins."

"SHIT! *I forgot them in the hotel!*" he says. He starts to move, then slowly processes that I'm not going to wait for him if he goes back to the hotel. He turns back around.

"It's cool," he says a moment later. "I don't need 'em."

"What about your sunglasses?" I ask.

"What do you mean?"

"You gonna wear them in the water?"

"SHIT! I didn't even think about that!" he says to me. I can see his brain ticking again, trying to figure a way out of this one.

"Do you think I should leave 'em with the lifeguard?"

"No."

"If I hide them, you think someone's gonna rip 'em off?"

"Yes."

"Shit," he says with a nervous laugh, "I guess that wasn't too smart of me, huh?"

I don't say anything. I just start towards the water while Mark the geek runs into the bushes for something. I hope it's to hide his sunglasses, but I'm not sure and I'm not looking back. If it isn't, I don't want to know.

Catching up to me at the water's edge, he says to me, "Hey, I got a quick question."

"What?" (No sunglasses. Thank God.)

"When there's two guys on the same wave, how do you know who gets it?"

Okay. This is important. But it's also a little bit complicated. So I try and tell him as simply as possible that whoever is inside has the wave. Which is pretty much true most of the time, but not all of the time. It's not cut and dried. Because if someone stands up first, the wave is theirs. If someone's local, it's theirs. If someone's meaner, it's theirs. Sometimes it's just basic human territoriality. And how do you teach that?

It doesn't matter, though. Because Mark the geek cannot comprehend what I mean by the inside of a wave. It might as well be quantum mechanics. I try slower explanations. I try drawing pictures in the sand. I try everything but publicly acting it out back in the hotel lobby. Until finally I come up with an analogy I think he'll get. There's this old video game called Pole Position—a Sega race car game that essentially uses the same principle of inside position on a track to parallel inside position on a wave.

"It's like Pole Position," I tell him. "Have you played that?"

"Pole Position? Yeah, that's a great game!"

"You know how to tell who's got right of way on the track?"

"Yeah, yeah, yeah! I get it! The inside guy! Pole Position! We used to have it at our community center when I was . . ."

"It's the same thing out there," I interrupt. "Okay? Same thing. Just think Pole Position. And try to stay out of people's way, okay?"

"Got it, big guy!" he says.

I turn around for the water, then stop. I look back at Mark the geek. He's standing in the sand, putting on his leash, and sunburning before my eyes.

"And be mellow out there, okay?"

He's telling me yeah yeah sure sure Pole Position while I'm already on my way out. I paddle out fast. Much faster than he can go finless on his sponge. I figure the more distance, the better. The more likely I can blend in. Your first entry into any surfing lineup is critical. It's like walking into a bar in an old Sergio Leone spaghetti western. The saloon doors swing open and you're backlit in the dust. Everyone stops drinking and talking. All they see is the silhouette of your hat and gun. In the water, you get instantly sized up on your paddling, your look, your board, your position. And if it's crowded, this initial entrance can mean the difference between an unreal session and a kook nightmare.

People have this idea of surfing as friendly and amiable. Which I imagine it originally was. It just never will be again. There are just too many people now. Too much attitude. Too much male insecurity. Like driving the 405 at rush hour, everything becomes a competition, complete with cell phones, lane changes, and short tempers. Paddling out is like trying to run the 10 West–to–605 South interchange. You need to show your confidence and ability, and you need to do it fast. Which means I'm separating myself as much as possible from Mark the geek. I mean, I'd like to help him and all, and if this was my home break I might even be able to get away with it. But this is town, and it's crowded as usual. The vibe is hostile. And I've only got seven days here, stuck between Denny's and Pizza Hut for $499. It's not much, but I want to make the most of it. Like they say, I'm still looking out for *número uno.*

I'm out ten minutes before Mark the geek finally scratches up to me. He comes paddling up out of breath, sputtering, "Wow! Did you see those last waves? They were huge, man!"

I ignore him, staring straight ahead and putting on my best bad-ass Asian male face. After nineteen years of practicing, I've finally found a place to use it. Mark reads my face and he reads me ignoring him. And, amazingly, he seems to actually get the word. He clues in. He shuts up. Slowly, he calms down. I feel him gradually stop looking over and imitating me. My eyes stay looking ahead and the crowd ignores him. We're in between sets and things are going fine.

Things are going fine.
Things are going fine.
Things are going fine.

The pack is restless, but stable. Aggressive, but under control. No one is owning it. No noticeable pecking order. I'm scanning the horizon, looking for bumps. When out of nowhere, this pasty sweater-packing kid sits up, looks around at me and these twenty-five local guys, and screams out,

"HEY GUYS! HOW'S THE POLE POSITION OUT HERE?"

Every head instantly turns towards us. Oh God. You think I practiced *my* bad-ass Asian male face? What is this guy thinking? I'm wondering whether to tell him to paddle in or just pretend he's not with me, wait a minute, and beat him up with the rest of the gang. Pretending like I don't know him, I casually glance over at this Housner kid with a moderate look of disdain. And he's beaming back at me! He's actually *stoked.* Like he just lost his virginity or something. Like he just finished his first beer. He's smiling ear to ear and nodding his chin at me.

"WHAT'S UP, KIP! HOW'S *YOUR* POLE POSITION, HUH? YEAH! RIGHT ON!"

And the place this takes me to is more than fear, more than anger, more than embarrassment. I reach utter bewilderment. Straight and 100% pure. Unfiltered. No traffic lights and the roads are open and I have no idea what to do. I'm stuck. I can't comprehend this kid's complete and absolute unawareness. His unabashed pride in making idiotic comments. His total ignorance about his public persona. Any more than I can fathom putting nude-women mud flaps on my car or wearing a BAD BOY CLUB T-shirt, and actually believing that a desirable woman might not find this behavior repulsive, juvenile, or insecure. I am beyond understanding. The matador has gone to bed and the bull is goring him in his sleep. The killer bees are swarming. I'm standing in the middle of a golf course during a freak summer thunderstorm. We're all looking at a landscape where physics no longer makes sense. We want to trust our eyes, but how can we?

Everyone around me is running for shelter, leaving clubs and carts scattered across the green. But I stay where I am. How am I supposed to believe what I'm seeing? Lightning strikes the ground next to me, burning steam off the grass and causing the sheep to stand on their hind legs. I feel the electricity pulse through my body and I see a dozen golfers' eyes peeping out from behind the safety of a country club window. But the sheep don't come back down. They just start walking on two legs. First a bit shakily. Then with more confidence. Pretty soon you forget they ever crawled. You forget they ever grazed. Pretty soon the storm passes and everything is back to normal again. We walk together along precisely manicured Ikea traffic paths, viewing cheap, overpriced furniture without feeling manipulated. We vote for racist conservatives and beautiful women settle for mediocre men. I sit alone and write, and admit, that I admire a boy's ability to not comprehend.

ך

Six years later, I'm in some indistinguishable crisis-management therapy. I sit across from a bearded Freudian psychologist, looking past him and out the window at Moonlight Beach in Encinitas. The Freud guy asks about my relationship with my mother. He asks about my relationship to the public as a performer. He asks about all the parallels in my life of helping others—as leader, activist, teacher, lifeguard, role model. The bearded man means well. As well as he can, given healthcare plans that limit sessions to five meetings unless I'm willing to start SSRI treatment. Some of his directions make sense. Others go nowhere. One that leads somewhere is when he asks me if I can sit—just sit for a minute, without thinking about what others are thinking of me. It's like some Zen koan or nursery rhyme.

Can you exist without thinking of what others are thinking of you?

Moonlight is a special beach to me. In one day, I make eighteen rescues there. On another, I arrest a man for possession. The entire beach boos me as I walk him back, handcuffed, to the main tower. It's just a job. In one night, sheriffs stop Holly Sanders and me for parking and making out after hours on the cliff above. She kisses too hard, but I learn to like it. She's a beginning art student while I'm in graduate school. When we meet she wears Christian stigmata on her bare palms and feet. When we break up she becomes a lesbian. Analyze that one, Freud boy.

I tell him no. I can't just sit and not think about what others are thinking of me. And he enters this line of questioning that runs toward the performing persona taking over. Like that movie *Magic,* where the dummy starts taking over the ventriloquist. This is one of his directions that goes nowhere. I can see it coming and I can dodge it like slow-pitch softballs. I know the bearded man means well, but where are we really going to get with two sessions left? How much of you really wants to help me, and how much just wants to fill out your Pacificare question-naire and get your $75? Do you really listen to me or do you just go through the motions? Do you really want to know what goes on in my head when I'm not helping others? Wouldn't you rather hear about me and Holly Sanders? How we lay in bed together naked in Cardiff, kiss-ing hard and burning past recognition, when her virgin soul whispers,

"We can do it if you'd like to."

Like to? Like it's a question? My dick is gonna explode. Wouldn't you rather listen to why I balk at the idea of being her first, because for some reason, part of me thinks it's too important for her? And how she tells me with her eighteen-year-old freshman wisdom that every first time with someone should be equally special? What can I say to that? She's right and we both know it. Wouldn't you rather hear how I don't enter her, but instead move behind her, envelop her, and how we fall asleep for our one and only night together? How to this day I don't know if I did the right thing or not? Because why should I have to carry the trust and duty of the entire male gender? That maybe we aren't all assholes. That maybe we aren't all pigs. If I don't show her, who will? Is sweetness something to be remembered by? Is it something acted? Is it my respon-sibility to prove the existence of a passionate Asian man? To show the size of my cock? To show public aggression? If I don't show her, who will?

It's just a job.

It's just a job.

It's just a job.

I admire a kid who can be a geek and not know it. I admire a woman who holds every fuck to the same level. I hold her from behind and we fall asleep, unjoined, waking at dawn in the same position. To this day, I have never slept more peacefully than a single night with a virgin named Holly. What does that tell you?

Amid nineties pop punk and a lifetime of questioning, I read a newspaper one sunrise later. A *Los Angeles Times* front-page article about a shark-attack fatality in Santa Barbara. Looking down in the morning light, I read about the man. I read about the history, the odds, the situation. And I come to the time of the attack. And I realize, without surprise, that this is the exact time I felt a thought. This is the exact time I asked a seemingly random question about shark attacks off the Channel Islands. And I realize I understand more than I understand. It's not a scary realization because it's not a scary thing. It's natural.

I killed a dog in high school. Ran it over in my '82 Celica on Grand Avenue in Covina. The dog steps from behind a bush and is instantly illuminated in my headlights. I lock the brakes and scream. My tires screech at 45 mph and for half a second I see the big dog's pointed ears and glowing eyes, frozen and reflected in my headlights. A half-second later I feel the shudder of its impact. It rocks the car. For several seconds which feel like minutes, I feel the dog passing through me. Through my legs. Through my body. Rising as the dog dies and moves on. This was a scary thing at the time that left me unable to drive home. I sat on the curb shaking, and called my father to come pick me up. I had never felt life's essence before. And I had never seen my father ashamed of me. These are two powerful feelings to experience in a single night.

Four of us return from surfing to the camp store in Jalama. Steve and Bill order hamburgers. Cindy and I order breakfast burritos. Beans. Eggs. Salsa. Cheese. The store man tells us an urchin diver was attacked this morning. Got his leg bit right off.

"Happens sometimes," he mumbles to himself.

Steve and Bill's hamburgers come. They start eating. Bill ravages his, taking handfuls of fries between bites. Steve eats his hamburger slowly, and more distraught, because he thinks he might know the victim. He pauses between bites to wonder aloud what the man's name is. Cindy and I eat our breakfast burritos somewhere between Bill speed and Steve dismay, until our tongues taste the flesh. Hopelessly sickened, we instantly feel the meat settle into our stomachs. It breaks down into its various proteins, vitamins, trace minerals, fat, and cholesterol. We toss the remains in the trash. Going back into the camp store, we talk to the man who had told us no meat, until his wife emerges from the kitchen and argues that chili has meat.

"Do you understand?" she tells us. "Chili has meat."

"We understand," I tell her, "But your husband told us beans, egg, salsa, cheese. Not chili."

"You don't understand. *Chili means meat.*"

And I tell her, "I understand that. But we didn't know they had chili in them . . ."

"That's what chili means—meat! Chili means meat!"

"Okay. Fine. Chili means meat. But your husband didn't tell us the burritos had chili in them . . ."

"So if you order something with chili, it means you're ordering something *with meat!*"

We circle each other a while longer, like buzzards, until her husband walks out and says, "We'll make you some new ones without the chili. No charge. My fault." Which is all I wanted. All that's fair. But it sends his wife, who's gonna make our food, into this completely maniacal tirade. I mean, she's about to go Postal.

"YOU'D NEVER GET AWAY WITH THIS IN McDONALD'S!" she screams. "YOU HEAR ME? THEY WOULDN'T STAND FOR IT IN McDONALD'S!"

But Cindy and I don't say anything. About chili meat or McDonald's policy or the fact that she caused me to ingest a cow's body for the first time in seven years. I know it's never a good idea to argue with the person who's cooking your food.

Two chililess burritos come and we begin eating. Bill digs through the trash and finds Cindy's half-eaten burrito. He goes inside and pays the store man for the extra food and eats it. It is the right thing to do. Cindy and I are looking for meat in our beans while Steve still wonders aloud about the eaten man who could have been his friend. Somewhere a great white digests a man's leg and wetsuit and continues swimming. How does it feel to eat a man? How does it feel to eat a cow? How does it feel to eat a shark?

When you drive freeways and turn your head to look at someone, they turn to look at you. You wake when someone watches you sleep, and seals hurtle past the danger zone from thirty to eighty feet to reach the shelter of the rocks. Body surfing at Point Panic, I swim in through the channel towards the stairs. And after thousands of hours in the water, I get struck with pure fear. It walks through me like bare feet on snow, crunching icily through my neck and shoulders while I lie with my foot caught in a steel trap. I panic to the stairs, suddenly primitive, scampering out of the water on all fours. But even with my feet touching the safety of the wet stone, I still expect a monster behind me. I still expect a hunter. I turn around in slow motion, waiting for foam and the wet slap of a fin.

But everything moves normally. Above me, young boys pry shell-fish off the rocks for bait. Tourists snap pictures. Business types eat their lunches in the sun. Everything is where it's supposed to be. I take a deep breath, stand up, and slowly start to regain composure. I walk up the stairs and back to my car. Reaching it, I look down at my leg and find blood dripping in a constant flow. From knee to ankle to ground to water. A tiny, steady stream trailing behind me. Slow and paced at fifty beats a minute, it pours as long as it needs to. It pours as long as I let it. With my face bloodied from safety glass, I swim next to the shark and suckle my mother's nipple after my first car accident. I repack the torn muscles of my right leg, tie the wound with some loose bandan-nas, and I'm still here. I have always been here. I'm still standing by the car, watching the pigment flow down my leg, and waiting for the all-clear sign. By the time I leave, the entire parking lot will be rained red.

If you look, you know which car ride to take and which water is safe. If you listen, you know when a man is being eaten. If you pay attention, you can hear pigs crying. If you open yourself, you can feel your enemies cursing you and a former lover thinking of you and mak-ing a song request on the radio. You know your own life and your own death and your own blood type. O-negative, I am a universal donor. Giving blood to anyone, but only able to receive my own. There is a time when you realize the importance of your body's purpose and com-position. Its scent. Its touch. Its taste. Its vision. There is a time you relearn how to see and experience. To feel your blood. To smell your breath. To taste your spit. I taste my spit every day.

impatiens

Twenty-five

There are only so many things you can do something about. Everywhere you go, you see people you can help and dogs you can adopt from the pound. Row after row of brown eyes and cocked ears. You see people looking for guidance as much as you look for it yourself. You see people emulating others and emulating you, as if you have some further grasp of contentment or happiness or meaning. When you leave the shelter, do you sometimes wonder if it's better not to visit at all? Do you wonder who it is you're supposed to emulate? Do you wonder who picks your heroes?

I'm talking to one of my former junior lifeguards. He was my kid for a summer when he was ten. Now he's thirteen and has just gotten expelled for dealing herb at his junior high. His mother is an old friend of mine. She called me and told me about his trouble at school, asking if I could fly out to visit for a few days and talk with the boy. "Put some sense into him," as she put it. Apparently she remembers how straight he was when he was my junior guard and has some faint hope this magic time can return. But there are other elements operating now. Things like a second divorce, several moves, and flaming thirteen-year-old hormones to name a few. So I agreed to come. It's a different time now, and someone has to tell her. I'm just hoping that that someone doesn't have to be me.

Mason is too embarrassed to tell me about the pot episode himself, and he doesn't know I know. For all he knows, I'm just visiting his mom. He hangs around pretending he isn't paying attention as me and Mom catch up talking on the couch. We talk about our friends, who's gotten married and who's gotten divorced. Later she leaves for night school. I read the paper in the kitchen as Mason talks on the phone to one of his girlfriends. Deep inside he wants to talk to me about the various things a thirteen-year-old needs to talk about to an older man. But he can't let on he wants to ask. I let him stew with it while I sit around reading the paper and he talks to the girl on the phone. He raises his voice periodically, saying things like, "So you want me, baby?" while he glances over to see if I'm noticing. I just read the paper and wait for his questions. This one's a lock.

The boy's Japanese father left when he was six months old, so he grew up getting raised by his white mother and his aunt. He's small for

234

his age, probably six inches shorter than his average classmate, and he's moved from L.A. to an all-white area of Minnesota. Combine these factors and you get the selling pot and attempted womanizer conditions spelled out pretty clear. He gets off the phone and hangs around nonchalantly at the table where I'm reading, waiting for me to ask the so-who-was-that-on-the-phone–type questions, which never come. Sometimes the more silent you are, the more people listen to you.

The kid waits around like a seagull watching you eat a bagel. No crumbs here. No reward. No curiosity. It's killing him. Finally he can't take it anymore and strikes up a conversation, intending to steer it back so he can talk about his upcoming sexual conquest. I'm just reading the comics.

"So you a player?" he asks me.

To a kid lookin' up to me, life ain't nothin' but bitches and money.

I respond without putting the paper down or looking up.

"Player?"

"Yeah, you know . . . like with the bitches. *The ladies . . .*"

I mumble something about whatever and keep reading the paper. The kid's going completely up the wall.

"With the ladies, man," he says perturbed. "Y'know? *Scoring with the ladies?*"

"Mmm," I mutter. *Calvin and Hobbes* is pretty funny today. Calvin is pretending his parents are really secret heroes in the basement.

"C'mon! You a player with the ladies or not?"

In the last panel, Calvin's sighing over his parents and their otherwise uneventful lives. I think Watterson's a genius at capturing the random way six-year-old kids think. I'm thinking maybe part of Watterson

"Come on, Kip! I know you are!"

must have stayed behind here, stuck at six. It's the only way to explain it. You look at the way some people think, and you know part of them is left behind at some age. I figure I'm good at thinking and recognizing the way a thirteen-year-old young man worries about women and sex and what other men might be thinking about him,

"Did you hear that chick on the phone, man? I got game!"

so I'm thinking maybe part of me stayed behind here stuck at thirteen. It's the only way to explain it. Maybe I should be writing a comic strip about a thirteen-year-old superhero who fights off hordes of pubescent girls on the phone. We could call it "Teenage Phone Boy"— he's an operator.

"KIP, COME ON, MAN! I'M TALKING TO YOU!" Mason yells.

"What? What?" I'm saying, as I put the paper down and look him in the eyes. "What are you babbling about?"

He hesitates for a second. All this search for attention and he does-n't have a clue what to do with it now that he has it.

"The girl—the girl on the phone . . . ," he says. "Did you hear?"

"What, so you talked to a girl on the phone—that's big news?"

"No, man," he says, slowly gathering his confidence and arrogance. "She was saying she wants me, man. She wants to *do* me!"

He's got my attention for real now. I lost my virginity at fifteen and I thought I was young. I remember how scary it was with our pants pulled down around our knees and our socks and shoes on, downstairs on the carpet in the living room. I remember the girl was fourteen and had already been with two guys, one in a van. I lied and told her I had been with other girls, too. Mason just turned thirteen. I wonder how scary it is for him.

"I take it you've had sex?" I ask him.

The kid smiles the smile of finally getting on top of the conversation.

"That's for me to know and for you to find out," he says over his shoulder, walking away.

"All right," I mumble, and go back to the comics.

Mason stops at the door to the kitchen with his smile gone. What's up? Don't you wanna know? He hesitates for a while, looking at me reading the paper and ignoring him. Then he goes to the refrigerator casually, pours himself some Kool-Aid, and meanders back toward the table again. It's like watching him count to 100 really slow. I'm on to *Doonesbury*. Lately there's been too much to read and not enough reward, but this one's about J.J. the performance artist and those are usually pretty funny. Mason sits down with his Kool-Aid, quietly watch-ing me, and waits for me to ask him questions.

"How many partners?" I ask casually.

"What, like all the way, or . . ."

"Never mind," I interrupt, and open up the paper again.

"*Two*," he says hurriedly.

We sit for a while longer. *Doonesbury* isn't that funny today.

"How old were you?" I ask.

"Like the first time or . . ."

"Never mind," I interrupt.

"*Eleven.*"

This pattern of give and take goes on for a while until we settle into a groove. He wants me there for him and I want to be there for him. We both understand this. The atmosphere gradually becomes more casual and relaxed.

"You know how old I was before I had sex?" I say, sounding more and more like old men have sounded to me.

"C'mon, Kip . . ." Mason tells me, laughing. "These are the *nineties.*"

⸙

Mason and I are driving to a theater workshop I'm conducting for "At-Risk Teens." Which is a euphemism for we-don't-know-what-to-do-with-them-and-they-might-cause-trouble. Mason visited a few times and tried it on for size. The class is about twelve kids ages twelve to seventeen. Mostly colored, all confused. We stop at a traffic light and Mason comments about a graffiti tag on some wall alongside.

"TLC's the bomb, man. He's up everywhere."

I don't say anything. I'm thinking about what kind of exercises to do with the students today and what kind of crap radio they have here

"He's cool, huh?"

in Minnesota. I mean, every other station is classic rock. And I like Clapton as much as the next guy, but how much Yes and Pink Floyd and

"Kip, did you see it? Huh? Did you see it?"

Genesis can you take in an hour? Switch. Same thing. Switch.

"KIP, I'M TALKING TO YOU, MAN!"

"What? What?" I say, making a left turn into the community center.

"He's bad, huh?"

"Who?"

"TLC, man! He's up everywhere. That guy's king!"

I switch the radio a last time and click it off. I park Mason's mom's Honda in one of the unenforced twenty-minute zones and shut it off. Class starts at 3:00 and it's 2:58. I usually like to be there about ten minutes early to get things set up, but there was some nasty traffic today. I'm getting my bag out of the back seat and looking for a cassette that isn't there. Maybe it fell under the seat.

"KIIIIP!" Mason whines.

"What?" It's not under the seat either. Did I leave it back at the house?

"He's cool, huh?"

"Who?"

"TLC!—COME ON, MAN! THE TAGGER! YOU KNOW YOU THINK SO!"

I look at this boy for a while. Just turned thirteen. Multiple partners and every bit of gangbanger attire you can imagine except for the beeper, and that's only because Mom won't let him. I mean, this kid's boxers come up to his nipples. His pants are so baggy he's gotta take two steps in them before they move. And he's totally fried and frazzled trying to find out if his senses match with any of mine. I love it.

"I guess he's all right," I say, walking ahead of Mason towards the main door of the community center, ". . . for a coward."

"What?" the kid says defiantly, as I open the door and say hi to Joanne at the front desk. She tells me the kids are all waiting in the multipurpose room. Good group. Here on time. I stop to get a Gatorade out of the machine. $1. Insert quarters, nickels, or dimes. I've got seventy . . . no, eighty cents. Mason catches up.

"What you talkin' about coward?" he says.

"You got twenty cents?" I ask him.

"What?"

"Twenty cents," I repeat. *"Do you have twenty cents?"*

Mason fishes in his pockets and pulls out a handful of change. He hands me a quarter. I plug it in and start to decide between original lemon-lime, mandarin orange, tropical punch, lemonade, and cool blue ice. The red stuff is out because it looks like red dye #4. The blue stuff looks like Drano.

"What do you mean he's a coward?" Mason rephrases.

"Who?" I say, picking original lemon-lime. When all else fails go with what you know. The machine's out. Now it's either orange or lemonade.

"TLC, man! What you gotta say shit on him for?"

I stop for a second and select mandarin orange. Somehow lemonade Gatorade just doesn't sound right.

"Who's TLC?"

The machine spits it out with a **kerclunk** and I head down the hall to the multipurpose room.

"C'mon, Kip—the tagger!" he says, running alongside me to catch up. "Come on, man. He's bad! What you saying shit on him for, huh?" he says, grabbing hold of my arm agitatedly.

"Why you always gotta say shit on him?"

I stop outside the door. Through the window I see my At-Risk class playing around with the various air hockey and pool table distractions that bureaucrats think will keep kids away from drugs, sex, and crime. Mason's hand is locked around my upper arm, shaking it hurriedly like there's a fire or something. Not a good move, kid. I'm looking in the window at my students.

"Let go of my arm, Mason."

"C'mon, Kip. I'm talking to you, man!" he says. He's got both hands shaking and tugging on me now. My bag is starting to slip off my shoulder. I can feel the strap inching down with each jerk on my arm. It's gonna fall any second.

"I said let go of my arm."

"You tell me why you gotta . . ."

That's it. I snap around and look him straight in the eyes.

"WHAT IS YOUR PROBLEM?"

Mason's startled. He flinches for a second and lets go of my arm. I'm right in his face. Eye to eye. You got something to say, Mason? Say it. He stares back at me for a second without saying anything. His hands disappear into his enormous front pockets. His gaze shifts and he shuffles his shoes. They're old-school Air Jordans. The ones with all the accomplishments embossed on the soles.

'83 SLAM DUNK CHAMPION

'87 SCORING TITLE

'91 MVP CHAMPIONSHIP

"You got something to say or not?"

"I just wanna know why you always gotta talk shit on him," he mumbles, looking away.

An adult decides what to do. A child reacts. I'm somewhere in between, as I've always been. I'm angry with Mason, no doubt. Part of me wants to shake him silly. Part of me wants to see him get his ass kicked the next time he tags. I know that won't do anything but make him want to tag back, hit back, or shoot back—depends on where he is in life and what he has access to. Part of me wants to figure out where I am with this whole thing. I mean, how can this kid have been around me so long and still think like this? Do you listen to anything I say or see anything I do? Or have I just been wasting my breath and wasting my time? Maybe you need to have your ass kicked. Maybe you need to get pushed. Maybe you're a lost cause. I don't even know anymore.

"What?" I ask him. "Speak up."

"I said," Mason replies, looking back at me and enunciating each individual word sarcastically, like I'm geriatric, *"why you always gotta talk shit on him?"*

"You want to know why?" I say. I lean in over him and stare him down. Mason rolls his eyes with a gimme-a-break look and stares past me in complete thirteen-year-old defiance. Don't even try it, boy. I'm not your parent, I'm not your schoolteacher, and I'm not some rent-a-cop shopping mall security guard. I *invented* this shit. You want to push *me*? I move right in his punk-ass face. We're nose to nose. We're breath to breath. *Oh, do I have your attention now?* Mason looks back at me and I'm not blinking. He's uncomfortable, but he can't back off now.

"I'll tell you why. Your boy's gotta run from everybody. He's got to hide from the cops. He's got to hide from the building owners . . ." I step back and continue, breaking into a whiny baby voice *"and then when it's dark, and no one's around, you run up to the little wall and spray your initials on it . . ."*

"It's not his initials!" Mason snaps back. "It's . . ."

". . . and then you run away and spray some more initials . . ."

"I said it's his tag!"

"I DON'T CARE WHATEVER PUSSY-ASS NAME YOU CALL IT!" I say loud enough for some of the other kids to turn around through the window. They can see both of us and Mason knows it. He's embarrassed. I don't care. You want to kick my ass, boy? Come here and try it. Come on.

"Look at me! I sprayed my name on the wall!" I say in the baby voice again.

"Shut up," he mumbles.

"Oooh look, I can do it in different colors . . ."

"Shut up!"

"I can do it in blaaaaack . . . I can do it in greeeen . . . I can . . ."

"SHUT UP!"

The kids on the other side of the door have stopped playing air hockey and stopped talking. Mason is looking down at his shoes again, furious. He knows everyone is watching and waiting to see what he's gonna do. He may be close to crying. He may be close to hitting me. I don't know and I can't tell. I'm just waiting. What you got, Mason? You want to spend time with me? You want me to care about you? You want me to kick your ass? You want me to leave you alone? This is what it's about. Make a decision.

Mason is looking at his shoes with his hands in his pockets. He's not saying anything. I lean in closer to him.

(Oh, you don't like that, do you?)

I feel him tense up. I move even closer, cheek to cheek. I put my mouth to his ear, and whisper

"TLC's a pussy."

I go in the door leaving the thirteen-year-old Hapa kid outside. He doesn't strike out, he doesn't say anything, and he doesn't follow me in. I know Mason tags. I know he smokes. I know he carries a knife at least. I know he treats girls like shit, and these girls keep coming back for more. I know he does a lot of things that remind me of a lot of things I've done, and he's gone through a lot of things I've gone through. He's going through more now, and I don't have the heart to tell him how much more I see waiting for him down the line. Maybe it's a different time now and things are better. Maybe things will just work out. Maybe Mason will remember the things I tell him, or the things I do after I fly back to L.A. and his life goes back to girls and phone calls and talking large. When I was him, I didn't remember any of these things. Look what happened.

✂

"Take out a piece of paper," I tell the class. They're sprawled out all over the room on couches, chairs, or the floor. Twelve kids today—six Asians, four Chicanos, one black, two whites. All various forms of teenagers, and all of us with something in common.

"I want you to write down the worst thing anyone could ever say to you," I tell them. They look up, confused. "You got it?" I say, still perturbed about Mason. "Just write down the absolute worst thing you could ever imagine hearing from someone."

"You mean like real stuff or . . . ?"

"Just start writing," I interrupt. They start writing.

Mason walks in the door, composed and badass again. He high-fives a couple other boys wearing Raiders paraphernalia and kicks it on one of the couches next to a beautiful Hmong girl already doing her exercise.

"Join up with the group," I tell him and toss him a pen.

"Whatever," he mumbles, and starts whispering what-are-we-doing kind of things to the Hmong girl with the biggest breasts. I'd do the same thing. A few seconds later he starts to write.

Something changes between where these kids are at now and where they are in college. Because when I give out this assignment in college, I get uncommitted, hollow responses like "You were never there for me" or "I don't love you" or "You're a bad person." As if these are anywhere close to the worst things you could ever hear. I can blast you worse than that and I don't even know you. There's no commitment whatsoever, and without commitment there's no point in doing the assignment. I mean, how hard can it be? These teenagers do it in a minute. I look around the room. Most of them are finished writing and are waiting to see what I'm going to do next.

"Now, turn the page over and write the best thing anyone could ever tell you."

ત્ર

A friend of mine named Eric went through vet school at U.C. Davis. Afterwards he moves back down to San Diego and tries to set up a practice. He rents a space, hires a lab assistant and secretary, advertises locally for new clientele, and tries to get up and running as a business. At $60k in debt over student loans, he figures he's got about three months to put it in the black, or fail. Slowly, he develops a small base of clients. During his second month in practice, a man brings his prize rottweiler to the office. The dog has some kind of tumor on its right rear leg. The assistant is out, so Eric takes the dog in the back and gives it an injection to knock it out, like he's done hundreds of times in training and dozens of times in practice. As he pushes the plunger of the hypodermic needle he suddenly sucks in his breath, realizing he's pulled the wrong drug. Mistakes happen. The dog dies instantly. This is where I stop telling the story and ask, "So what do you do?"

My old man's a TV repairman. He has an ultimate set of tools.

. . .

I can fix it.

Basically it comes down to two main choices, each with its own set of variations. You can tell the truth or you can lie. Everything else is just an offshoot. If you tell the truth, you're out of work in California at a minimum. Your schooling is shot. Your practice is shot. Your reputation is shot. If you lie, there are more variations, but the end result is you have to live with it. All the stories my junior lifeguards come up with, like getting another look-alike dog and switching them, or pretending to pass out, still amount to lying and living with it. And what's curious about what happens when I ask the "So what do you do?" question is that the basic difference between where we are as kids and where we are as adults shows itself straight up. When I ask my ten-year-old junior guards, 90 percent say they'd tell the truth. When I ask my twenty-year-old college students, 90 percent say they'd lie. Go figure.

ત્ર

The At-Risk kids fall somewhere in between. They finish their assignment and are waiting to read it. No fear and no hesitation. Sixteen-year-old Nicole wants to go first. She's a shy and quiet girl with braces and acne who's going to blossom into a real heartbreaker as she matures and gains confidence. She holds her ripped-out spiral notebook paper and starts reading.

"You can't play the drums worth shit. You probably slept with the band teacher to get first chair. Ha! You like it when I unsnap your bra in the middle of band class, don't you? Ha! You like it when I back you up into the corner. Aren't you scared? Aren't you terrified? Let's see you play the drums now, you weak, silly, flaky blonde girl. Girls play the bells and boys play the drums. Girls should stay in the house barefoot and pregnant, you little feminazi. It's a male-dominated instrument so just get used to it."

Nicole puts her spiral notebook page down and hides under her bangs. I ask the class what they think. Everyone is a bit blown away. There's uncomfortable silence until one of the boys bursts out, "You're a *stud,* Nicole!" Everyone laughs a bit and it lightens the mood. Nicole laughs a little herself and the class starts to talk more. It turns out she actually filed a sexual harassment complaint to her high-school counselor about the boy drummers in her band class. When she did, the counselor told her, "Well you know, Nicole . . . it *is* a male-dominated instrument." That was a year ago. Maybe it's a different time now and things are better.

I ask Nicole to turn her page over and read the other side—read the best thing anyone could ever say to you. She says it plain out.

"Nicole, you play the drums better than anyone I know."

ϒ

"When you can acknowledge something," I tell them, "when you're able to say it out loud, you start to take away some of its power." If this is the worst thing you can ever hear, how bad can it really be? They're just words, right?

"Who wants to go next?" I ask.

Mason stands up.

"I do."

He's got his Raiders cap on backwards and jeans three sizes too big. I mean you can swim in them. He strikes a pose and starts to read.

"YOU BANANA. FORTUNE COOKIE. HONG KONG CHING

CHONG DONKEY KONG JAP. YOU YELLOW ZEBRA PARTY-MIX KUNG FU TOYOTA-SELLING LITTLE MONKEY. THAT'S NOT YOUR DAD, RIGHT? YOUR MOM HAD SOMEONE ELSE'S KID, YOU FREAK. HOW COME DAVID DUKE ISN'T HELPING THE KKK LYNCH YOUR DAD? YOUR MOM COULDN'T GET A WHITE MAN SO SHE HAD TO GO TO CHINATOWN. I THINK WE BET-TER TEACH YOUR PARENTS A LESSON, BOY. YOU HEAR ME? I THINK WE BETTER TEACH YOUR PARENTS A LESSON."

Mason flashes some wannabe gangbanger sign and sits down, reborn badass. He's tapped in. The class is stark quiet again.

"Why don't you read the other side of your page?" I ask.

"It's not that long," he says quietly.

"Read it anyway."

"I totally respect you and your parents' cultures."

I can talk about other things here. I can talk about how I tried to bring the assignment together, or how we created a group performance out of it for their At-Risk parents to watch. But what I want to talk about is how we ended our two-week workshop. Some fellow performance friends of mine came up with an idea for closure on the last summer day of our workshop. We stand together in a circle in the multi-purpose room and toss some stuffed panda bear to each other randomly. The rules are simple. When you toss it to another person in the circle, you tell them something you see in them. It starts out predictably simple and innocuous,

"I see you as happy."

"I see you as a dancer."

"I see you being successful."

and slowly progresses further and more honestly as we go. People start actually sharing what they feel and what they see, because there's an element of trust in the room. Every one of us knows the other would tell the rottweiler owner we killed his dog and we're very, very sorry. It's my fault. I take full responsibility. What would you like me to do?

This continues for five or ten minutes until the ritual naturally diminishes and the panda bear gets put down. Everyone has said what they see to at least ten other people and has heard as much about them-selves. The space is relaxed and people are comfortable. It is the kind of situation where we've all put ourselves in the same boat together, like *Gilligan's Island* or a hunger strike. The game closes with us going around the circle and each of us saying the one thing we remember most out of everything we've just heard. This is telling, not so much in what's been said, but more for what's stayed inside. It is about recognizing power and about stepping into it. Standing next to mountains. Chopping them down (with the edge of our hands). Nicole remembers me telling her "I see you becoming a heartbreaker." Mason remembers me telling him "I see you becoming a man."

Pick up all the pieces, make an island,
Might even raise a little sand.

When we depart, Nicole and Mason and I hug each other for the last time and the three of us cry a little, but not much. Mason doesn't cry much because crying doesn't go well with the gangbanger attire. Nicole doesn't cry much because for the first time in her life she knows no man is ever going to unsnap her bra again without answering for it. Knowing this feels good. I don't cry much because I'm the adult and the professor and the teacher, and we're not really allowed to.

I don't know what either of these kids does these days. I'm sure Nicole still plays the drums and wears makeup. I'm sure Mason still smokes and tags and probably more. I'm also sure that, somewhere inside, he at least knows it's possible to be a man without doing these things. That's something I'm not sure he knew before. I don't know if his mom thinks I helped him or not.

ٮ

Mason and I are still sitting at the kitchen table with Kool-Aid and Calvin.

I start to say "So, your phone girl . . ."

"I got *game!*" he interrupts. "I'm tellin' you she wants me!"

"Oh, she does?"

"Straight up," he says smiling. "Says she wants to fuck me."

I let him sit a second. He's waiting for me to high-five him or ask what her body's like or maybe what he's going to do about it.

"So that's a good thing?" I ask.

"Hell *yeah!*" he snickers. "What are you thinkin'?"

"You going over there?"

"Yeah, you wanna give me a ride?"

I let him sit again. Now that he's opened up and asked a favor, he's

put me in as an accomplice. He's hanging around the table, nonchalantly tapping his knees frantically under the table at Mach 2. I can feel
the linoleum shaking.

"Who's the girl?" I ask, ignoring his question.

"I dunno . . . Susie somebody. I never met her."

"How old?"

"She's like my age."

"Mmm," I say, and get quiet again. Mason watches me and I watch
him wondering what I'm wondering. Come on, Mason, if you were me
what would you say to you right now? If you need someone to kick
your ass, I'll kick your ass. If you need someone to tell you right from
wrong, I'll tell you right from wrong. But you've got to ask for it. I'm
waiting.

"So . . . what?" he says softly. "You gonna give me a ride or not?"

(There it is.)

I go off on Mason the way you'd expect me to go off on a younger
image of me. I ask him what the girl's really saying to him, what she's
really saying about herself. I ask him how he'd feel if he heard his sister
talking like that on the phone. I ask him all the questions no one asks
me but therapists I pay and angry women I offend. But Mason is too
caught up in his own boner to listen to what I'm saying. To him, the
whole world right now revolves around whether or not I'm going to
give him a ride in his mom's Honda. To him, there's a bigger picture
here and no one is telling him I'm on his side. To him, no one is telling
him they love him but confused thirteen-year-old girls with absent
fathers. And you can't react if you can't hear someone. You can't react
if you don't read their letters. Maybe part of it will stay inside and burn
after I go back to L.A. Probably not, but maybe.

To some people, the whole world revolves around whether or not
my work offends them, whether or not I use the words "Oriental" or
"bitch" or "pussy" or "white trash." As if it doesn't exist if it's not in here.
To some people, any man talking straight about sex or race or women
is part of the problem. Maybe we're all a little too caught up in our own
boners for our own good. Maybe we're all a little too caught up in our
own boners to notice anything else around us. Maybe all we see outside
of ourselves and our own private circles are approaching opponents and
future attackers. I'm not here to hurt you. Think about it. If you want
to change things in this world, you don't start by ignoring them. None
of us is thirteen anymore.

Twenty-six

Occasionally people listen. Our lives overlap and we tune to each other like schooling fish. For a moment, we sense some kind of meaning in our existence besides work, money, or sex. For a moment, we sense a purpose bigger than avoiding embarrassment or affording titanium sunglasses. This can occur as easily in a church service as by playing poker with your friends on a hot summer evening. You never know. Maybe it happens lying in bed on the phone, falling in and out of conversation and sleep together with the line still connected. There are long periods of silence, slow breathing, and comfort over the next eight hours. In the morning, you wake to the sound of a busy tone and the feeling of your lover across town. You turn your call-waiting back on and hang up.

I've listened to a monk chant over me, watched a *santero* bless my beads, and gone to Catholic confession. But I still feel the right ritual eluding me. I still feel like I teach better sitting in my office with a student than I do in some classroom or lecture hall. I still feel my art lives and works better as an extension of my being, that without my voice the words only hint and imply. And I'd still rather watch a sumo tournament on TV than go to a faculty meeting. Actually, I'd rather do almost anything than go to a faculty meeting. I think most people would.

Much of my work over the past few years has taken me around the country and abroad as a visiting artist. I've been fortunate in that regard. Even if it means getting trapped in a London subway, or bombing onstage as a stand-up comedian in Kuala Lumpur, it's all experience that informs my future work. And I've used each of these times to try to figure out the things I'm always trying to figure out—where it is I am and what it is I'm doing. I know my life walks a daily path between euphoria and suicide, and I know why it does. Past the comforts of Pledges of Allegiance and daily breads. Past the conveniences of written speeches and generic interviews. It's all an integral part of how I work and how I relate to others. I need that challenge of not being completely prepared and not knowing the answers. I need that uncertainty to push me, to scare me, and to surprise me. I need situations where I have to come through. Sounds like I'm ready for the Marines.

I did a talk recently at RISD—the Rhode Island School of Design—where everything seemed to come together. RISD is your basic art school, which means half the students don't want to be there and the other half pretend they don't want to. Nothing's changed from when I went to art school, really. You come in with fresh ideas, fresh attitude, and fresh presence. But as soon as you realize making art is full of the same tragedies of human interaction as any other field, it becomes something new altogether. The same jealousies, the same insecurities, the same pretensions, gossip, and occasional backstabs are as much a part of the art world as of any other working environment or social club. Most people just accept the conditions and join in, hunting the same game as everybody else. The art they study, emulate, and eventually value recycles back into the same perpetuating system. Most of it never comes close to transcending the pettiness. Most of it doesn't touch the world we live in. Most of it doesn't even try.

I admit it. I hate most art. Most every museum and gallery I've been into has sucked away any semblance of life, passion, or adventure from the work they've got on display. All that's left are sterile receptacles. There's no experience. It all tastes the same, like dorm food. It's all lasagna and shepherd's pie and chili mac. It's just got fancier title cards and stuffier critics. My real world is a long, long way from here. I don't want to go to the Guggenheim and see Rauschenberg's *Bed* sitting on a wall ten feet away from me, mounted in some wood-and-Plexiglas box. I don't want to stay outside velvet ropes delineating proper viewing space, and I don't want security guards in blue blazers and walkie-talkies telling me "no flash photography." I don't trust any curator who can't play with kids, and I don't trust any curator who doesn't stop to pet a dog. Nothing here makes me believe anymore, and believing is what I look to art for. That's what I want it to do. I want art to make me believe.

When I get scheduled to do these visiting-artist talks, I'm never quite sure what they're expecting of me. I never know if they're looking for me to really push the students or if they just want me to entertain them. So I usually try to do a bit of both. It's taken me a long time to develop the confidence to talk about what matters to me without feeling stupid. And it's taken me a long time to realize the things I find interesting are justifiably relevant, and justifiably important. I mean, I'm glad the term "pop culture" has finally achieved some kind of academic legitimacy. But it's also nice to be able to tap into all the comic books I've read, all the movies I've watched, and all the music I've listened to—and to actually use this knowledge without some underlying sense of embarrassment. I don't bluff anymore. Like growing up in Covina, it's a badge of honor now. Yeah, I grew up in the seventies. I actually sat down and watched *The Love Boat* and *Three's Company*. I know David Banner, Steve Austin, *Electro Woman & Dyna Girl,* and every sequel to *Planet of the Apes.* Which one you want to talk about?

The RISD gig is set up nicely—200 students required to be there for a three-hour class. No parameters of what I have to cover or what I have to show. They just bring me in, turn me on, and let me go. I'm introduced to the A/V tech, who tells me his fellow students are excited. They know what I'm about, he says. They know my work and they're interested in what I have to say.

"That's good," I tell him. "'Cause I don't know what I'm gonna talk about yet."

The A/V guy likes that. Or he's laughing anyway.

"Cool," he smiles.

Together we walk into a lecture hall filled with college art students. Two hundred chairs, 200 sketchbooks, and 400 black socks. He hands me a laser pointer, a wireless microphone, and says "Good luck." I look in front of me and all that's there is a captive audience and a stage. Beautiful. Give me three hours and I'll change the world, or at least give it a shot. At least for the moment, this is where I am supposed to be.

I turn on my mic and say hi to my audience. They don't say anything back. Just open their pens and get ready to take notes. So I lean into the mic and try it again, a little slower.

"*Hi . . .*"

"Hi," they finally respond. Some of them even laugh a little. For art students, a surprising number of them seem pretty human. Must be a new moon. So now what? They've all written the date and "Kip Fulbeck" at the top of a blank notebook page. Their pens are hovering like news copters.

"You're not gonna need to take notes. Relax."

It takes a second to register. Maybe I should have checked with their professor about that. Too late now anyway. Their pens go down, and for a moment they wonder what to do with their hands. A few bags rustle. A few backpacks zip. Their hands find a comfortable spot and their attitude gingerly steps down a notch, still wary. Toes first, then heel. Then the other foot. I figure it's a good enough place to start and we begin our conversation.

I talk to my audience the same way I'd talk to anyone I care about, or to anyone whose opinion I value. Students usually get a little surprised by this at first, but I've found in the end it works out pretty well. I guess like most of us, they aren't used to someone talking to them as if they mattered. Which is a little bit sad when you think about it. But like picking up trash at the beach or buying 25¢ lemonade from a neighborhood kid's cardboard stand—when no one else is doing it, all the more reason to.

Since I'm at an art school, I start by talking about how scary the whole art school experience was for me. How I never thought I actually belonged there. I'm glad to see some of them nodding their heads in unison. Because, in reality, nobody really belongs in art school. We don't need any more artists. We've got enough artists in the world. We need more teachers, more guardian angels, more eco-terrorists. We need more people with bigger vision and a better perspective on the world. And, unfortunately, an artist's vision is usually very narrow. You find this out your first day when you arrive out of uniform. Everyone looks like an artist but you. And you figure it's just a matter of time until everyone finds out you're an impostor and calls you on it. You think maybe you should paint your shoes or dye your hair. Maybe you should start smoking and wearing black clothes and hanging out at gourmet coffee houses, snapping your fingers for exclamation. Maybe you should start making snide leftist comments and esoteric references to Foucault and Baudrillard during movie trailers. Maybe you should join in and hunt the same game as everyone else.

Oh yeah, you're on the swim team or something. So are you on some kind of scholarship or what? What do you mean my smoke bothers you? Nobody tells me not to smoke in my studio. You got that? Nobody. If you don't like it, go outside. Don't you have a swim meet or something to go to? You have to miss class for what? What's an NCAA? What time do you get up, anyway? When? And you don't drink coffee? You've got to be kidding me. So is all your work about sports or what? Are you good enough for the Olympics? Why not? What's half a second? That's doesn't sound like very much. There—see? Half a second. Boom. Gone.

And somewhere in this sharing of experience, somewhere in the acknowledgment of the horrors of art school and fitting in, this RISD audience and I get introduced to each other. Somewhere in this three-hour evening of show and tell, we start to trust each other a little. It's like a long distance spin-the-bottle game, and we've already been playing an hour. Almost everyone has kissed almost everyone else. If you came walking in right now, it would look like a real bad impersonation of *My So-Called Life*. Except it's real, we're pretty far out to sea, and there's 200 of us playing Angela or Brian.

"Uh, Brian? Brian, look at me. Um, that letter I told you about. Um, Rickie said you wrote it. And I have to know because . . ."

Know what? There's nothing to know. Okay, what—what Rickie probably meant is that, see . . . Jordan Catalano asked me to, like, proofread it for grammatical errors.

"You proofread a love letter? Is this like a game to you?"

Um, hardly . . .

"But you admit that you were involved."

I'm not admitting anything.

"This is a joke, right? That the, the two of . . . Oh God. I can't believe I fell for it. It's obviously a total lie."

No, I meant every word.

"Brian?"

I didn't write it.

"But Brian, you said . . ."

Forget what I said. Forget this whole conversation.

"How?"

You liked it though, right? It made you, like, happy?

"Yeah."

Because that's probably all that, y'know, matters.

"To who?"

To, y'know, the person . . . who wrote it.

We're reading our lines well, but the script's too tight. We all got too much sleep last night. The plane ride's too long. The water's too shallow. The students start stretching their legs, involving themselves more. They begin asking me some basic, fundamental questions. The kind you might expect, but never seem to get. And what do you know? After all the hundreds of questions about editing strategies and visual representations and multi-layering, an audience and I are actually swimming in the same direction. If I knew how it was we got to this point, I'd tell you. If I knew how to replicate it, I'd do it every time. But I can't really say how it happened. I was only driving half the time.

A student raises his hand and asks what inspires me, and I answer by talking about my first KISS concert at twelve. No more bluffs. No more evasive maneuvers. And no more black outfits. I talk about screaming my head off when Gene Simmons blew fire and I talk about wearing my black-and-white LOVE GUN WORLD TOUR baseball jersey to Mesa School the next day. I talk about discovering Coltrane's live version of "Spiritual" playing over the speakers in some cockroach-infested sushi bar, and finally realizing that Clapton's "Layla & Other Assorted Love Songs" was all recorded for the same woman. I talk about seeing Spalding Gray for the first time, watching *Rashomon* for the twentieth time, and reading *Calvin and Hobbes* to my lover in bed.

The students listen to my answer, thinking of their own inspirations in what they do. They engage deeper and relax a bit at the same time. They start asking questions without worrying about them being stupid or embarrassing. It's like we got a full scholarship to boot camp and the drill sergeant didn't show up. It's kindergarten minus the poop and nap time. School starts to work.

"Did you always know you'd become an artist?" one of them asks.

"No. Actually, when I enrolled at UCLA I thought I was gonna be a brain surgeon."

They start laughing.

"I'm serious," I say. "That's really what I thought I was gonna do—neurosurgery."

This makes them laugh even more. This one I'm not gonna win. Next question.

"Where do you get your ideas?"

"That's like saying 'How do you pick your mate?' or 'Why do you like that kinda dog?' You just move towards the things that call to you. I mean, I like blue . . . I like pugs . . . I like the pedal placement on German cars . . .

"Everywhere you go, you should be able to look at what's around you and think about making art. Everything around you should be able to affect you, okay? Art isn't about affecting others. It's about letting yourself feel. This thing about 'Well, I have to get out of my environment for inspiration' and so forth? Bunch of crap. If the environment you spend your time in isn't stimulating or pleasing, change your environment.

"I mean, I can't believe how some of you guys live. I've been in your dorm rooms, okay?"

Laughter again.

"You know what I'm talking about. I mean, you spend, what—*at least* eight hours there a day, right? I'm not saying you got to be some kind of neat freak or something, but you got to get past the idea that you go to school to make art. Get it? *You got to get past the idea that you have to go to school to make art.* That's why kids draw so great until they're like nine or ten or something. It's before they learn about good art and bad art—they're just doing what comes natural. It's like we go to school to learn how not to do it a certain way, then you guys come back to school and try to learn how to do it all over again. I don't know, man . . . How much you guys pay to go here?"

I'm shaking my head, keeping a straight face. This place feels all right.

"I don't know . . . I forgot the question, anyway. Simple stuff. Bring flowers into your room, eat vegetables. That sort of thing."

"What's the best advice you can give us?"

"Better than the vegetables?"

252

"About making it as an artist."

"I don't know about making it as an artist, but I'll tell you the best advice I can give you, period. You gotta learn how to figure out systems."

I watch 200 brows crinkle. Let's go out further.

"It's not about making art, okay? It should be. But it's not. There's a lot of great artists flipping hamburgers and working shopping malls.

"Look, no matter where you go—school, job interview, social gig, department store, whatever. When you walk in a room, there's a system going on. It's already in operation and you gotta figure it out. You got power dynamics, sexual dynamics.

"Let me put it this way. You walk into some company and there's a beautiful receptionist, okay? She's got the whole thing going—you know what I'm saying? You want to know the absolute worst thing you can do? Pick up on her. Get it? 'Cause every straight guy in that corporation *has already tried*. You're not walking into some blank situation. You just been watching too many movies. Either this girl's got a boyfriend, she's dating someone in the company, or she's dated a whole bunch of guys in the company. For all you know she's the boss's daughter. And not one of these things is gonna help you—it's only gonna mess you up. You don't want some car salesman selling you a car when he's pissed off at you for hitting on Monica or Susan or Jackie or whatever her name is. You don't want her ex-boyfriend watching you flirt with his shit. And you don't want her thinking that all you want is to get into her jeans. I mean, she spends every day dealing with guys like that.

"Every situation has power players, okay? Someone's in control. Someone looks up to someone else. Someone used to sleep with someone who's sleeping with someone down the hall. This guy doesn't get along with that guy. This person hates that person. Whatever. There's history there. You walk in. You figure it out."

I think it's starting to sink in. Maybe.

"All right, look. Concrete example. Every school's got some guy that knows the building inside out. It's always a guy. He's the guy with all the keys on his belt? You know who I'm talking about? Okay. This guy knows everything about everything, right? But just because he doesn't have some title or salary or something, there's a lot of people there that don't treat him so well. *Especially* students.

"You just got to treat him right. That's it. Figure it out. If you want something done or you're in a jam, who you gonna turn to? No one gonna solve your problem faster. Plus, he's probably used to people treating him like a slave, so hang out with the guy a little. Y'know, listen to him. Ask about his pet. Bring him a candy bar. Write him a thank you note.

"That's pretty much it. Figure out how the system works and make sure you're in with the right people. And I'm not saying be two-faced or fake either. But instead of going in and looking for who's got the biggest name or best contacts or whatever, look for the people who live their lives a little more honestly. Y'know, the kind who don't spend their lives talking behind people's backs. People who aren't afraid of doing the right thing. Try to surround yourself with them."

This gets them silent for a few seconds. They're either taking it in or rolling their eyes at me. I can't tell because I can't see the back half of the room too well. I was originally trying not to tangent too much here, but I've got a live mic and a breathing audience that's willing to swim outside. So we're a little far out and the rip's starting to flow. It's under control. And it was worth the risk. Just swim parallel. I mean, how many chances do you get like this?

They're still quiet, waiting for me to continue rambling like I'm doing a solo show at a non-profit theater company. No more questions. No more interaction. Sure, I could keep going. But that's not what I'm here for. It's too easy.

Semper fidelis.

Carpe diem.

E pluribus unum.

Time to call headquarters and bring them back in. Multiple 906. Straight out. No backup.

Spot victim. Pop buoy. High step. Dolphin. Sight after each wave.

I look into the audience and they're still not saying anything. With me or not, they're just treading water and waiting.

Upon reaching victim, immediately assess physical and psychological condition.

"All right. Let's try this," I tell them. "How much longer do we have? . . . Okay. Here's the deal. You guys ask the questions. I answer them in one sentence or less. Kinda like *Jeopardy.* Cool?"

A couple of heads in the first couple of rows nod. Good enough.

"Okay . . . shoot."

Always maintain a constant visual assessment.

Hands go up. Ball's in. Game's on.

Go.

Two o'clock. Fourth row.

"What's your best talent?"

(Jewish-looking kid. Black jacket. Baggy jeans. Acne. Virgin.)

"What do you *think,* Einstein?" I laugh, shaking my head. "Figuring out systems. You just walk in or something?"

"That was more than a sentence."

"All right, I'm warming up," I say, shifting my weight from side to side like Sugar Ray. "Ready. Go."

More hands.

Eleven o'clock. Front row.

"What one compliment would mean the most to you?"

(White guy. Curly hair. Heavy set. Played high school football. Occasionally refers to beer as "brewski.")

"Your work is musical."

Go.

Straight out. Twelfth row.

"Did you ever think about making a feature film?"

(White girl. Bright red hair. Natural brunette. Facial piercings. At least three tattoos not visible. One of them a flower.)

"I work better alone."

"What about the possibility of reaching a bigger audience?" she says. "Don't you think a film would do that better?"

"You only get one sentence," I say.

"That's *you.*"

"So you get as many as you want?"

"Yep."

"That's not fair."

"Okay," the piercing girl continues, "have you ever thought about using film to reach a bigger audience?"

"Was that 'okay' with a comma or a period?"

"What?"

"If it's a period, that's two sentences."

She rolls her eyes a bit and smiles a beautiful smile. She'd look great if she took half that shit out of her face.

"Just answer the question," she says.

"What's the magic word?"

"Money."

"I'd rather throw bombs from the sidelines," I say, laughing.

Go.

Eleven-thirty. Third row.

"What CD is on your CD player right now?"

(Asian guy. Chinese. Rave poser. Color-tinted glasses indoors. Berates popu-

lar movies.)

"Um . . . Albert King. 'Funky London.' Good question."

"Two sentences," he says with a smirk.

I check off an imaginary scoreboard in the air with my right hand.

ding

"One for you."

Go.

Ten o'clock. Front row.

"Are you in love?"

(White female. Re-entry student. Thirties. Sensible shoes.)

"I want to be."

"Does that mean you are?"

"It doesn't mean I'm not."

Go.

Ten o'clock. Eighth row.

"How do you write?"

(Latino guy. Skinny. Puerto Rican. Gay. Doesn't know it.)

"That's a tough one. I'm gonna need more than a sentence here. You guys get another point."

ding

"I'm not a real 'work ethic' kind of writer," I continue. "You know, I'm not the four-to-six-hours-a-day type. I mean, sometimes I am, but it comes in spurts. Sometimes I go for weeks or months without doing crap, and then all of a sudden it just comes to me and I go for three days straight, trying to get it out.

"I don't know . . . writing process . . .

"I usually wake up around 6:30 and check the surf. If it's good, I go out. If it's not, I usually go back to bed. Sometimes I run if it's sunny . . .

"I think I'm pretty good with deadlines. Actually, let me change that. I think I suck *without* deadlines. Ask my agent. I usually try and set myself up working with people I care about and respect. And at the same time I try to get people around me who can push me. It's that system thing again. I mean, if there's a choice between surfing and making art? I don't really think about it very long, you know?"

The Latino guy nods, still with me. Cool.

Go.

One o'clock. Twenty rows plus.

"How do you keep from getting nervous in front of crowds?"

(Asian Indian girl. Hard to see in the dark. Guy next to her sits there

because she's pretty.)
"You don't."
Go.

Two-thirty. Tenth row.
"Who's your favorite guitarist?"
(Neo-beatnik guy. Showers sporadically. Dirty corduroys. Comes from money. Hairy everywhere.)
"Living or dead?"
"Dead."
"Stevie Ray."
Go.

Two o'clock. Fourth row.
"What do you want your art to do?"
(Same Jewish-looking kid. Black jacket. Still a virgin. Virgin until forty.)
"I want it to fuck my audience."

Shit. Got carried away. I look across this sea of art students with their mouths open. For $30,000 a year, I don't think they've had a lot of their professors or visiting artists tell them that. No one's even laughing. I don't know whether they're too stunned to or they want to but they're afraid of getting in trouble. I spot a couple of faculty members sitting together in the back. We just had dinner together a couple hours ago. Lentil soup and blackened tuna and stuff. The system was easy. The power players were stuffy and starched. The non-tenured professors and lecturers were lively, engaging, and devoted. Business as usual.

I try to dig my way out. I talk about how I don't really mean "fuck" in the sexual sense. But I just don't have any other way to describe it. We don't have another verb in the English language to articulate what I want my art to do. I'm trying to explain this to them, but deep down I know it's a lost cause. Like everywhere I go, people have made up their minds long before I ever got there. Their decisions are set and locked in. All the old guard can see now is a giant erection walking around the stage with a live mic and a laser pointer. All the students see is something else. Constant visual assessment. Everything is where it's supposed to be. And everything is more than I am. Time stops. For this moment, at this place, we are closer to each other than to anyone else in our worlds. And like the last kiss with your lover before they drive north, you want it to last forever. No more bottles. No more rips. You want to embrace the things you love. You want to keep them with you. You want to keep laughing together. For now, at this particular moment, it's really where I am and it's a good place to be. If I could keep hold of it after the lights go down and the audience leaves, I'd have it made. But like I said, I only drove halfway.

Twenty-seven

I write most of this manuscript at my desk in Santa Barbara. I moved out of the married-student housing complex a couple of years back and bought a house in an area south of downtown called The Mesa. My neighbors now are mostly retired folks and younger couples starting to build their families. They seem to have the same loves and desires as anyone else. On Sunday afternoons they wash their cars. On Thursday mornings they recycle their glass and plastic. They walk their golden retrievers and yellow labs on retractable leashes, picking up after them with plastic bags. There are two parks within walking distance and a right-hand point break a half mile down the road. It's supposed to be a good place to live and raise children. Decent schools, safe neighborhood. That sort of thing.

Next to me is a phone-answering machine, a Panasonic that sends faxes as well as takes messages. There's a small green light on the lower left-hand corner which blinks when it has messages waiting. Sometimes it's blinking. Sometimes it's not. Either way, I check it when I come home. My mail is full of phone bills and real estate advertisements and brightly colored mail order computer catalogs you can't get rid of. My e-mails and phone calls are filled with friends wanting to get some food or get in the water or play some music, colleagues needing favors or offering favors, student groups asking me to speak or show my work. Sometimes there are other messages. Sometimes not. The window to the left of my desk faces the Pacific, and skylights above me flood the room with natural light. Overall, it's not a bad way to live a life. And not a bad way to make a living. Like they say, anybody else would be happy.

I look around me. In front of me are a television and a computer with Internet access. To my right are a stereo with a remote control and a collection of Coltrane CDs. *The Paris Concert, Quartet, First Meditations, Bye Bye Blackbird.* Downstairs there are running shoes, a punching ball, a jump rope, and a random assortment of freeweights. In the next room are a Fender Strat, a PRS Custom 22, and an acoustic cutaway Takamine. There are books to be read, artworks to be made, and manuscripts to be written. Taken together, they are all the never-ending temptation of keeping busy. There are always things to do. There is always work to be done. There are always distractions to keep you from grasping where you really are, what you're really doing, and what you're really looking for.

I look out the window at the water. I've spent my life letting it console me after falling. I know the comfort of feeling it enter my eyes and my nose and my ears. I know the safety of feeling it silence the world around me—how for the shortest of moments, I am touched and held everywhere at once again. I know how to move effortlessly through it, and how to harness its energy for play. I know its grip on my body and its taste on my tongue. Taken together, these are all the wonders of a lifetime affinity and kindred spirit. But what I really want, what I'm really looking for, is someone to keep me from falling in the first place. Someone to hear me when I'm ready to read. It's just a matter of timing, I keep telling myself. Everything is just a matter of timing.

I like to think of my artwork as immortal. I like to imagine it having the power to change the world. Maybe it does, in some small way. But like they say in Counseling 101, only if the world really wants to change. And for the most part, art doesn't work that way. Art on its own doesn't have the power to reach and move and seduce and ignite. It has potential. Nothing more. We carry these things in ourselves like organs. We search for our own catalysts when we're ready, and we do so only when and if we really want to. In this equation I have control only over my part of the process. And that's a hard thing to accept. No man likes to talk about impotence. No man wants to admit inability because we're supposed to be in charge of our own destinies and the destinies of those around us. But it doesn't work that way. I know deep down that no matter how much I put into this—no matter how passionately I compose or how densely I layer, no matter how much of my soul I invest in here, a person can only come to me when she lets herself.

Sometimes I torment myself a bit too much over this in my writing—wondering if it really is just an exercise in futility or some kind of hamster wheel I'm running in. I don't want to search only for the sake of searching. I'm not a rodent or a canary. I don't want to spend my life spinning wheels, calling out to Rapunzel, or chasing Amy. I don't want to spend my life trying to find my way home. I want to know my songs can reach someone, but that's the one thing you can never know as an artist. It's always a gamble. And the stakes are always different. Playing dollar chips and talking about love are easy things to laugh at. I know that. I'm not asking you to take me seriously. I'm just asking you to let me play. How easy is it to roll your eyes? How easy is it to keep your days busy to the point of exhaustion? (And what do you do at night then?) Can you read and not really read? Or can you just simply ignore? It's just a matter of patience, I tell myself. Everything is just a matter of patience. Things take time. Absence makes the heart grow fonder. Time heals all wounds. Good things come to those who wait.

Shhhhhh . . . shhhhhh . . .

Three years into writing this manuscript, I met the woman I want to spend my life with. I don't know if you'd call it fate or luck, or if it had something to do with my being thirty-two years old. But for the first time in my life, I just knew. Could I have really grown up? Or would this have happened whenever I met her in my life? I still don't know if it was her, me, or us—if it was something about who she was to me, where I was in my own life, or the way the two of us were together. But at the time, none of that mattered. I just knew it was real.

It happened faster than the movies, without any kind of preparation or buildup. I was standing in line behind her at a neighborhood bagel shop. And when she turned around to face me, I couldn't breathe. Just like that. Very simple. No fanfare, no soundtrack, no slow motion. I know it sounds silly, but it just hit me. It was like standing next to a moving train, or peering over the edge of an enormous cliff and feeling the wind rise up at you. It's like I got faced with something so much larger, so much more powerful than anything I had ever experienced in my life, that I completely forgot how to inhale for a second.

She smiled and walked past me, sat down at a table outside, and started reading a newspaper. So, naturally, I bought myself a paper and followed her out. I mean, what are you gonna do? Walk away? Get on with your life? Go to *work?* I sat down at the table next to her with my newspaper and my bagel bag, like a six-week-old puppy that can't stop wagging its tail. And our lives together began. For the next half hour she gave me every sign a girl could give a guy. She made eye contact. She smiled at me. She raised her sunglasses up so I could see her beautiful brown eyes. And for the next half hour I couldn't muster up the balls to smile back or even look at her directly. I just kept sneaking glances, pretending to read the paper, and cursing myself. I was frozen. I was absolutely and truly caught. The connection was so much bigger than me that all I could do was hide in my sports section and take shy glimpses of it.

When she finally got up to go, I prepared to watch the chance of my lifetime swim away. And I faced the very real possibility of living with this forever—of looking in the mirror every single day, and knowing I didn't run after life when it brushed by me and winked. Of knowing I didn't even try. Of knowing I just stood on the cliff. But she didn't leave me or disappear. She just walked up and said "Hi." I looked up, stunned for a second in disbelief. Is this how it happens? Is it this easy? Where's Ed McMahon and my check? Somehow I remembered how to swallow. I ran my tongue over my teeth to check for leftover bagel bits, stood up as my mother had taught me to do when a lady enters the room, and asked her to sit down. It's all I knew how to do. It's all I *could* do.

We talked for a while. I don't remember about what. All I remember is eyes and smiles and the euphoria inside me. All I remember is feeling my life suddenly come into sharp, almost frightening focus. I tried to control it—but it kept rushing out of me, magnifying off her, and coming back for more. It was like a chemical reaction or an unexpected change in the weather. The sun came out and I had no cover, no glasses, no sunscreen. I left the hair dryer plugged in and it fell in the bathtub water. I didn't mean to. I stuck a fork in the toaster. I dripped water on the magnesium. I mixed chocolate and peanut butter and everybody in town loved it. Within ten minutes, I knew why it was I began writing in the first place. Within an hour, I was telling my roommate, "I think I just met the woman I'm gonna marry."

Sitting here at my desk, nine months later, I understand why I continue to write now. I see why I make art, and why I can't live honestly without doing so. It's part of who I am and what I need to do. It's part of reaching out. Making art is the most sacred activity we as human beings can undertake. Done genuinely, it transcends our individuality unlike any other pursuit. But like any other human endeavor, it is filled with countless, clueless impostors. For every Billie Holiday or Bob Marley we have a thousand *Star Search* candidates, their performances filled with clenched fists, scripted body angst, and snap-on abandon. For every marriage based in love we get 10,000 paper marriages reduced to mutual tolerating of each other and lives based on routine and rote. We measure value in terms of weeks or months or years together, as if it's somehow worth staying with someone just because you've put in time with them. For every passion followed, there are a million evenings spent watching odorless, tasteless Bob Sagat clones on America's funniest home-video shows and listening to Kenny G and Michael Bolton and Yanni. Aren't they all the same guy?

Sometimes all I see is what we could be doing, and what we could achieve together. Sometimes all I see is the possibility of transcending our daily activities and errands and affairs with something bigger than the two of us. This is vision I never asked for, and vision I never thanked anyone for, either. It's just there.

Her name isn't important, because everything I've written here has been for her. Everything here is her name. I've come to terms with that. When I write about marriage, she is the sun coming through the mini-blinds and the potted ficus in the morning. When I write about adapting to chaos, she is the stuffed-sock monkeys and the broken windows and the coffee. She's the one leaning on her knees with her elbows locked on the edge of the bed when I write about champagne and parades and abandon. She's the person I'd take a bullet for without hesitation, without decision—the person I'd cover with my body during a 7.0 earthquake. She is all the red ribbons and all the laughter and all the senses of desire and urgency and euphoria around me. It's not even a question, really. I'd drown in this girl time and time again without thinking. Sometimes, in life, I think we're supposed to drown a bit. Sometimes, maybe, a little more.

We fell in love in an hour. And we dated only a month. I wanted it to work, but there was simply more there than I could reach. More there than I could rescue. All the towers were closed. The storm hatches were battened and the city was evacuated. Everyone had already fled to higher ground. I was standing on the beach in my street clothes with no rescue buoy, no fins, and no backup. What could I do? There were the telltale nightmares of beautiful women mirrored in male attention. There was a life spent never, ever, having to ask for a ride home. There was a violent ex-boyfriend. Three years of alcoholism, abuse, and manipulation. Denial and self-blame and the inability to process feelings. And there were rivers and rivers of guilt and tears flowing into the ocean. I wanted to rescue her, but I couldn't enter without becoming infected myself. Everything around her was broken and churning and contaminated. Everything around her was toxic. Everything around her was battered.

I want the story to trail off magically, but it doesn't. It doesn't even end. Nine months later, the rivers have dried to trickles and the gutters are empty. The waters are calm again. You forget all the pain and frustration and helplessness. You forget the addictions and the confusion. You forget the floods.

All that's left is the love. Still palpable between us, though we see each other only in passing. The occasional chance meetings of our eyes caress each other now. Nothing else. We may want more, but we don't have the timing. And, like they say, timing is everything.

ٱ

A bouquet of flowers lives like a symphony, each species playing off of and complementing the other. Each individual strand drawing its own line and fragrance. Some rise singly while others support and lay a foundation. You choose by color and shape. By bloom, form, and scent. Each flower plays its own note in its own particular manner and at its own particular temperature. Every decision to give does the same. But the focus is always on the whole, and on the purpose. We all have our own individual reasons to give flowers. It's part of what makes this world worth living in.

You come to me now, bringing with you the beginnings of emotional freedom and independence. Given vision for the first time, you look back in disbelief at what you went through. You tell me, "He's out of my life," and for the first time I hear conviction in your voice. For the first time I hear the beginnings of strength. It happens quickly in me. It happens beyond my control. I listen with barely restrained excitement, for I feel the connection between us as powerful as ever. My hopes, once stifled and pushed away, return with a vengeance. My heart races again. I'm a sucker for happy endings, and I'm still waiting for ours. I want our epilogue to start. I want our sequel. And I want it better than *The Empire Strikes Back, Jaws 2,* or *An American Werewolf in Paris.* Where's our original soundtrack? Where's our sunset? Where's our credit roll? Looking at you, I feel the pull and the draw and the unbridled elation again. I feel our eyes beginning to dance. All that's missing are blueberry bagels and me being an idiot. Yes, I'm in love with you. I always have been. But windows come and go between us like moon phases. Why are you here? And what have you brought with you?

I try to think reasonably, though this has never been one of my strong points. I try to keep some semblance of my feet on the ground, and some clarity in my thinking. Listen to me. There is nothing I want more than to run back into your arms. But we both know that would only throw us back into chaos again. The small gifts you bear would be lost. Your life would continue in its reliance on men, and I'd fall back in my addiction to you. You may be everything to me. Or you may be nothing more than a flash of beauty in my life. But it's the only beauty I have ever seen. It's beauty I can't forget. As it is, my every action, my every thought is colored by the ways you make me feel. I carry hope and I hang on to patience like water and Power Bars because I've got nothing else to go on. Do you understand? I've got nothing else in my hands. I dream of you being healthy, of you being able to feel. I dream of you being able to go on with your life without the scars of what you've been through. I dream of you just being able to smile when you think about me. I dream of very simple things.

But I don't know how long that healing process takes, or if it's even possible. How much of you is still there now, even as you come to me—caught up in being the forgiver and the blame and the guilt? Can you ever really get away from it? How long does that process take? A month? A year? Ten years? I don't have the answers. I don't even have the comprehension. Everything is so far removed from any part of my reality that I don't know where to begin. It's like we're stuck on some Tomorrowland ride or a really stupid TV show. Amanda and Billy and Allison and Kimberly and Michael are all standing around giving bad advice on mating rituals and half of us are taking it. We should be on exhibit in some natural history museum, with a bunch of Cub Scouts and elementary school kids on field trips watching us through the glass in amazement.

That's not real, is it?

Sometimes nature just goes through the motions, and all we can do is sit around and watch it. It's out of our hands. We're totally powerless. We watch male lions kill off their rivals' cubs on the Discovery Channel. Then we run to the kitchen at commercial and fix a snack. We watch orcas torture seals before eating them, tossing them in the air like rag dolls. Then we take our boats back to shore and drop our film off at Rite Aid. We watch men play fish to exhaustion, then gill them, gut them, and throw them in the refrigerator. A year later we go through the freezer when no one is home, sniff the folded newspaper packages, and toss them in the trash.

I don't want to go through motions with you. I'm not searching for the sake of searching. I'm still here because together we have the potential for something wonderful—something most people never even dream of. And I'm not ready to give that up. I've waited nine months, and chances are I'll have to wait years more with no promises and no money-back guarantees. That's a huge gamble. It always is, but this time the stakes are more precious. We could lose each other in a crowd as quickly as any kid at Disneyland. There's not a thing I can do about it. We could pass our evenings watching recycled sitcoms and having things go *okay*. We could spend a lifetime of Saturday nights with other partners, wondering what to do with each other. *You want to get something to eat? You want to see a movie? You feel like staying home? Are you listening to me?* We could spend a lifetime of health-club memberships, big screen TVs, and two-week vacations, knowing we let this one chance swim away without even reaching. We could wake up every single morning, look at ourselves in the mirror, and know we let it go by.

This is the gamble. And all my cards are out. The rules are pretty simple, and as usual they favor the house. I'm on my last stack of chips here. No more cash. No more credit. No more ATM. Everything's on the table and the dice are rolling. All our attention and hope rest on two spinning cubes, the gentle slope of a table, and a few random laws of physics. The rest depends on chance, luck, fortune, and fate. I don't get much of a say here. If you know I'm waiting for you, you only pretend to heal. If I don't let you know, you think I'm abandoning you. Either way, I stand to lose. Either way, I can only hope you have what it takes within yourself. Everything else is out of my hands. And that's a weird place to be for me, because I'm used to running after what I want in life. I'm used to identifying my goals and tightening my focus. I'm used to working alone. But sitting at my desk overlooking the Pacific, I can't do any of these things. It's like I'm tapered and shaved, but there's no competition ahead of me. I don't know when my next race is, what it's for, or who it's against. I'm at the ball, but there are no other guests here. The caterers are still setting up. They're putting flower arrangements on the tables and the food is covered with Saran Wrap. I'm out of place and off course with nothing in front of me but open ocean and time. So I do the only things I'm able to. I hedge my bets as best I can. I wait quietly. And I write.

I dream of waking in the morning next to you and saying nothing. Of just knowing and feeling you there, without words. I make my living using words, but there is no place for them here. No place for them when we wake together. I trace my finger along your eyebrow and down the side of your face. I feel the undulations of your ribs and the rise and fall of your slow breathing. It's okay if you want to keep sleeping. I just want to watch you. I just want to make sure you're okay. Everything's okay, love. Everything's okay. Go back to sleep.

I dream of waiting to make love with you. I don't know for how long. Do you remember the one night we came so close in my bedroom? How everything just clicked? How we were right . . . there—before I gently pulled you off me? I know how hard it was for you to understand, after spending so much of your life fighting men off you. Were you offended? Did you feel rejected? I wanted you with every part of my physical being, believe me. But I just couldn't bring myself to enter you yet. Somehow, and I don't quite know how to explain this—I just felt like I loved you too much. You are the most beautiful woman I have ever seen, and I'm drawn to you like no one else in my life. But that's not why I want to make love with you. I know you couldn't understand that then, but can you now? I never thought I'd have the strength, or even the desire, to stop something as powerful as our draw—especially after spending so much of my life trying to get women into bed with me. Somehow, though, it was easy with you. Somehow it was right. Do you remember the next morning? You told me softly, "No man has ever stopped me before," and I told you the men in your life have been assholes. I don't want to be one of the men in your life. Because I'm not.

I dream of asking you to marry me on the 4th of July—wrapping my arms around you from behind and watching fireworks explode over the ocean. My head leans over your shoulder, and I feel our cold ears and cheeks against each other. Your hair, shorter than mine, lies against the nape of my neck. Mine falls along your shoulder and back. I slip a ring off your middle finger while you look into the night sky, and replace it with a diamond on your wedding finger. The sky is lit up with blue and orange and red bursts of light. I've kept the ring with me all day. It just kept getting heavier and heavier, until it felt like a golf ball in my pocket. All the way through dinner and our walk down to the waterfront, I kept feeling for it to make sure it was still there. Did you wonder why I kept wiping my hands on my pants? Did you wonder why my hands were so sweaty all night? Did you wonder why I couldn't stop smiling?

I want you to not even notice the switch. To be so caught up in the rapture of the nighttime explosions and my body surrounding you. To feel safe in my hold amidst a sea of strangers. Until you wonder why it is I put your ring back on your other finger. When you reach to switch it back and your fingers touch the stone, do you realize immediately? Or do you have to look? Do you turn to kiss me in the dark? Or do you just sink deeper into my body? I wonder whether you smile or cry, and if you knew I had the ring with me all this time. Did you know I've had the ring since I met you? Does knowing that make you smile more? Or cry more?

I dream about you every time I wake up, and you stay with me through my daily hours. But I can't stop by your work. I can't run into you on the street. I can't drop off a gift for your family on Christmas Eve. I can't be around you this way—not if we're not together. It's just wrong and I can't do it. When I watch you, it is so hard not to run into your arms. I can't see you on campus and not want to pull you to me. I can't look into your eyes and not want to kiss them softly. I can't talk to you without wanting to cry in joy for the way you make me feel. When we laugh together, when we touch each other in the dark, when I let my hair down and it falls in your face and you come to its shelter—you make me feel the same way I do when I make art. Can you understand that? This is how I feel when I make art. This is why I'm here. I don't know how else to explain it. Nothing in this world makes me feel half the person I am when I'm with you. You make me feel more alive, more important, than anything else in my known existence. When I'm with you, I feel for the first time like I'm doing what I am supposed to be doing. And I've never felt like that outside the water before. If you ask me if I love you, I'll tell you that's a silly question. If you ask me to keep loving you, I'll tell you I don't have a choice. If you ask me to drown, I'll tell you I already have.

A flash of beauty is a strange way to put it. It doesn't come close to the way you affect my life. I just don't have any other words to use. Don't get me wrong—I think you're exquisitely beautiful. There's not a thing I'd change about you physically. Not one tiny thing. But that doesn't do justice to how I feel when I see you. Because I see "beautiful" women every day of my life. It's part of my job. Every day of my life I'm surrounded by eighteen-to-twenty-two-year-olds in sundresses and beach cruisers. Every single quarter that I teach, beautiful students get crushes on me. Every time I speak or perform in public, beautiful women in the audience fall into infatuation. *It doesn't mean anything compared to you.* Can you see that? Does that make any sense? It doesn't mean anything compared to you. Every woman in the world can want to share their life with me, and I can still spend mine lonely without you.

I always thought it would be a few years before you realized what you lost. A few years before you realized what it is I offered you. Yes, I might have every surface attribute a woman could look for in a man—looks, career, passion, a beautiful home, a love of children. But these are all completely meaningless without the emotion. You instill in me an unconditional love. A sense of purpose surrounding you. And that's what I brought to the table. When it comes to being a partner, all my other attributes are worthless without it. Without you, everything is hollow. I've tried so many times before. I've offered every other part of me to a dozen women in my life, and all it's ever done was come back and bite me three months, six months, or a year later. It's not that they were bad people. They were wonderful. And it's not that I was shallow or unfeeling or callous. If I could have given more, I would have. I just wasn't able to.

When these relationships end up on the wayside, filled with blame and hurt and abandonment, you search for reasons why. You wonder why it is you fell out of love with someone, or how it was you suddenly discovered yourself going through the motions. Living day to day, crossing off errands. Afterwards, you assess blame and responsibility. You craft scenarios to tell your mutual friends. You return keys and spare clothes, and you change answering-machine messages. You throw away letters and dead flowers. You put glass vases away in cupboards. I always thought it was a fault of mine. Something missing within me. That somehow I didn't have the discipline or the willpower to push through. That I was somehow wrong for wanting something beyond satisfaction and security. That it was unrealistic to expect or even want the laughter to continue. But that's not the case. Maybe anyone else *would* be happy. But I'm not anyone else. You aren't either.

Parsley, sage, rosemary, and thyme.

Nine months later, you come to me. We sit three feet apart from each other in separate chairs, talking about where we are in our lives apart, and where we are in our lives together. I hear some of the things you're saying. But mostly I feel the pull and the draw and the euphoria. Mostly I just want to come to you. The three feet between us is the longest three feet in the universe, but I could be there in the blink of an eye. You know that. But you also trust that I won't, and I feel this from you. It's like I've got nothing inside me but your trust and my desire. The rest of me just gets to look at you. I see the courage it took for you to come here and I see the tears welling in your eyes. I look down at my hands and there's nothing in them but sweat. What do you have in yours, clenched together there in your lap? What have you brought with you?

Somewhere in the conversation I swallow for the first time, and tell you how I feel. There are some things you need to know, and some things I need to say to you. Because above all else, I want to be the one man in your life who stands out. I want to be the one man who never wanted you for your beauty or your sex or your stunningness. I want you to know, beyond any doubt, that my love for you was, and is, absolutely real. Whether we end up together or not, I need to be the one man in your life who lives apart from the rest.

"You are," you tell me quietly.

(Does knowing that make you smile more? Or cry more?)

Part of me wants to smile. The other part of me wants to cry. Either way I don't think I'll be able to stop. The curtains should be closing and the audience should cautiously be starting to applaud now. Fade out.

I've been blessed with many things. A supportive family and dozens of friends who would do anything for me. I have good health, a beautiful face and body, and more talents than I deserve. I come to this place with a gift for putting words together, and for transferring my desires and passion to the page. I also bring whatever advice I have to the table. Sometimes it's relevant. Sometimes it's not.

I also come here as an artist, an athlete, and a tenured professor at the University of California. Call me whatever else you want. I've got a résumé a mile long. Gimme that and a guitar pick and I'll play you a G major. There are more important things that go unwritten and unrecognized—the changing of my students' lives, traveling the world and hugging strangers, throwing Frisbees with neighborhood kids, making sure an old lady can start her car in a dark airport parking lot. I've lost myself playing music until the calluses tear off my fingers. I've grown sunflowers, caressed a dolphin, and hugged Magic Johnson. In the water I've pulled into the tube, shot out, and screamed in pure exhilaration. I've loaned money to friends knowing it will never come back, then watched it get returned to me with gratitude. I've carried bugs outside in the rain and let them go in the grass. I've sat vigil while one of my former junior guards was in a coma, and I was standing next to him when he opened his eyes. Throughout my life I've tried to treat others' hearts gently, but I haven't always done so. I've spent a lot of time hurting a lot of people. But I've rescued countless more. In the end, these are important things in the scope of life. These are the things I want listed on my vitae. They're part of what makes this world a place worth living in. But they're not the only things I want, or the only things I'm looking for.

I spend my every waking day rescuing people. Students, friends, strangers. My days are spent saving others. I've pulled 200 people out of the water—counseling them about their artwork, their loves, hatreds, and angers, with water still dripping from their eyes. Sometimes I loan them a towel to put around their shoulders, or to dry off with. Sometimes they experience my artwork, and I have the opportunity to convince them there's more to our existence than details and convention and routine. It's my job and I'm good at it. But in the morning, when I'm alone, I don't want to be a rescuer anymore. I don't want to be an inspiration or a role model. I don't want to be a guide. I just want to be found. When it's still warm outside in late summer, I sleep alone with the Pacific to my right, a night sky above, and a garland of flowers below me. This is where I am now. I imagine you here with me, on my left. But as much as I may want you to walk in my bedroom door, I know you can't come to me yet. And when the time does come that you're finally able to, I can't even say where I'll be. I hope I'm still here, though. That would be a good thing.

Sometimes nature just goes through the motions, and all we can do is sit around and watch it happen. And sometimes we have everything we need to chase after what we want in life. Everything is just a matter of timing. I know what I've got in my hands right now. I know what I'm looking for, and I know what I have to offer. But I can only guess what you have in yours. I don't know where you are, who you're with, or how you're sleeping. And I don't know what you're holding behind your back. If I ask really nice, will you show me?

Sources

Aliens, written and directed by James Cameron (Brandywine Productions, Twentieth Century Fox Film Corporation, 1986). *Apocalypse Now,* written by Joseph Conrad (novel) and Francis Ford Coppola, Michael Herr, and John Milius (screenplay), directed by Francis Ford Coppola (Zoetrope Studios, 1979). *Austin Powers: The Spy Who Shagged Me,* written by Mike Myers, directed by Jay Roach (Eric's Boy, Moving Pictures, New Line Cinema, Team Todd, 1999). *Barb Wire,* written by John Arcudi (novel), Ilene Chaiken (story), Chuck Pfarrer (screenplay), and Chris Warner (comic), directed by David Hogan (Dark Horse Entertainment, PolyGram Filmed Entertainment, Propaganda Films, 1996). *Basic Instinct,* written by Joe Eszterhas, directed by Paul Verhoeven (Canal Plus, Carolco Pictures, TriStar Pictures, 1992). *The Blair Witch Project,* written and directed by Daniel Myrick and Eduardo Sánchez (Haxan Entertainment, 1999). *The Breakfast Club,* written and directed by John Hughes (A&M Films, Universal Pictures, 1985). *Chasing Amy,* written and directed by Kevin Smith (Miramax Films, View Askew Productions, 1997). *The Craft,* written by Peter Filardi (story) and Andrew Fleming and Peter Filardi (screenplay), directed by Andrew Fleming (Columbia Pictures Corporation, Sony Pictures Classics, 1996). *The Empire Strikes Back,* written by George Lucas, Leigh Brackett, and Lawrence Kasdan, directed by Irvin Kershner (Atari Games, Lucasfilm Ltd., 1985). *Enter the Dragon,* written by Michael Allin, directed by Robert Clouse (Concord Productions Inc., Warner Bros. Pictures, 1973). *The Exorcist,* written by William Peter Blatty (novel and screenplay), directed by William Friedkin (Hoya Productions, Warner Bros. Pictures, 1973). *Fast Times at Ridgemont High,* written by Cameron Crowe (novel and screenplay), directed by Amy Heckerling (Refugee Films, Universal Pictures, 1982). *Fatal Attraction,* written by James Dearden (also earlier screenplay) and Nicholas Meyer, directed by Adrian Lyne (Paramount Pictures, 1987). *Full Metal Jacket,* written by Gustav Hasford (novel, *Short Timers*) and Gustav Hasford, Michael Herr, and Stanley Kubrick (screenplay) (Natant Films, Warner Bros. Pictures, 1987). *Gamera vs. Monster X,* written by Nisan Takahashi, directed by Noriaki Yuasa (American-International Television, Saiei Studios, 1970). *Goodfellas,* written by Nicholas Pileggi (novel, *Wiseguy: Life in a Mafia Family*) and Nicholas Pileggi and Martin Scorsese (screenplay), directed by Martin Scorsese (Warner Bros. Pictures, 1990). *The Graduate,* written by Charles Webb (novel) and Calder Willingham and Buck Henry (screenplay), directed by Mike Nichols (Embassy Pictures Corporation, 1967). *The Island of Dr. Moreau,* written by H. G. Wells (novel) and Al Ramrus and John Herman Shane (screenplay), directed by Don Taylor (American International Pictures, Cinema 77, Major Productions, 1977). *Jaws,* written by Peter Benchley (novel) and Carl Gottlieb and Peter Benchley (screenplay, with uncredited contributions by John Milius, Howard Sackler, and Robert Shaw to Quint's *S. S. Indianapolis* monologue), directed by Steven Spielberg (Universal Pictures, Zanuck/Brown Productions, 1975). *Lord of the Flies,* written by William Golding (novel) and Peter Brook (screenplay), directed by Peter Brook (Two Arts Ltd., 1967). *Mallrats,* written and directed by Kevin Smith (Alphaville Films, Universal Pictures, View Askew Productions, 1995). *The Matrix,* written and directed by Andy Wachowski and Larry Wachowski (Groucho II Film Partnership, Silver Pictures, Roadshow Productions, 1999). *My So-Called Life,* created by Winnie Holzman, produced by Marshall Herskovitz, Scott Winant, and Edward Zwick (Bedford Falls Production Company, a.k.a. Productions, ABC Television, 1994–95). *North Shore,* written by Randall Kleiser, Tim McCanlies, and William Phelps, directed by William Phelps (Universal Pictures, 1987). *The Princess Bride,* written by William Goldman, directed by Rob Reiner (Act III Productions, Buttercup Films Ltd., The Princess Bride Ltd., 1987). *Psycho,* written by Robert Bloch (novel) and Joseph Stefano (screenplay), directed by Alfred Hitchcock (Shamley Productions, 1960). *Pulp Fiction,* written by Roger Avery and Quentin Tarantino, directed by Quentin Tarantino (A Band Apart, Jersey Films, Miramax Films, 1994). *Rashomon,* written by

Ryunosuke Akutagawa (stories "Rashomon" and "In a Grove") and Shinobu Hashimoto and Akira Kurosawa (screenplay), directed by Akira Kurosawa (Daiei Studios, 1950). *Reality Bites,* written by Helen Childress, directed by Ben Stiller (Jersey Films, Universal Pictures, 1994). *Rocky,* written by Sylvester Stallone, directed by John G. Avildsen (Chartoff-Winkler Productions, 1976). *The Shining,* written by Stephen King (novel) and Stanley Kubrick and Diane Johnson (screenplay), directed by Stanley Kubrick (Hawk Films, Peregrine, Producers Circle, Warner Bros. Pictures, 1980). *The Silence of the Lambs,* written by Thomas Harris (novel) and Ted Tally (screenplay), directed by Jonathan Demme (Orion Pictures Corporation, Strong Heart/Demme, 1991). *Star Trek,* created by Gene Roddenberry (Desilu Studios, Paramount Pictures, NBC Television, 1965–69). *Swingers,* written by Jon Favreau, directed by Doug Liman (The Alfred Shay Company Inc., 1996). *Taxi Driver,* written by Paul Schrader, directed by Martin Scorsese (Bill/Phillips, Columbia Pictures Corporation, Italo-Judeo Productions, 1976). *This Is Spinal Tap,* written by Christopher Guest, Michael McKean, Rob Reiner, and Harry Shearer, directed by Rob Reiner (Spinal Tap Productions, 1984). *Trading Places,* written by Timothy Harris and Herschel Weingrod, directed by John Landis (Cinema Group Ventures, Paramount Pictures Corporation, 1983). *The Treasure of the Sierra Madre,* written by B. Traven (novel) and John Huston (screenplay), directed by John Huston (Warner Bros. Pictures, 1948). *The Usual Suspects,* written by Christopher McQuarrie, directed by Bryan Singer (Bad Hat Harry, Blue Parrot, Gramercy Pictures, PolyGram Filmed Entertainment, Rosco Film, Spelling Films International, 1995). *Vacation,* written by John Hughes, directed by Harold Ramis (Warner Bros. Pictures, 1983). *Wild at Heart,* written by Barry Gifford (novel) and David Lynch (screenplay), with uncredited contributions by L. Frank Baum, author of *The Wonderful Wizard of Oz* (PolyGram Filmed Entertainment, Propaganda Films, 1990).

"Big Mouth Strikes Again," written by Johnny Marr and Morrissey (Warner–Tamerlane Publishing Co., BMI, 1986). "Blister in the Sun," written by Gordon James Gano (Gorno Music, ASCAP, 1982). "Boys Don't Cry," written by Robert Smith, Lol Tolhurst, and Michael Dempsey (APB Music Co. Ltd., 1979). "Communication Breakdown," written by John Baldwin, John Bonham, Jimmy Page, and Robert Plant (Superhype Publishing Inc., ASCAP, 1969). "The Four-Legged Zoo," written by Bob Dorough (Capitol Records, 1973). "Fuck Tha Police," written by Ice Cube and Lorenzo Patterson (Ruthless Attack Muzick, ASCAP, 1988). "Gangsta Gangsta," written by Ice Cube, Lorenzo Patterson, and Eric Wright (Ruthless Attack Muzick, ASCAP, 1988). "Good Vibrations," written by Mike Love and Brian Wilson (Irving Music Inc., BMI, 1966). "Helter Skelter," written by John Lennon and Paul McCartney (Sony/ATV Songs LLC, BMI, 1968). "Hit Me with Your Best Shot," written by Edward Schwartz (Sony/ATV Songs LLC, BMI, 1980). "I Know What Boys Like," written by Christopher Butler (Merovingian Music, BMI, 1982). "Institutionalized," written by Louis Mayorga and Michael Muir (American Lesion Music, You'll Be Sorry Music, BMI, 1983). "Just the Two of Us," written by Ralph MacDonald, William Salter, and Bill Withers (Bleunig Music, Cherry Lane Music Publishing, ASCAP, 1980). "Little Girls," written by Danny Elfman (Little Maestro Music, BMI, 1981). "Love Shack," written by Catherine Pierson, Fred Schneider, Keith Strickland, and Cynthia Wilson (EMI Blackwood Music Inc., Man Woman Together Now Inc., BMI, 1989). "Mental Hopscotch," written by Warren Cuccurullo and Terry Bozzio (Private Parts Music, Private Life Music, ASCAP, 1982). "Never Say Never," written by Benjamin Bossi, Larry Carter, Deborah Iyall, Peter Woods, and Frank Zincavage (Talk Dirty Music, BMI, 1981). "Scarborough Fair/Canticle," written by Paul Simon and Art Garfunkel (Paul Simon Music, BMI, 1967). "She Blinded Me with Science," written by Jonathan Michael Kerr and Thomas Morgan Robertson (Lost Toy People Inc., Zomba Enterprises Inc., ASCAP, 1982). "Stray Cat Strut," written by Brian Seltzer (EMI Longitude Music, Rockin' Bones Music Inc., BMI, 1981). "Tonight's the Night," written by Rod Stewart (EMI April Music Inc., Warner Bros., 1976). "There Is a Light That Never Goes Out," written by Johnny Marr and Morrissey (Warner–Tamerlane Publishing Co., BMI, 1986). "Turning Japanese," written by David Fenton (Glenwood Music Corporation, EMI Music Publishing Inc., ASCAP, 1980). "Voodoo Chile," written by Jimi Hendrix (Experience Hendrix LLC, ASCAP, 1968). "Wouldn't It Be Nice?," written by Tony Asher, Mike Love, and Brian Wilson (Irving Music Inc., BMI, 1966).